triumphlearning™

Mathematics
4

Coach®

Table of Contents

Domain 1

Number and Operations in Base Ten

Domain 1: Diagnostic Assessment for Lessons 1–10

Domain 1: Cumulative Assessment for Lessons 1–10

Domain 1: Diagnostic Assessment for Lessons 1–10

1. Frankie read that three hundred sixty-seven thousand, five hundred sixty-two people live in his city. Which is another way to write this number?

   A. $300,000 + 60,000 + 7,000 + 500 + 60 + 2$

   B. 367,000,562

   C. $3 + 6 + 7 + 5 + 6 + 2$

   D. 367,652

2. How many times greater is the 4 in the hundreds place than the 4 in the ones place in this number?

   536,494

   A.　　1

   B.　　10

   C.　　100

   D. 1,000

3. A spring was 8 centimeters long at first. Now it is stretched to be 72 centimeters long. How many times as long is the spring now as it was at first?

   A. 6

   B. 7

   C. 8

   D. 9

4. Each CD that Rashaun bought last year cost $16. He bought 42 CDs last year. How much money did Rashaun spend on CDs last year?

   A. $672

   B. $472

   C. $462

   D. $96

5. What is the missing number in this sentence?

   $$4 \times (5 \times 12) = (\square \times 5) \times 12$$

   A. 1

   B. 4

   C. 5

   D. 12

6. Which number sentence is the same as this sentence?

   $$15 \times 5 = \square$$

   A. $(10 + 5) \times (5 + 5)$

   B. $(10 \times 5) + (5 \times 5)$

   C. $(10 \times 5) \times (5 \times 5)$

   D. $(10 + 5) + (5 + 5)$

7. Anna spent $36 on 9 notebooks. Each notebook cost the same amount of money. How much did each notebook cost?

   A. $3

   B. $4

   C. $6

   D. $7

8. On Saturday, David read 96 pages of his book. That is 8 times the number of pages he read on Friday. How many pages of his book did he read on Friday?

   A. 8

   B. 9

   C. 12

   D. 14

9. Multiply.

$$3 \times 800 = \boxed{}$$

10. Mr. King has 155 oranges to pack into boxes. Each box can hold 8 oranges. He will keep any extra oranges for himself. How many full boxes of oranges does Mr. King pack?

   A. Write a number sentence for the problem. Use a variable to represent the quotient.

   B. Solve the number sentence you wrote for Part A. Explain your answer.

Read and Write Whole Numbers

Getting the Idea

A **whole number** can be written in different forms:

base-ten numeral: 134,582

number name: one hundred thirty-four thousand, five hundred eighty-two

expanded form: 100,000 + 30,000 + 4,000 + 500 + 80 + 2

Place value is the value of a digit in a number based on its location.

You can use a place-value chart to find the value of each digit.

The digit 3 is in the ten thousands place. It has a value of 30,000.

Hundred Thousands	Ten Thousands	Thousands	,	Hundreds	Tens	Ones
1	3	4	,	5	8	2

The value of a digit is 10 times the value of the digit to its right.

The models below represent the number 2,222.

The 2 in the thousands place has a value of 2,000.
That is 10 times the value of the 2 in the hundreds place.

The 2 in the hundreds place has a value of 200.
That is 10 times the value of the 2 in the tens place.

The 2 in the tens place has a value of 20.
That is 10 times the value of the 2 in the ones place.

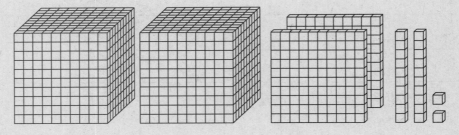

$2{,}000 \div 200 = 10$

$200 \div 20 = 10$

$20 \div 2 = 10$

Example 1

A singer on a show received 45,698 votes from viewers. What is the value of the 5 in 45,698?

Strategy   Use a place-value chart.

Step 1   Write each digit of the number in a chart.

Ten Thousands	Thousands	,	Hundreds	Tens	Ones
4	5	,	6	9	8

Step 2   Find the value of the 5.

The 5 is in the thousands place.

The value of the 5 is 5,000.

Solution   **The value of the 5 in 45,698 is 5,000.**

Example 2

A company has 312,775 employees. What is the number name for 312,775?

Strategy   **Use place value. Look at the comma.**

Step 1   Find the value of the digits before the comma.

There are 312 thousands.

Write *three hundred twelve thousand.*

Step 2   Find the value of the digits after the comma.

There are 775.

Write *seven hundred seventy-five.*

Step 3   Write the number name.

Put a comma after the thousands.

three hundred twelve thousand, seven hundred seventy-five

Solution   **The number name for 312,775 is *three hundred twelve thousand, seven hundred seventy-five*.**

Example 3

How can you write the number 954,362 in expanded form?

Strategy   **Use a place-value chart.**

Step 1   Write each digit of the number in a chart.

Hundred Thousands	Ten Thousands	Thousands	,	Hundreds	Tens	Ones
9	5	4	,	3	6	2

Step 2   Write the value of each digit.

9 hundred thousands = 900,000

5 ten thousands = 50,000

4 thousands = 4,000

3 hundreds = 300

6 tens = 60

2 ones = 2

Step 3   List the values. Use a + between each value.

900,000 + 50,000 + 4,000 + 300 + 60 + 2

Solution   **In expanded form, 954,362 is 900,000 + 50,000 + 4,000 + 300 + 60 + 2.**

Coached Example

Laura bought a new home for $239,807.

Write the expanded form and the number name for this dollar amount.

Write the value of each digit.

What is the value of the 2? _____

What is the value of the 3? _____

What is the value of the 9? _____

What is the value of the 8? _____

What is the value of the 0? _____

What is the value of the 7? _____

The expanded form of 239,807 is _____.

Find the value of the digits before the comma.

There are _____ thousands.

Write the value in words.

_____

Find the value of the digits after the comma.

There are _____.

Write the value in words. _____

Place a comma after the thousands.

The number name for 239,807 is

_____.

Lesson Practice • Part 1

Choose the correct answer.

1. A toy store had 27,436 customers last week. Which digit is in the thousands place in 27,436?

   A. 2

   B. 3

   C. 4

   D. 7

2. Which is another way to show this number?

   thirteen thousand,
   one hundred nineteen

   A. 13,119

   B. 13,190

   C. 13,191

   D. 13,911

3. In 2009, there were 15,095 airports in the United States. What is the value of the digit 9 in 15,095?

   A. 9,000

   B. 900

   C. 90

   D. 9

4. Which number has the digit 6 in the thousands place and in the tens place?

   A. 13,662

   B. 44,668

   C. 76,361

   D. 86,629

5. Which is the number name for 240,048?

   A. two hundred four thousand, four hundred eight

   B. two hundred four thousand, forty-eight

   C. two hundred forty thousand, four hundred eight

   D. two hundred forty thousand, forty-eight

6. How many times greater is a digit in the thousands place than that same digit in the hundreds place?

   A. 1

   B. 10

   C. 100

   D. 1,000

7. A phone company serves 475,931 households. Which shows the expanded form of 475,931?

    A. 400,000 + 70,000 + 50,000 + 9,000 + 300 + 10

    B. 400,000 + 70,000 + 5,000 + 900 + 30 + 1

    C. 40,000 + 7,000 + 5,000 + 900 + 30 + 1

    D. 100,000 + 30,000 + 9,000 + 500 + 70 + 4

8. Which shows the expanded form of 945,025?

    A. 900,000 + 40,000 + 5,000 + 20 + 5

    B. 900,000 + 40,000 + 5,000 + 200 + 50

    C. 90,000 + 40,000 + 50,000 + 20 + 5

    D. 900,000 + 40,000 + 500 + 20 + 5

9. A school collected 15,838 plastic bottles to be recycled.

    A. Write the number of bottles in expanded form.

    _____

    B. How many times greater is the 8 in the hundreds place than the 8 in the ones place? Explain your answer.

    _____

    _____

    _____

    _____

Lesson Practice • Part 2

Choose the correct answer.

1. The estimated population of Alaska in 2013 was seven hundred thirty-five thousand, one hundred thirty-two. When written using base-ten numerals, which two place values have the same digit?

   A. thousands and tens

   B. thousands and hundreds

   C. ten thousands and tens

   D. ten thousands and hundreds

2. Dinosaur National Monument in Colorado and Utah has an area of 210,283 acres. What is 210,283 written in expanded form?

   A. 200,000 + 1,000 + 200 + 80 + 3

   B. 200,000 + 10,000 + 200 + 80 + 3

   C. 200,000 + 10,000 + 2,000 + 80 + 3

   D. 200,000 + 10,000 + 2,000 + 800 + 3

3. Which number has a 4 that is ten times as many as the 4 in 657,482?

   A. 354,792   C. 542,971

   B. 458,217   D. 625,245

4. Alisa wrote the number 237,468. Then she wrote a number that has 1 more in the ten-thousands place and 3 fewer in the hundreds place. Which number did Alisa write?

   A. 227,498

   B. 238,438

   C. 247,168

   D. 337,438

5. Lake Superior has an area of 20,600 square miles. What is the number name for 20,600?

   A. twenty thousand, sixty

   B. twenty thousand, six hundred

   C. twenty-six thousand

   D. two hundred thousand, six

6. Which number has a 7 in both the hundred thousands and thousands places?

   A. 587,709

   B. 677,384

   C. 718,792

   D. 727,436

7. The longest bridge in the United States is one hundred twenty-six thousand, fifty-five feet long. What is that length written using base-ten numerals?

   A. 126,550 feet

   B. 126,505 feet

   C. 126,055 feet

   D. 120,655 feet

8. In the number five hundred four thousand, two hundred seventeen, which place has a value of 0?

   A. hundreds

   B. thousands

   C. tens

   D. ten thousands

9. The Sun has a mean radius of four hundred thirty-two thousand, two hundred miles.

   A. Write the mean radius of the Sun using base-ten numerals.

   _____

   B. Write the mean radius of the Sun in expanded form.

   _____

   C. Which place in the mean radius of the Sun is the digit in a place value exactly ten times as many as another place value?

   _____

10. Which shows the number sixty-five thousand, three hundred fifty-three? Circle all that apply.

   A. 65,353

   B. 605,353

   C. 60,000 + 5,000 + 300 + 50 + 3

   D. 65,533

   E. 65,000 + 30 + 50 + 3

11. Draw a line from each number to its number name.

   A.   348 •

   B. 36,480 •

   C. 4,080 •

   D. 148,008 •

   E. 108,048 •

   • one hundred forty-eight thousand, eight

   • three hundred forty-eight

   • one hundred eight thousand, forty-eight

   • thirty-six thousand, four hundred eighty

   • four thousand, eighty

12. Select True or False for each statement.

   A. In 652,908, the digit 6 is in the hundred thousands place.   ○ True   ○ False

   B. In 161,782, the digit 6 is in the thousands place.   ○ True   ○ False

   C. In 502,168, the digit 6 is in the tens place.   ○ True   ○ False

   D. In 502,619, the digit 6 is in the hundreds place.   ○ True   ○ False

13. Circle the number that makes the statement true.

In 1,888, the 8 in the tens place is

| 10 |
| 100 |
| 1,000 |

times greater than the 8 in the ones place.

In 5,555, the 5 in the hundreds place is

| 10 |
| 100 |
| 1,000 |

times greater than the 5 in the ones place.

14. Find the value of the digit 9 in each number. Write the number in the correct box.

| 694,887 | 429,203 | 97,700 | 109,804 | 194,678 | 19,087 |

9,000	90,000

15. Draw a line from each underlined digit to its value.

A.   2̲68   •   •   2,000

B.   2̲87,900   •   •   20,000

C.   40̲2,961   •   •   200,000

D.   2̲7,041   •   •   2

E.   35,89̲2   •   •   200

Compare and Order Whole Numbers

Getting the Idea

You can compare numbers using place value.

Use these symbols to compare numbers.

The symbol > means **is greater than**.

The symbol < means **is less than**.

The symbol = means **is equal to**.

Example 1

Which symbol makes this sentence true? Write >, <, or =.

65,912 ◯ 65,879

Strategy **Use a place-value chart. Start with the digits in the greatest place.**

Step 1   Write the numbers in a place-value chart.

Ten Thousands	Thousands	,	Hundreds	Tens	Ones
6	5	,	9	1	2
6	5	,	8	7	9

Step 2   Compare the digits in the ten thousands place.

Both numbers have 6 in the ten thousands place.

Compare the next greatest place.

Step 3   Compare the digits in the thousands place.

Both numbers have 5 in the thousands place.

Compare the next greatest place.

Step 4   Compare the digits in the hundreds place.

9 hundreds are greater than 8 hundreds.

So, 65,912 is greater than 65,879.

Step 5   Choose the correct symbol.

> means is greater than.

Solution **65,912 ⊘> 65,879**

Example 2

A city's budget for maintaining its parks for one year was $718,325. The town spent $718,352 that year. Did the city spend more or less than the budgeted amount?

$718,325 ◯ $718,352

Strategy   Line up the numbers on the ones place.
Then compare the digits from left to right.

718,325

718,352

Step 1   Compare the digits in the hundred thousands place.

Since 7 = 7, compare the next greatest place.

Step 2   Compare the digits in the ten thousands place.

Since 1 = 1, compare the next greatest place.

Step 3   Compare the digits in the thousands place.

Since 8 = 8, compare the next greatest place.

Step 4   Compare the digits in the hundreds place.

Since 3 = 3, compare the next greatest place.

Step 5   Compare the digits in the tens place.

Since 2 < 5, then 718,325 < 718,352.

Solution   **The city spent more than the budgeted amount.**

When you order numbers, find the greatest number and the least number.

Compare two numbers at a time, and then order the numbers.

Example 3

Order the following numbers from least to greatest.

527,877   528,371   527,918

Strategy   **Line up the numbers on the ones place.**
                 Start comparing the digits in the greatest place.

                 527,877
                 528,371
                 527,918

Step 1 Compare the digits in the hundred thousands place.
        All the digits are 5s.

Step 2 Compare the digits in the ten thousands place.
        All the digits are 2s.

Step 3 Compare the digits in the thousands place.
        Since 8 > 7, then 528,371 > 527,877 and 527,918.
        528,371 is the greatest number.

Step 4 For the remaining numbers, compare the digits in the hundreds place.
        Since 8 < 9, then 527,877 < 527,918.

Solution   **The order of the numbers from least to greatest is 527,877;**
                 527,918; 528,371.

Coached Example

Which symbol makes this sentence true? Write >, <, or =.

693,041 ◯ 693,582

Use a place-value chart. Write the numbers in the chart.

Hundred Thousands	Ten Thousands	Thousands	,	Hundreds	Tens	Ones

Compare the digits in the hundred thousands place.

Are the digits in the hundred thousands place the same? _____

Compare the digits in the ten thousands place.

Are the digits in the ten thousands place the same? _____

Compare the digits in the thousands place.

Are the digits in the thousands place the same? _____

Compare the digits in the hundreds place.

Are the digits in the hundreds place the same? _____

0 hundreds is _____ than 5 hundreds.

So, 693,041 is _____ than 693,582.

Which symbol should you use? _____

693,041 ◯ 693,582

Lesson Practice • Part 1

Choose the correct answer.

1. Which sentence is true?

   A. 78,412 > 79,421

   B. 67,905 < 76,905

   C. 19,058 > 21,037

   D. 52,915 < 52,836

2. Which symbol makes this sentence true?

   237,352 ◯ 237,452

   A. >

   B. <

   C. =

   D. +

3. Which list orders the numbers from greatest to least?

   A. 67,358   72,185   72,581

   B. 72,581   67,358   72,185

   C. 72,581   72,185   67,358

   D. 72,185   72,581   67,358

4. The table shows the seating capacities of the stadiums of four baseball teams.

   Stadium Seating Capacity

Team	Seating Capacity
Diamondbacks	49,033
Orioles	48,876
Rangers	49,200
Twins	48,678

   Which team's stadium has the greatest seating capacity?

   A. Diamondbacks

   B. Orioles

   C. Rangers

   D. Twins

5. The numbers are ordered from greatest to least. One number is missing.

   582,364   __?__   578,264

   Which number is missing?

   A. 573,095

   B. 575,195

   C. 578,263

   D. 578,493

6. Which number is greater than 128,278 and less than 129,384?

   A. 128,209

   B. 128,728

   C. 129,394

   D. 129,438

7. Which digit makes this sentence true?

$$48,185 < 4\boxed{},242$$

   A. 8

   B. 7

   C. 6

   D. 0

8. The table shows the number of ice cream cones sold at Bennie's Ice Cream Parlor each year for four years.

Ice Cream Cone Sales

Year	Ice Cream Cones
2007	11,296
2008	11,474
2009	12,107
2010	12,044

   A. In which year was the greatest number of ice cream cones sold? Explain how you found your answer.

_____

_____

_____

   B. In which year was the least number of ice cream cones sold? Explain how you found your answer.

_____

_____

_____

Lesson Practice • Part 2

Choose the correct answer.

1. Carlos wrote a 6-digit whole number with 3 as the digit in the greatest place. Sofia wrote a 5-digit whole number with 6 as the digit in the greatest place. Which sentence is true?

   A. Carlos wrote the greater number because any 6-digit whole number is greater than any 5-digit whole number.

   B. Sofia wrote the greater number because her number has the greater digit in the greatest place of each number.

   C. Sofia wrote the greater number because any 5-digit whole number is greater than any 6-digit whole number.

   D. Who wrote the greater number cannot be determined until the other digits in the numbers have been revealed.

2. Which sentence is true?

   A. $375,802 > 378,028$

   B. $417,364 < 417,297$

   C. $462,095 = 462,059$

   D. $503,137 < 503,321$

3. Which digit does **not** make this sentence true?

   $$308,426 > 30\boxed{},512$$

   A. 2   C. 6

   B. 8   D. 7

4. The table shows the populations of four U.S. cities in 2013.

   City Populations

City	Population
Garland, TX	234,566
Glendale, AZ	234,632
Irvine, CA	236,716
Reno, NV	233,294

   Hialeah, FL, has a population of 233,394. How many of the cities in the table have a greater population than Hialeah?

   A. 1   C. 3

   B. 2   D. 4

5. Amber is comparing two 5-digit whole numbers that are not equal. She compares the digits in each number. What is the least number of place values that the greater number must be greater than the lesser number?

   A. 0   C. 2

   B. 1   D. 5

6. Cloud Peak in Wyoming has an elevation of 13,171 feet. Gannett Peak, also in Wyoming, has an elevation of 13,810 feet. Kings Peak in Utah has an elevation greater than Cloud Peak and less than Gannett Peak. Which could be the elevation of Kings Peak?

A. 13,837 feet

B. 13,902 feet

C. 13,146 feet

D. 13,534 feet

7. Eric scored 374,055 points the first time he played a computer game. Christina tried the game next and scored 374,505 points. Which sentence is true?

A. $374{,}055 > 374{,}505$

B. $374{,}055 = 374{,}505$

C. $374{,}505 < 374{,}055$

D. $374{,}505 > 374{,}055$

8. The table shows the areas, in square miles, of four states.

State Land Areas

State	Area (in square miles)
Alabama	52,420
Arkansas	53,179
Louisiana	52,378
North Carolina	53,819

A. Compare the areas of Alabama and Louisiana. Write two sentences comparing the two areas using > and <.

_____

B. Compare the areas of Arkansas and North Carolina. Write two sentences comparing the two areas using > and <.

_____

C. Which of these states has the greatest land area?

_____

9. Circle the digit that makes the sentence true.

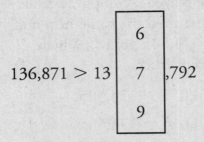

136,871 > 13 [6 / 7 / 9] ,792

10. Circle the symbol that makes the sentence true.

601,561 [> / < / =] 601,651

11. Use symbols from the box to complete the sentences.

46,702 ◯ 36,702

348,679 ◯ 345,981

116,020 ◯ 116,200

67,890 ◯ 67,890

> < =

12. Select True or False for each sentence.

A. 67,513 > 68,531 ◯ True ◯ False

B. 58,815 < 85,815 ◯ True ◯ False

C. 18,902 > 22,903 ◯ True ◯ False

D. 32,501 < 32,851 ◯ True ◯ False

13. Compare each number to 26,708. Write the number in the correct box.

| 26,698 | 25,780 | 28,680 | 62,708 | 27,270 | 16,807 |

Greater than 26,708	Less than 26,708

14. Use numbers from the box so that each group of numbers is ordered from greatest to least.

188,712 _____ 178,702

198,699 _____ 187,690

177,202 _____ 177,020

202,190 _____ 199,100

| 177,200 |
| 189,999 |
| 199,611 |
| 178,710 |

15. Look at each list. Are the numbers in order from least to greatest? Select Yes or No.

A. 46,762   45,689   48,896   ○ Yes   ○ No

B. 89,706   97,607   98,706   ○ Yes   ○ No

C. 65,892   65,982   65,998   ○ Yes   ○ No

D. 28,800   28,080   28,008   ○ Yes   ○ No

Multiplication Facts

Getting the Idea

You can **multiply** to find the total number of equal groups.

Here are the parts in a multiplication sentence.

$$5 \quad \times \quad 4 \quad = \quad 20$$

factor   factor   product

You can use an array to show multiplication. An **array** has the same number of objects in each row.

Example 1

What multiplication sentence does this array show?

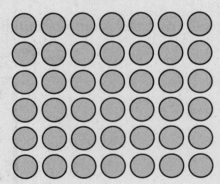

Strategy   **Count the number of rows. Then count the number of counters in each row.**

Step 1   Count the number of rows and the number of counters in each row.

There are 6 rows and 7 counters in each row.

Step 2   Find the number of counters in all.

There are 42 counters in all.

Step 3   Write the number sentence.

The factors are 6 and 7 and the product is 42.

$6 \times 7 = 42$

Solution   **The array shows $6 \times 7 = 42$.**

You can also use repeated addition to solve a multiplication problem. Repeated addition is adding the same number over and over again. Multiplication is a shortcut for repeated addition.

To find 3×4, you can add 4 three times: $4 + 4 + 4 = 12$

Repeated addition is similar to skip counting.

To find 3×4, you can skip count by 4 three times: 4, 8, 12

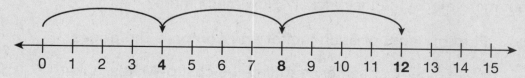

Example 2

Stephanie baked 4 pies for her school's bake sale. She cut each pie into 8 slices. How many slices did Stephanie make in all?

Strategy   **Use repeated addition.**

Step 1   Write the multiplication sentence for the problem.

She made 4 pies. Each pie has 8 slices.

Find 4 groups of 8.

$4 \times 8 = \boxed{}$

Step 2   Write the repeated addition for the multiplication sentence.

4×8 is the same as adding 8 four times.

$4 \times 8 = 8 + 8 + 8 + 8$

Step 3   Find the sum.

$8 + 8 + 8 + 8 = 32$

Solution   **Stephanie made 32 slices of pie in all.**

A **variable** is a letter or symbol used to represent a value that is unknown.

You can use a variable to represent an unknown value in a number sentence.

Example 3

Darren bought a T-shirt for $5. Matt bought a jacket that cost 6 times as much as Darren's T-shirt. Wilmer bought a jacket that cost $22 more than Darren's T-shirt. Who spent more money on their jacket? How much more?

Strategy   **Find the cost of each jacket and compare the prices.**

Step 1   Write a number sentence to find the cost of Matt's jacket.

Let m represent the cost, in dollars, of Matt's jacket.

Matt's jacket cost 6 times as much as $5.

Multiply: $5 \times 6 = m$

Step 2   Find the value of m.

$5 \times 6 = 30$

Matt spent $30 on his jacket.

Step 3   Write a number sentence to find the cost of Wilmer's jacket.

Let w represent the cost, in dollars, of Wilmer's jacket.

Wilmer's jacket cost $22 more than $5.

Add: $5 + 22 = w$

Step 4   Find the value of w.

$5 + 22 = 27$

Wilmer spent $27 on his jacket.

Step 5   Find the difference in costs.

Matt spent $30 and Wilmer spent $27.

$30 - $27 = $3

Solution   **Matt's jacket cost $3 more than Wilmer's jacket.**

You can use a multiplication table to help you learn basic multiplication facts.
The factors are along the first column and the top row.
The box where the row and the column meet is the product.

Columns

×	0	1	2	3	4	5	6	7	8	9	10	11	12
0	0	0	0	0	0	0	0	0	0	0	0	0	0
1	0	1	2	3	4	5	6	7	8	9	10	11	12
2	0	2	4	6	8	10	12	14	16	18	20	22	24
3	0	3	6	9	12	15	18	21	24	27	30	33	36
4	0	4	8	12	16	20	24	28	32	36	40	44	48
5	0	5	10	15	20	25	30	35	40	45	50	55	60
6	0	6	12	18	24	30	36	42	48	54	60	66	72
7	0	7	14	21	28	35	42	49	56	63	70	77	84
8	0	8	16	24	32	40	48	56	64	72	80	88	96
9	0	9	18	27	36	45	54	63	72	81	90	99	108
10	0	10	20	30	40	50	60	70	80	90	100	110	120
11	0	11	22	33	44	55	66	77	88	99	110	121	132
12	0	12	24	36	48	60	72	84	96	108	120	132	144

Rows

Example 4

Naomi is 11 years old. Naomi's great grandmother is 9 times Naomi's age.
How old is Naomi's great grandmother?

Strategy   **Use a multiplication table.**

Step 1   Write the multiplication sentence for the problem.

Naomi is 11. Her great grandmother is 9 times Naomi's age.

Find 11 groups of 9.

$11 \times 9 = n$

Step 2   Look at the 11s column.

Step 3   Find the 9s row.

Step 4   Find the box where the 11s column and the 9s row meet.

The number 99 is in the box.

So, $11 \times 9 = 99$.

Solution   **Naomi's great grandmother is 99 years old.**

Coached Example

Kate gives her dog 3 biscuits each day.
How many biscuits does Kate give her dog in 7 days?

Write the multiplication sentence for the problem.

Find _____ groups of _____ biscuits.

_____ × _____ = ☐

Use the multiplication table.

Find the _____s column.

Find the _____s row.

Find the box where the row and the column meet.

The number _____ is in the box.

So, _____ × _____ = _____.

Kate gives her dog _____ biscuits in 7 days.

Lesson Practice • Part 1

Choose the correct answer.

1. Multiply.

   $7 \times 5 = \boxed{}$

   A. 35

   B. 36

   C. 42

   D. 49

2. Which multiplication sentence does this repeated addition show?

   $3 + 3 + 3 + 3 + 3 + 3$

   A. $3 \times 3 = \boxed{}$

   B. $5 \times 3 = \boxed{}$

   C. $6 \times 3 = \boxed{}$

   D. $7 \times 3 = \boxed{}$

3. Multiply.

   $12 \times 6 = \boxed{}$

   A. 6

   B. 18

   C. 60

   D. 72

4. A small potted plant costs $4. A large potted plant costs 5 times as much. How much does the large potted plant cost?

   A. $9

   B. $16

   C. $20

   D. $25

5. A blue shirt costs $7. A green shirt costs 3 times as much. How much does the green shirt cost?

   A. $10

   B. $21

   C. $24

   D. $28

6. For a park cleanup, there were 6 volunteers on each team. There were 4 teams. How many volunteers helped clean up the park?

   A. 36

   B. 32

   C. 28

   D. 24

7. A dime is worth 10 cents. How much are 7 dimes worth?

    A.   7 cents

    B. 17 cents

    C. 35 cents

    D. 70 cents

8. Which multiplication fact has the greatest product?

    A. $6 \times 9 = \square$

    B. $5 \times 10 = \square$

    C. $4 \times 11 = \square$

    D. $3 \times 12 = \square$

9. A school bus has 12 rows of seats. Each row can fit 4 students.

    A. Write a number sentence that shows how many students can sit on the bus.

    _____

    B. How many students can sit on the bus? Explain how you found your answer.

    _____

    _____

    _____

Lesson Practice • Part 2

Choose the correct answer.

1. David has 8 eggs in his refrigerator. He bought 2 packages of 12 eggs each. How many eggs does David have now?

   A. 20

   B. 22

   C. 28

   D. 32

2. Avery has 4 drama DVDs. She has 5 times as many comedy DVDs as drama DVDs. She has 6 DVDs that are neither drama nor comedy. How many DVDs does Avery have in all?

   A. 20

   B. 26

   C. 30

   D. 34

3. There are 8 carrot sticks in a blue bag. There are 4 times as many carrot sticks in a green bag. Which multiplication sentence can be used to find the total number of carrot sticks, c, in the green bag?

   A. $8 \times 4 = c$

   B. $4 \times c = 8$

   C. $c \times 8 = 4$

   D. $c \times 4 = 8$

4. Which describes the number sentence $3 \times 9 = 27$?

   A. 3 is 9 times as many as 27.

   B. 3 is 9 more than 27.

   C. 27 is 3 times as many as 9.

   D. 27 is 3 more than 9.

5. Janice wears uniform number 6. Lily's uniform number is 4 times as great as Janice's. Addison's uniform number is 20 more than Janice's uniform number. Which sentence about the uniform numbers is true?

   A. Lily's number is 4 greater than Addison's.

   B. Janice has the greatest number.

   C. Lily and Addison have the same number.

   D. Addison's number is 2 greater than Lily's.

6. Katrina biked 5 miles on Monday. She biked 3 times as many miles on Tuesday. How far did she bike in the two days?

   A. 30 miles   C. 15 miles

   B. 20 miles   D. 13 miles

7. Each package contains 6 table tennis balls. Daniel bought 3 packages of table tennis balls. He already had 9 table tennis balls. Which equation represents how to find b, the total number of table tennis balls that Daniel has?

A. $6 + 3 + 9 = b$

B. $6 \times 3 + 9 = b$

C. $6 + 3 \times 9 = b$

D. $6 \times 3 \times 9 = b$

8. In a game, Jaxon scored 4 times as many points as Colt. Colt scored 7 points. Which number sentence can **not** be used to find the number of points Jaxon scored?

A. $4 \times 7 = \square$

B. $7 + 7 + 7 + 7 = \square$

C. $7 + 4 + 7 + 4 = \square$

D. $7 \times 4 = \square$

9. Students were asked to name their favorite subject. Eight students chose science. Three times as many students chose reading as science. The number of students that chose reading is 6 more than the number of students that chose math.

A. How many students chose math?

_____

B. Explain how you found your answer to Part A.

_____

_____

10. Find each product. Write the multiplication sentence in the correct box.

| $9 \times 4 = \square$ | $6 \times 6 = \square$ | $3 \times 8 = \square$ |

| $4 \times 6 = \square$ | $2 \times 12 = \square$ | $3 \times 12 = \square$ |

24	36

11. Circle the unknown factor that makes the sentence true.

$$7 \times \begin{array}{|c|} \hline 6 \\ 7 \\ 9 \\ \hline \end{array} = 63$$

12. Select True or False for each statement.

A. 5×8 is the same as $8 + 8 + 8 + 8 + 8$.   ○ True ○ False

B. 3×3 is the same as $3 + 3 + 3$.   ○ True ○ False

C. 6×7 is the same as $7 + 7 + 7 + 7 + 7 + 7 + 7$.   ○ True ○ False

D. 4×2 is the same as $2 + 2 + 2$.   ○ True ○ False

E. 6×4 is the same as $4 + 4 + 4 + 4 + 4 + 4$.   ○ True ○ False

13. Draw a line from each multiplication sentence to the number line that shows its product.

A. $2 \times 3 = \boxed{}$ •   •

B. $4 \times 2 = \boxed{}$ •   •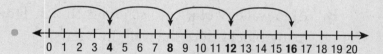

C. $1 \times 6 = \boxed{}$ •   •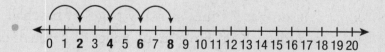

D. $3 \times 5 = \boxed{}$ •   •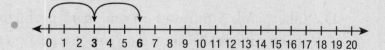

E. $4 \times 4 = \boxed{}$ •   •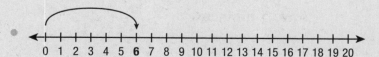

14. Look at each multiplication sentence. Is the product correct? Select Yes or No.

A. $4 \times 5 = 20$ ◯ Yes   ◯ No

B. $8 \times 11 = 88$ ◯ Yes   ◯ No

C. $8 \times 7 = 48$ ◯ Yes   ◯ No

D. $12 \times 4 = 48$ ◯ Yes   ◯ No

E. $5 \times 9 = 54$ ◯ Yes   ◯ No

15. Which multiplication fact has a product greater than 35? Circle all that apply.

A. $6 \times 6 = \square$

B. $8 \times 9 = \square$

C. $9 \times 3 = \square$

D. $5 \times 6 = \square$

E. $4 \times 9 = \square$

F. $7 \times 7 = \square$

16. Draw a line from each word problem to its solution.

A. Maria is 9 years old. Her mother is 4 times Maria's age. How old is Maria's mother?   •   • 56

B. Akio walks 9 blocks to school each day. How many blocks does she walk in 6 days?   •   • 36

C. Ken has 8 pages of baseball cards in his album. Jason has 7 times as many pages of baseball cards as Ken. How many pages of baseball cards does Jason have?   •   • 25

D. Lila spends 5 minutes on one math problem. If she spends the same amount of time on each problem, how many minutes will it take Lila to solve 5 problems?   •   • 54

Multiply Greater Numbers

Getting the Idea

You can multiply greater numbers by using basic facts and regrouping. Sometimes using models can help you multiply.

Example 1

Multiply.

$3 \times 24 = \square$

Strategy   **Use an array model.**

Step 1   Use an array.

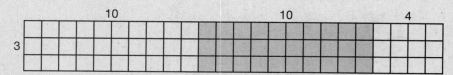

Step 2   Decompose 3×24 into the sum of lesser numbers.

$3 \times 24 = (3 \times 10) + (3 \times 10) + (3 \times 4)$

Step 3   Find the partial products and then add.

$3 \times 24 = 30 + 30 + 12$

$3 \times 24 = 72$

Solution $3 \times 24 = 72$

Example 2

Washington Elementary School has 4 sections of seats in the cafeteria. Each section has 48 seats. How many seats in all are in the cafeteria?

Strategy   **Multiply by the ones. Then multiply by the tens.**

Step 1   Write a multiplication sentence for the problem.

The cafeteria has 4 sections of seats.

There are 48 seats in each section.

There are n seats in all.

$4 \times 48 = n$

Step 2 Write the problem in vertical form.

$$\begin{array}{r} 48 \\ \times\ 4 \\ \hline \end{array}$$

Step 3 Multiply the ones: $4 \times 8 = 32$.

Write the 2 and regroup the 3 tens.

$$\begin{array}{r} 3 \\ 48 \\ \times\ 4 \\ \hline 2 \end{array}$$

Step 4 Multiply the tens: $4 \times 4 = 16$.

Add the regrouped tens: $16 + 3 = 19$.

Write the 19.

$$\begin{array}{r} 3 \\ 48 \\ \times\ 4 \\ \hline 192 \end{array}$$

Solution **There are 192 seats in all in the cafeteria.**

Example 3

Tasha bought 7 rolls of paper streamers for the school dance. Each roll is 328 inches long. How many inches of paper streamers did Tasha buy in all?

Strategy **Multiply each place by 7, regrouping when necessary.**

Step 1 Write the problem vertically.

$$\begin{array}{r} 328 \\ \times\ \ 7 \\ \hline \end{array}$$

Step 2 Multiply the ones.

$7 \times 8 = 56$

Write the 6 and regroup 5 tens.

$$\begin{array}{r} 5 \\ 328 \\ \times\ \ 7 \\ \hline 6 \end{array}$$

Step 3 Multiply the tens and add the regrouped tens.

$7 \times 2 = 14$

$14 + 5 = 19$

Write the 9 and regroup 1 hundred.

$$\begin{array}{r} 15 \\ 328 \\ \times \quad 7 \\ \hline 96 \end{array}$$

Step 4 Multiply the hundreds and add the regrouped hundreds.

$7 \times 3 = 21$

$21 + 1 = 22$

Write the 22 hundreds.

$$\begin{array}{r} 15 \\ 328 \\ \times \quad 7 \\ \hline 2{,}296 \end{array}$$

Solution   **Tasha bought 2,296 inches of paper streamers.**

Example 4

Mrs. Rivera earned $1,635 each week for 4 weeks. How much money did she earn in all?

Strategy   **Multiply each place by 4, regrouping when necessary.**

Step 1 Write the multiplication sentence for the problem.

She earned $1,635 each week for 4 weeks.
Use n for the unknown product.

$1{,}635 \times 4 = n$

Step 2 Write the problem vertically.

$$\begin{array}{r} 1{,}635 \\ \times \quad 4 \\ \hline \end{array}$$

Step 3   Multiply the ones.

$4 \times 5 = 20$

Write the 0 and regroup 2 tens.

$$
\begin{array}{r}
2 \\
1,635 \\
\times \quad 4 \\
\hline
0
\end{array}
$$

Step 4   Multiply the tens and add the regrouped tens.

$4 \times 3 = 12$

$12 + 2 = 14$

Write the 4 and regroup 1 hundred.

$$
\begin{array}{r}
1\,2 \\
1,635 \\
\times \quad 4 \\
\hline
40
\end{array}
$$

Step 5   Multiply the hundreds and add the regrouped hundreds.

$4 \times 6 = 24$

$24 + 1 = 25$

Write the 5 hundreds and regroup 2 thousands.

$$
\begin{array}{r}
2\,1\,2 \\
1,635 \\
\times \quad 4 \\
\hline
540
\end{array}
$$

Step 6   Multiply the thousands and add the regrouped thousands.

$4 \times 1 = 4$

$4 + 2 = 6$

Write the 6 thousands.

$$
\begin{array}{r}
2\,1\,2 \\
1,635 \\
\times \quad 4 \\
\hline
6,540
\end{array}
$$

Solution   **Mrs. Rivera earned $6,540 in all.**

When multiplying two-digit numbers, first multiply a factor by the ones digit of the other factor. Then multiply the same factor by the tens digit of the other factor. Finally, add the partial products to find the final product.

Example 5
Multiply.

$$45 \times 28 = \boxed{}$$

Strategy   **Multiply each place value. Regroup when necessary.**

Step 1   Write the problem in vertical form.

$$\begin{array}{r} 45 \\ \times\ 28 \\ \hline \end{array}$$

Step 2   Multiply 45 by the ones digit of 28: 8 ones × 45.

Regroup.

$$\begin{array}{r} 4 \\ 45 \\ \times\ 28 \\ \hline 360 \end{array}$$ ← partial product

Step 3   Multiply 45 by the tens digit of 28: 2 tens × 45.

Write a 0 in the ones place because you are multiplying the tens.

Regroup.

$$\begin{array}{r} 1 \\ 45 \\ \times\ 28 \\ \hline 360 \\ 900 \end{array}$$ ← partial product

Step 4   Add the partial products.

$$\begin{array}{r} 45 \\ \times\ 28 \\ \hline 360 \\ +\ 900 \\ \hline 1{,}260 \end{array}$$

Solution   **45 × 28 = 1,260**

Coached Example

A student ticket to a theme park costs $34. A class of 26 fourth-grade students went to the theme park. How much did the tickets for the students cost in all?

Write the multiplication sentence for the problem.

A student ticket costs $ _____.

A class of _____ students went to the park.

Find _____ × _____ = ☐ .

Write the problem in vertical form.

Multiply 34 by the _____ digit of 26.

_____ ones × 34. Regroup.

What is the first partial product? _____

Multiply 34 by the _____ digit of 26.

_____ tens × 34. Regroup.

What is the second partial product? _____

Add the two partial products.

_____ + _____ = _____

The tickets for the students cost $_____ in all.

Lesson Practice • Part 1

Choose the correct answer.

1. Multiply.

    48
    × 8

    A. 384

    B. 364

    C. 352

    D. 324

2. Multiply.

    9 × 37 = ☐

    A. 323

    B. 333

    C. 343

    D. 433

3. A tour group of 68 people has an overnight stay at a hotel. Each person will receive a 3-pancake breakfast. How many pancakes will the hotel serve to the tour group?

    A. 184

    B. 194

    C. 204

    D. 214

4. Hiro brushes his teeth 3 times each day. How many times will he brush his teeth in a month with 31 days?

    A. 11

    B. 33

    C. 93

    D. 930

5. Multiply.

    74
    × 11

    A. 85

    B. 747

    C. 814

    D. 7,474

6. Multiply.

    4,962 × 6 = ☐

    A. 27,401

    B. 27,410

    C. 29,766

    D. 29,772

7. An auditorium has 68 rows of seats. There are 56 seats in each row. How many seats are there in all?

   A. 3,808

   B. 3,768

   C. 3,408

   D. 3,048

8. A baseball cap and T-shirt set costs $9. What will be the total cost for 1,086 sets?

   A. $8,688

   B. $9,765

   C. $9,774

   D. $10,317

9. A pie company made 57 apple pies and 38 cherry pies each day for 14 days.

   A. How many apple pies does the company make in all? Show your work.

   B. How many cherry pies does the company make in all? Show your work.

Lesson Practice • Part 2

Choose the correct answer.

1. Multiply: 15×9

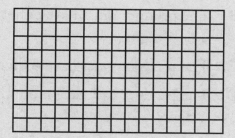

- **A.** 95
- **B.** 125
- **C.** 135
- **D.** 149

2. Each model of the most popular laptop computer at Laps R Tops sells for $1,279. There were 6 such computers that sold yesterday. Another computer sold for $729. How much money was earned in computer sales yesterday?

- **A.** $2,008
- **B.** $5,653
- **C.** $7,674
- **D.** $8,403

3. Multiply: 18×13

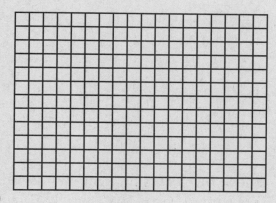

- **A.** 234
- **B.** 224
- **C.** 214
- **D.** 204

4. Mr. Vasquez has a CD cabinet with 16 shelves. Each shelf holds 54 CDs. What is the greatest number of CDs that Mr. Vasquez can fit in the cabinet?

- **A.** 358
- **B.** 844
- **C.** 854
- **D.** 864

5. Ike's Bike Shop sold 8 mountain bikes yesterday. Each mountain bike sold for $475, except one that was $350. How much money was earned in bike sales yesterday?

A. $3,275

B. $3,450

C. $3,675

D. $4,150

6. Riley is going to multiply two 2-digit whole numbers. Which sentence is true?

A. The product can have less than 3 digits.

B. The product must have either 3 or 4 digits.

C. The product must have 4 digits.

D. The product can have more than 4 digits.

7. Block Bus Tours brought 36 busloads of people to a national park. Tickets to enter the national park cost $8 each. Each bus carried 64 passengers.

A. How many people did Block Bus Tours transport to the national park? Show your work.

_____

B. How much money did the passengers spend on park tickets? Show your work.

_____

8. Select True or False for each multiplication sentence.

A. $7 \times 36 = 252$ ○ True   ○ False

B. $78 \times 6 = 428$ ○ True   ○ False

C. $54 \times 9 = 486$ ○ True   ○ False

D. $5 \times 25 = 225$ ○ True   ○ False

E. $3 \times 91 = 273$ ○ True   ○ False

9. Draw a line from each multiplication sentence to the array model that shows its product.

A. $3 \times 15 = \square$ •

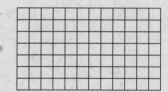

B. $4 \times 21 = \square$ •

C. $7 \times 12 = \square$ •

D. $6 \times 23 = \square$ •

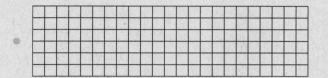

10. Circle the digit that makes the multiplication sentence true.

$$25 \times 77 = 1, \boxed{\begin{array}{c} 7 \\ 8 \\ 9 \end{array}} 25$$

11. Is the number a partial product for the problem 85×62? Select Yes or No.

A.   170   ◯ Yes   ◯ No
B.   160   ◯ Yes   ◯ No
C.   500   ◯ Yes   ◯ No
D. 5,100   ◯ Yes   ◯ No

12. Multiply to check each product. Write the sentence in the correct box.

$6 \times 3{,}245 = 18{,}270$	$74 \times 16 = 1{,}164$	$15 \times 52 = 780$
$8 \times 758 = 6{,}064$	$4 \times 129 = 486$	$4 \times 1{,}654 = 6{,}616$

Correct Product	Incorrect Product

13. Which problem has an answer of 2,288? Circle all that apply.

A. Rama runs 14 miles each week. How many miles does Rama run in 13 weeks?

B. Liang's mother makes 286 muffins for her bakery each day. How many muffins does she make in 8 days?

C. There are 88 tables in the school lunchroom. Each table has 26 students. How many students are in the school lunchroom?

D. Trinh rides his bike 96 miles a month. How many miles does Trinh ride in one year (12 months)?

E. Tad raises worms for composting. He places the worms into kits of 143 worms each. How many worms are in 16 kits?

Multiplication Properties

Getting the Idea

There are some mathematical properties that can help make multiplication easier for you. Properties are rules.

> **Commutative Property of Multiplication**
> The order of the factors can be changed.
> The product does not change.
>
> $$12 \times 18 = 18 \times 12$$
> $$216 = 216$$

Example 1

Which number makes this number sentence true?

$$13 \times \boxed{} = 23 \times 13$$

Strategy   **Use the commutative property of multiplication.**

Step 1   Look at the number sentence.

The left side of the equal sign shows $13 \times \boxed{}$.

The right side of the equal sign shows 23×13.

The equal sign means that they have the same product.

Step 2   Think about the commutative property of multiplication.

The order of the factors does not change the product.

$$13 \times 23 = 23 \times 13$$

Solution   **The number 23 makes the number sentence true.**

> ## Multiplicative Identity Property of 1
> When you multiply any number by 1, the product is that number.
>
> $$1 \times 57 = 57$$

Example 2

Which number makes this number sentence true?

$\boxed{} \times 1 = 82$

Strategy **Use the multiplicative identity property of 1.**

Step 1 Look at the number sentence.

The left side of the equal sign shows $\boxed{} \times 1$.

The right side of the equal sign shows 82.

Step 2 Use the multiplicative identity property of 1.

Any number multiplied by 1 is that number.

Since one of the factors is 1, the other factor is 82.

$82 \times 1 = 82$

Solution **The number 82 makes the number sentence true.**

> **Associative Property of Multiplication**
> Factors can be grouped in different ways.
> The product will be the same.
>
> $$(12 \times 7) \times 14 = 12 \times (7 \times 14)$$
>
> $$84 \times 14 = 12 \times 98$$
>
> $$1{,}176 = 1{,}176$$

Example 3

Multiply.

$$8 \times (12 \times 10) = \boxed{}$$

Strategy **Use the associative property of multiplication.**

Step 1   Think about the associative property of multiplication.

  The grouping of the factors does not change the product.

Step 2   Regroup the factors.

  $$8 \times (12 \times 10) = (8 \times 12) \times 10$$

Step 3   Use mental math to multiply.

  Multiply inside the parentheses. Then find the final product.

  $$(8 \times 12) \times 10 = \boxed{}$$

  $$96 \times 10 = 960$$

Solution $8 \times (12 \times 10) = 960$

Coached Example

A bag has 5 packets of jellybeans. Each packet has 14 jellybeans. Joey bought 2 bags. How many jellybeans did Joey buy in all?

$5 \times 14 \times 2 = \boxed{}$

Use the _____ property of multiplication to change the order of the factors.

_____ $\times$ _____ $\times$ _____ $= \boxed{}$

Use the _____ property of multiplication to group the factors.

(_____ $\times$ _____) $\times$ _____ $= \boxed{}$

Multiply inside the parentheses.

(_____) $\times$ _____ $= \boxed{}$

Multiply that factor and the other factor.

_____ $\times$ _____ $=$ _____

So, $5 \times 14 \times 2 =$ _____

Joey bought _____ jellybeans in all.

Lesson Practice • Part 1

Choose the correct answer.

1. What is the missing number in this sentence?

$$31 \times 43 = 43 \times \square$$

 A. 1
 B. 12
 C. 31
 D. 43

2. Which correctly shows the commutative property of multiplication?

 A. $85 \times 0 = 0$
 B. $7 \times 13 = 91$
 C. $8 \times 17 = 17 \times 8$
 D. $1 \times 39 = 39$

3. What is the missing number in this sentence?

$$68 \times \square = 68$$

 A. 0
 B. 1
 C. 67
 D. 68

4. Which correctly shows the multiplicative identity property of 1?

 A. $27 \times 3 = 3 \times 27$
 B. $29 \times 1 = 29$
 C. $0 \times 18 = 0$
 D. $2 \times (35 \times 4) = (2 \times 35) \times 4$

5. Which number sentence is true?

 A. $32 \times 4 = 4 \times 32$
 B. $32 \times 4 = 4 + 32$
 C. $32 \times 4 = 324$
 D. $32 \times 4 = 32 \div 4$

6. What is the missing number in this sentence?

$$12 \times (5 \times 13) = (\square \times 5) \times 13$$

 A. 5
 B. 7
 C. 12
 D. 13

7. Multiply.

$$10 \times (9 \times 21) = \boxed{}$$

   A. 90

   B. 189

   C. 210

   D. 1,890

8. Multiply.

$$(18 \times 5) \times 12 = \boxed{}$$

   A. 60

   B. 90

   C. 216

   D. 1,080

9. A bus has 12 rows of seats. Each row can fit 6 passengers.

Mr. Kane ordered 5 buses to take people to a baseball game.

$$12 \times 6 \times 5 = \boxed{}$$

   A. Use the commutative property of multiplication to change the order of the factors.

      _____

   B. Use the associative property of multiplication to group the factors.

      _____

   C. How many passengers in all can Mr. Kane take to the baseball game?

      _____

Lesson Practice • Part 2

Choose the correct answer.

1. What is the missing number in this sentence?

$$27 \times 6 \times \boxed{} = 162$$

   A. 0

   B. 1

   C. 6

   D. 27

2. Which correctly shows the associative property of multiplication?

   A. $15 \times (6 \times 12) = (15 \times 6) \times 12$

   B. $15 \times (6 \times 12) = 15 \times (12 \times 6)$

   C. $15 \times 6 \times 12 = 15 \times 6 \times 12 \times 1$

   D. $15 \times 6 \times 12 = 12 \times 6 \times 15$

3. Multiply: $7 \times 4 \times 5$

   A. 55

   B. 63

   C. 108

   D. 140

4. What is the missing number in this sentence?

$$(28 \times 6) \times 10 = 28 \times (\boxed{} \times 10)$$

   A. 6   **C.** 28

   B. 10   **D.** 168

5. The Zephyrs and Pilgrims are tied after the second half. The Zephyrs scored 32 points in the first half and 27 points in the second half. The Pilgrims scored 27 points in the first half. How many points did the Pilgrims score in the second half?

   A. 5   **C.** 32

   B. 27   **D.** 59

6. Which describes the relationship between a factor and the product when multiplying by 1?

   A. The product is 1 less than the factor.

   B. The product is 1 more than the factor.

   C. The product is equal to the factor.

   D. The product is double the factor.

7. Each box contains 6 packs of flavor ice. Each pack contains 24 individual flavor ices. Mrs. Mitchell bought 5 boxes. How many individual flavor ices did Mrs. Mitchell buy?

    A. 720

    B. 604

    C. 174

    D. 150

8. Which correctly shows the commutative property of multiplication?

    A. $48 \times (5 \times 7) = (48 \times 5) \times 7$

    B. $48 \times (5 \times 7) = 48 \times (7 \times 5)$

    C. $48 \times (5 \times 7) = 48 \times 1 \times 5 \times 7$

    D. $48 \times (5 \times 7) = 48 \times 35$

9. Mrs. Mooney wrote the problem $5 \times 13 \times 20$ on the board.

    A. Rewrite the problem using the commutative property of multiplication.

    _____

    B. Using your answer to Part A, rewrite the problem using the associative property of multiplication.

    _____

    C. Find the product. Show your work.

    _____

    _____

    _____

10. Which number sentence shows the commutative property of multiplication? Circle all that apply.

    A. $18 \times 6 = 6 \times 18$

    B. $8 \times 19 = 19 \times 8$

    C. $11 \times 5 = 55$

    D. $56 \times 1 = 56$

    E. $4 \times 91 = 91 \times 4$

    F. $0 \times 23 = 0$

11. Circle the factor that makes the sentence true.

$$14 \times \boxed{\begin{array}{c} 14 \\ 23 \\ 32 \end{array}} = 32 \times 14$$

12. Select True or False for each statement.

    A. 15×18 is equal to 18×15.   ○ True ○ False

    B. 33×13 is equal to 13×33.   ○ True ○ False

    C. 16×7 is equal to $7 + 16$.   ○ True ○ False

    D. 56×12 is equal to $56 \div 12$.   ○ True ○ False

    E. 13×1 is equal to 1×13.   ○ True ○ False

13. Draw a line from each number sentence to the missing number that makes it true.

    A. $23 \times 1 = \boxed{}$ •   • 1

    B. $(32 \times 23) \times 13 = 32 \times (23 \times \boxed{})$ •   • 13

    C. $10 \times \boxed{} = 31 \times 10$ •   • 23

    D. $32 \times 1 = \boxed{} \times 32$ •   • 31

    E. $7 \times (32 \times 10) = (7 \times 32) \times \boxed{}$ •   • 10

14. Circle the factor that makes the sentence true.

$$11 \times (4 \times 18) = \left(\boxed{\begin{array}{c} 1 \\ 4 \\ 11 \\ 18 \end{array}} \times 4\right) \times 18$$

15. Is the number sentence true? Select Yes or No.

A. $10 \times (8 \times 12) = (10 \times 8) \times 12$ ○ Yes ○ No

B. $561 \times 1 = 561$ ○ Yes ○ No

C. $(16 \times 5) \times 12 = 16 \times (5 + 12)$ ○ Yes ○ No

D. $45 \times 17 = 17 \times 45$ ○ Yes ○ No

E. $5 \times (19 \times 3) = (5 \times 19) + 3$ ○ Yes ○ No

16. Which number sentence can be used to solve the problem? Circle all that apply.

Each page in a photo album holds 3 photos. There are 16 pages in an album. Max needs 8 albums for his photo collection. If all the pages of the albums are filled, how many photos are in Max's collection?

A. $(16 \times 3) + 8 = \boxed{}$

B. $16 \times 3 \times 8 = \boxed{}$

C. $(16 \times 3) \times 8 = \boxed{}$

D. $16 + 8 \times 3 = \boxed{}$

E. $3 \times (16 \times 8) = \boxed{}$

Distributive Property of Multiplication

Getting the Idea

The distributive property of multiplication can help you multiply numbers using mental math. The property uses the expanded form of numbers.

Area models can help you understand the distributive property of multiplication.

Distributive Property of Multiplication

When you multiply a number by a sum, you can multiply the number by each addend of the sum and then add the products.

$$5 \times 14$$

$$5 \times (10 + 4)$$

$$(5 \times 10) + (5 \times 4)$$

$$50 \quad + \quad 20 = 70$$

$$5 \times 14 = 70$$

$$5 \times 10 = 50 \qquad 5 \times 4 = 20$$

Example 1

Fred has 3 shelves of books. Each shelf has 18 books. How many books in all are on the shelves?

Strategy   **Use the distributive property of multiplication and mental math.**

Step 1   Write the multiplication sentence for the problem.

There are 3 shelves. There are 18 books on each shelf.
There are x books in all.

$3 \times 18 = x$

Step 2 Express 18 in expanded form.

$$18 = 10 + 8$$

Step 3 Rewrite the sentence with 18 in expanded form.

$$3 \times 18 = 3 \times (10 + 8)$$

Step 4 Distribute the 3 to each addend.

$$3 \times (10 + 8) = (3 \times 10) + (3 \times 8)$$

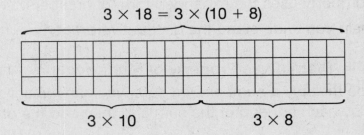

$$3 \times 18 = 3 \times (10 + 8)$$

$$3 \times 10 \qquad 3 \times 8$$

Step 5 Find each product.

$$(3 \times 10) + (3 \times 8) = x$$
$$30 \quad + \quad 24 \quad = x$$

Step 6 Add the products.

$$30 + 24 = 54$$

Solution **There are 54 books in all on the shelves.**

Example 2

Multiply.

$$12 \times 34 = \boxed{}$$

Strategy **Use the distributive property and mental math.**

Step 1 Express 34 in expanded form.

$$34 = 30 + 4$$

Step 2 Rewrite the sentence with 34 in expanded form.

$$12 \times 34 = 12 \times (30 + 4)$$

Step 3 Distribute the 12 to each addend.

$$12 \times (30 + 4) = (12 \times 30) + (12 \times 4)$$

Step 4   Find each product.

$(12 \times 30) + (12 \times 4) = \boxed{}$

$360 \quad + \quad 48 \quad = \boxed{}$

Step 5   Add the products.

$360 + 48 = 408$

Solution $12 \times 34 = 408$

Example 3

A Blu-Ray DVD costs $25. Ms. Ely ordered 15 Blu-Ray DVDs. How much did Ms. Ely spend in all on the DVDs?

Strategy   **Use an area model.**

Step 1   Make an area model.

Decompose 25 into $20 + 5$.

Decompose 15 into $10 + 5$.

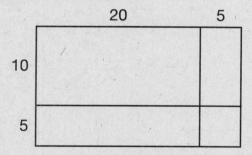

Step 2   Write multiplication sentences and find the product for each box.

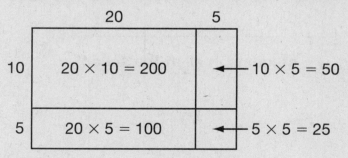

Step 3   Add the partial products

$200 + 50 + 100 + 25 = 375$

Solution   **Ms. Ely spent $375 in all.**

Coached Example

Monroe Elementary School has 32 classrooms. Each classroom has 24 students. How many students in all are at the school?

Write the multiplication sentence for the problem.

There are _____ classrooms.

There are _____ students in each class.

There are n students in all.

_____ × _____ = _____

Use the distributive property of multiplication.

Express 24 in expanded form.

24 = _____ + _____

Rewrite the sentence with 24 in expanded form.

$32 \times 24 = 32 \times$ (_____ + _____)

Distribute 32 to each addend.

$32 \times$ (_____ + _____) = (32 × _____) + (32 × _____)

Find each product.

(32 × _____) + (32 × _____) = n

_____ + _____ = n

Add the products.

_____ + _____ = _____

There are _____ students in all at the school.

Lesson Practice • Part 1

Choose the correct answer.

1. Which is true?

   A. $3 \times 78 = (3 \times 70) \times (3 \times 8)$

   B. $3 \times 78 = (3 \times 70) + (3 \times 8)$

   C. $3 \times 78 = (3 + 70) \times (3 + 8)$

   D. $3 \times 78 = (3 + 70) + (3 + 8)$

2. Which is true?

   A. $64 \times 14 = (64 \times 10) \times (64 \times 4)$

   B. $64 \times 14 = (64 \times 10) + (64 \times 4)$

   C. $64 \times 14 = (64 + 10) \times (64 + 4)$

   D. $64 \times 14 = (64 + 10) + (64 + 4)$

3. Which is true?

   A. $52 \times 23 = (52 \times 20) + (52 \times 3)$

   B. $52 \times 23 = (50 \times 20) + (2 \times 3)$

   C. $52 \times 23 = (52 \times 20) + (2 \times 3)$

   D. $52 \times 23 = (52 \times 20) \times (52 \times 3)$

4. Multiply.

   $16 \times 24 = \boxed{}$

   A. 96

   B. 324

   C. 326

   D. 384

5. Multiply.

   $23 \times 23 = \boxed{}$

   A. 115

   B. 246

   C. 529

   D. 1,024

6. A club charges $26 for a one-year membership. The club has 62 members. How much does the club collect in membership fees each year?

   A. $208

   B. $1,560

   C. $1,612

   D. $2,408

7. Rosa bought 15 cases of water for a school fair. Each case has 24 bottles. How many bottles of water did Rosa buy?

    A. 200

    B. 260

    C. 300

    D. 360

8. A manatee's heart normally beats about 55 times a minute. How many times does a manatee's heart beat in 60 minutes?

    A. 33,000

    B. 3,300

    C. 3,000

    D. 330

9. The art teacher bought 32 boxes of crayons. Each box has 64 crayons.

    A. Write a number sentence to find how many crayons the art teacher bought in all.

    _____

    B. Use the distributive property of multiplication to find the total number of crayons. Show your work.

    _____

    _____

    _____

Lesson Practice • Part 2

Choose the correct answer.

1. Use the area model to find the product.

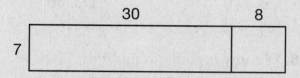

   A. 216

   B. 256

   C. 266

   D. 276

2. Which number makes this sentence true?

   $$54 \times 9 = (50 \times 9) + (\boxed{} \times 9)$$

   A. 4

   B. 9

   C. 50

   D. 54

3. Which correctly shows the distributive property?

   A. $42 \times 26 = (40 \times 20) + (2 \times 6)$

   B. $42 \times 26 = (42 \times 20) + (42 \times 6)$

   C. $42 \times 26 = (40 \times 20) + (42 \times 6)$

   D. $42 \times 26 = (40 \times 26) + (42 \times 26)$

4. Use the area model to find the product.

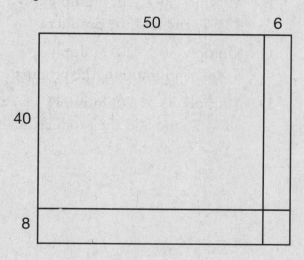

   A. 2,688

   B. 2,648

   C. 2,488

   D. 2,448

5. Tracy is using an area model to multiply 72×63. Which is not one of the correct partial products that she will find by using the area model?

   A. 6

   B. 120

   C. 240

   D. 4,200

6. Which explains one way to find the product of 38 × 27?

A. Multiply 38 × 20, multiply 38 × 7, and multiply the products.

B. Multiply 30 × 20, multiply 8 × 7, and add the products.

C. Multiply 30 × 20, multiply 8 × 7, and multiply the products.

D. Multiply 38 × 20, multiply 38 × 7, and add the products.

7. Which number makes this sentence true?

$$77 \times 86 = (70 \times 86) + (\boxed{} \times 86)$$

A. 7   C. 74

B. 70   D. 86

8. Jimmy is going to multiply 52 × 34. Which is **not** a way that he can use the distributive property to find the product?

A. 52 × 34 = (50 × 34) + (2 × 34)

B. 52 × 34 = (52 × 30) + (52 × 4)

C. 52 × 34 = (50 × 30) + (50 × 4) + (2 × 30) + (2 × 4)

D. 52 × 34 = (52 × 30) + (2 × 34)

9. There are 28 rows of seats on the bottom floor of an auditorium. Each row on the bottom floor contains 46 seats. There are 16 rows of seats on the top floor. Each row on the top floor contains 32 seats.

A. How many seats are on the first floor? Show your work.

_____

_____

B. How many seats are on the second floor? Show your work.

_____

_____

10. Select True or False for each number sentence.

    A. $48 \times 13 = (48 \times 10) \times (48 \times 3)$ ◯ True   ◯ False

    B. $48 \times 13 = (48 \times 10) + (48 \times 3)$ ◯ True   ◯ False

    C. $48 \times 13 = (48 + 10) \times (48 + 3)$ ◯ True   ◯ False

    D. $13 \times 48 = (13 \times 40) + (13 \times 8)$ ◯ True   ◯ False

    E. $13 \times 48 = (13 \times 40) \times (13 \times 8)$ ◯ True   ◯ False

11. Draw a line from each number sentence to the multiplication problem that can be used to solve it.

    A. $5 \times 15 = \square$ •   • $(12 \times 10) + (12 \times 6)$

    B. $15 \times 25 = \square$ •   • $(6 \times 10) + (6 \times 2)$

    C. $12 \times 16 = \square$ •   • $(15 \times 20) + (15 \times 5)$

    D. $6 \times 12 = \square$ •   • $(5 \times 10) + (5 \times 5)$

12. Circle the numbers that make the sentence true.

$$26 \times 62 = (26 \times \boxed{\begin{array}{c} 20 \\ 26 \\ 60 \\ 62 \end{array}}) + (\boxed{\begin{array}{c} 20 \\ 26 \\ 60 \\ 62 \end{array}} \times 2)$$

13. Select True or False for each number sentence.

    A. $3 \times 45 = (3 \times 40) + (3 \times 5)$ ◯ True   ◯ False

    B. $46 \times 14 = (46 \times 10) + (46 \times 4)$ ◯ True   ◯ False

    C. $5 \times 67 = (5 + 60) + (5 + 7)$ ◯ True   ◯ False

    D. $63 \times 22 = (63 \times 20) \times (63 \times 2)$ ◯ True   ◯ False

    E. $33 \times 33 = (33 \times 30) + (33 \times 3)$ ◯ True   ◯ False

    F. $71 \times 34 = (71 \times 30) + (3 \times 4)$ ◯ True   ◯ False

14. Use numbers from the box to complete the sentences.

$34 \times 43 = (34 \times \underline{\hspace{1cm}}) + (34 \times 3)$

$18 \times 18 = (18 \times \underline{\hspace{1cm}}) + (18 \times \underline{\hspace{1cm}})$

$43 \times 18 = (\underline{\hspace{1cm}} \times 10) + (43 \times \underline{\hspace{1cm}})$

4
8
10
40
43

15. Which number sentence can be used to solve the problem? Circle all that apply.

Mina bought 24 packs of napkins for the school party. There were 35 napkins in each pack. How many napkins did Mina buy?

A. $(24 \times 3) + (24 \times 5) = \square$

B. $24 \times 35 = \square$

C. $(24 \times 30) \times (24 \times 5) = \square$

D. $24 \times (30 + 5) = \square$

E. $(24 \times 30) + (24 \times 5) = \square$

F. $(24 + 30) \times (24 + 5) = \square$

16. Circle the operation sign that makes the sentence true.

$11 \times 88 = (11 \times 80) \begin{array}{c} + \\ - \\ \times \\ \div \end{array} (11 \times 8)$

Division Facts

Getting the Idea

You can **divide** to find the number of equal groups or the number in each group. Here are the parts in a division sentence.

54 ÷ 9 = 6

dividend   **divisor**   **quotient**

You can use an array to show division.

Example 1

Michael bagged 32 cans of soup in 4 bags. Each bag has the same number of cans. How many cans are in each bag?

Strategy   **Make an array.**

Step 1   Write the division sentence for the problem.

There are 32 cans in all. There are 4 bags.
There are n cans in each bag.

$32 \div 4 = n$

Step 2   Use 32 counters. Put the counters in 4 equal rows.

Step 3   Find the number of counters in each row.

There are 8 counters in each row.

Solution   **There are 8 cans in each bag.**

Division is the opposite, or the **inverse operation**, of multiplication. You can use a multiplication table to solve division.

×	0	1	2	3	4	5	6	7	8	9	10	11	12
0	0	0	0	0	0	0	0	0	0	0	0	0	0
1	0	1	2	3	4	5	6	7	8	9	10	11	12
2	0	2	4	6	8	10	12	14	16	18	20	22	24
3	0	3	6	9	12	15	18	21	24	27	30	33	36
4	0	4	8	12	16	20	24	28	32	36	40	44	48
5	0	5	10	15	20	25	30	35	40	45	50	55	60
6	0	6	12	18	24	30	36	42	48	54	60	66	72
7	0	7	14	21	28	35	42	49	56	63	70	77	84
8	0	8	16	24	32	40	48	56	64	72	80	88	96
9	0	9	18	27	36	45	54	63	**72**	81	90	99	108
10	0	10	20	30	40	50	60	70	80	90	100	110	120
11	0	11	22	33	44	55	66	77	88	99	110	121	132
12	0	12	24	36	48	60	72	84	96	108	120	132	144

Example 2

Frank is 72 years old. That is 8 times his granddaughter's age. What is Frank's granddaughter's age?

Strategy   **Use the multiplication table.**

Step 1   Write the division sentence for the problem.

Frank is 72 years old.

72 is 8 times his granddaughter's age.

His granddaughter is n years old.

$72 \div 8 = n$

Step 2   Look at the 8s column.

Step 3   Move down the column and look for 72.

Step 4   Move to the left and look for the row number.

The row is 9.

Solution   **Frank's granddaughter is 9 years old.**

You can solve multistep problems by using multiplicative comparison and additive comparison. To find the number in each group or how many groups, use multiplicative comparison to divide. To find the number left in a group, use additive comparison to subtract.

Example 3

There are 48 students on the track and field team. That is 6 times as many as the number of students that are on the tennis team and 30 more students that are on the softball team. Does the softball team or the tennis team have a greater number of students? How many more students does that team have?

Strategy **Find the number of students on each team and compare.**

Step 1 Write a number sentence to find the number of students on the tennis team.

Let t represent the number of students on the tennis team.

48 is 6 times as many as t.

Divide: $48 \div 6 = t$

Step 2 Find the value of t.

$48 \div 6 = 8$

There are 8 students on the tennis team.

Step 3 Write a number sentence to find the number of students on the softball team.

Let s represent the number of students on the softball team.

48 is 30 more than 18.

Subtract: $48 - 30 = s$

Step 4 Find the value of s.

$48 - 30 = 18$

There are 18 students on the softball team.

Step 5 Find the difference between the number of students on each team.

The softball team has 18 students and the tennis team has 8 students.

$18 - 8 = 10$

Solution **The softball team has 10 more students than the tennis team.**

Related multiplication and division facts create a **fact family**.

Related facts use the same numbers.

$$5 \times 6 = 30 \qquad 6 \times 5 = 30$$
$$30 \div 5 = 6 \qquad 30 \div 6 = 5$$

Example 4

A log is 49 inches long. Mr. Childs cuts the log into 7 equal pieces.
What is the length of one piece?

Strategy **Use a related multiplication fact.**

Step 1 Write the division sentence for the problem.

The log is 49 inches long.

It was cut into 7 equal pieces.

Each piece is p inches long.

$49 \div 7 = p$

Step 2 Use a related multiplication fact.

Related facts use the same numbers.

Since $7 \times 7 = 49$, then $49 \div 7 = 7$.

Solution **The length of one piece is 7 inches.**

Coached Example

Ms. Lopez has a total of 35 desks in her classroom. That is 5 times the number of desks in each equal row of desks. How many desks are in each row?

Write a division sentence for the problem.

Use *d* for the number of desks in each row.

There are _____ desks in _____ equal rows.

_____ ÷ _____ = _____

Use a related multiplication fact.

_____ × 5 = 35

Since _____ × 5 = 35, then 35 ÷ 5 = _____.

There are _____ desks in each row.

Lesson Practice • Part 1

Choose the correct answer.

1. Divide.

   $$45 \div 9 = \boxed{}$$

   A. 5

   B. 6

   C. 7

   D. 8

2. Vanessa used repeated subtraction to solve this division fact.

   $$96 \div 8 = \boxed{}$$

   How many times did she subtract 8 from 96?

   A. 9

   B. 10

   C. 11

   D. 12

3. Which division fact has a quotient of 4?

   A. $20 \div 2 = \boxed{}$

   B. $24 \div 6 = \boxed{}$

   C. $32 \div 4 = \boxed{}$

   D. $36 \div 3 = \boxed{}$

4. Which division fact is related to this multiplication fact?

   $$6 \times 8 = 48$$

   A. $48 \div 2 = 12$

   B. $42 \div 6 = 7$

   C. $48 \div 8 = 6$

   D. $56 \div 8 = 7$

5. Which fact does **not** belong in the same fact family as the others?

   A. $8 \times 2 = 16$

   B. $16 \div 4 = 4$

   C. $2 \times 8 = 16$

   D. $16 \div 2 = 8$

6. Michelle has 54 inches of ribbon. She cut the ribbon into 6-inch pieces. How many pieces of ribbon did Michelle cut?

   A. 6

   B. 7

   C. 8

   D. 9

7. Monica stores 36 paintbrushes in 3 cases. Each case has the same number of paintbrushes. How many paintbrushes are in each case?

A. 9

B. 11

C. 12

D. 16

8. A wooden board is 45 inches long before it is cut into short equal pieces. That is 5 times as long as each short piece. How long is each short piece?

A. 5 inches

B. 6 inches

C. 8 inches

D. 9 inches

9. Sixteen adults and 40 students attended a charity event. The adults and students sat at 8 tables.

A. Each table had the same number of adults. How many adults sat at each table?

_____

B. Each table had the same number of students. How many students sat at each table?

_____

C. How many people in all sat at each table? Show your work.

_____

Lesson Practice • Part 2

Choose the correct answer.

1. Ethan bought a computer game for $36 and a book for $6. How many times as much did the computer game cost as the book?

   A. 6

   B. 30

   C. 42

   D. 216

2. Which number makes both sentences true?

   $$7 \times \boxed{} = 56$$
   $$56 \div \boxed{} = 7$$

   A. 9

   B. 8

   C. 7

   D. 6

3. Doug baked 24 cookies. He kept 6 cookies for himself and gave 3 each to some friends. How many friends received cookies from Doug?

   A. 6

   B. 10

   C. 15

   D. 18

4. Brooklyn biked 54 miles last week. That was 9 times as many miles as she jogged last week. How many miles did Brooklyn jog last week?

   A. 486 miles

   B. 63 miles

   C. 45 miles

   D. 6 miles

5. Which number makes both sentences true?

   $$28 \div \boxed{} = 7$$
   $$7 \times \boxed{} = 28$$

   A. 3

   B. 4

   C. 5

   D. 6

6. Mrs. McGee gave her 5 grandchildren a total of $60 to share equally. Mr. McGee had already given the grandchildren $50 to share equally. How much money did each grandchild receive?

   A. $2

   B. $10

   C. $12

   D. $22

7. There are 32 pennies in a jar. That is 10 more than the number of nickels in the jar. The number of pennies is 4 times as many as the number of dimes in the jar. How many more nickels are there than dimes in the jar?

   A. 34

   B. 22

   C. 14

   D. 6

8. Evan had 15 books in a box when he was given 12 more. He put the same number of books on 3 shelves. How many books are on each shelf?

   A. 4

   B. 9

   C. 24

   D. 27

9. There are 36 windows in the Folsoms' house. The number of windows is 3 times as many as the number of closets and 4 more than the number of doors inside the house.

   A. How many closets are in the house? Show your work.

   _____

   _____

   B. How many more doors are there than closets in the house? Show your work.

   _____

   _____

10. Use numbers from the box to complete the other facts in the same fact family as $42 \div 6 = 7$.

   _____ ÷ _____ = _____

   _____ × _____ = _____

   _____ × _____ = _____

   | 6 |
   | 7 |
   | 8 |
   | 42 |

11. Which division fact is related to this multiplication fact? Circle all that apply.

$9 \times 8 = 72$

A. $72 \div 6 = 12$

B. $72 \div 8 = 9$

C. $63 \div 7 = 9$

D. $72 \div 9 = 8$

12. Select True or False for each statement.

A. $15 \div 3$ can be solved by $15 - 3 - 3 - 3 - 3 - 3$.	◯ True	◯ False
B. $24 \div 6$ can be solved by $24 - 6 - 6 - 6 - 6$.	◯ True	◯ False
C. $42 \div 7$ can be solved by $42 + 7 + 7 + 7 + 7 + 7 + 7$.	◯ True	◯ False
D. $25 \div 5$ can be solved by $25 - 5 - 5 - 5 - 5$.	◯ True	◯ False
E. $48 \div 8$ can be solved by $48 - 8 - 8 - 8 - 8 - 8 - 8$.	◯ True	◯ False

13. Draw a line from each division fact to its quotient.

A. $49 \div 7 = \boxed{}$ •   • 4

B. $18 \div 6 = \boxed{}$ •   • 9

C. $50 \div 5 = \boxed{}$ •   • 7

D. $72 \div 8 = \boxed{}$ •   • 3

E. $36 \div 9 = \boxed{}$ •   • 10

14. Look at each division sentence. Is the quotient correct? Select Yes or No.

A. $20 \div 4 = 5$ ◯ Yes   ◯ No

B. $30 \div 5 = 6$ ◯ Yes   ◯ No

C. $54 \div 6 = 7$ ◯ Yes   ◯ No

D. $35 \div 7 = 5$ ◯ Yes   ◯ No

E. $18 \div 6 = 2$ ◯ Yes   ◯ No

15. Find the fact families. Write each related fact in the correct box.

$6 \times 4 = 24$	$3 \times 8 = 24$	$24 \div 8 = 3$
$24 \div 6 = 4$	$4 \times 6 = 24$	$8 \times 3 = 24$

Fact family for $24 \div 3 = 8$	Fact family for $24 \div 4 = 6$

16. Which problem has an answer of 8? Circle all that apply.

A. Emily had 8 times the number of stamps that Bena had. Emily had 64 stamps. How many stamps did Bena have?

B. Ji Sun and her friends packed water bottles in boxes for the school field day. They packed a total of 144 bottles in 12 boxes. How many bottles were in each box?

C. Juan's sister is 32 years old. She is 4 times the age of Juan. How old is Juan?

D. Hector cut an 80-inch piece of wood into 10 small equal pieces. How long was each small piece?

E. Ella rode her bike 24 miles last week. That is 8 times as far as Charlie rode his bike last week. How many miles did Charlie ride his bike last week?

Divide Greater Numbers

Getting the Idea

Division problems can be written in another way.

$$\text{divisor}\overline{)\text{dividend}}^{\text{quotient}}$$

You can use models to help you divide.

Example 1

Divide.

$$56 \div 4 = \boxed{}$$

Strategy   Use counters to make an array.

Step 1   Use 56 counters. Put them in 4 equal rows.

Step 2   Count the number of counters in each row.

There are 14 counters in each row.

Solution   **56 ÷ 4 = 14**

Remember, inverse operations are operations that "undo" each other. Multiplication and division are inverse operations. You can use multiplication to check a division problem.

For Example 1, you can use $4 \times 14 = 56$ to check $56 \div 4 = 14$.

The product 56 matches the dividend 56, so the answer is correct.

When you divide greater numbers, divide each place of the dividend from left to right.

Example 2

Alex has 72 baseball cards that he wants to store in three cases. If he stores the same number of cards in each case, how many cards will be in each case?

Strategy **Write a division sentence, then solve.**

Step 1 Write a division sentence for the problem.

He has 72 cards. He has 3 cases. There are n cards in each case.

$72 \div 3 = n$

Step 2 Write the problem another way.

$3\overline{)72}$

Step 3 Divide.

$$\begin{array}{r} 2 \\ 3\overline{)72} \\ -6 \\ \hline 1 \end{array}$$

← Multiply: $3 \times 2 = 6$
← Subtract: $7 - 6 = 1$

Step 4 Bring down the 2 ones.

$$\begin{array}{r} 2 \\ 3\overline{)72} \\ -6\downarrow \\ \hline 12 \end{array}$$

Step 5 Divide.

$$\begin{array}{r} 24 \\ 3\overline{)72} \\ -6\downarrow \\ \hline 12 \\ -12 \\ \hline 0 \end{array}$$

← Multiply: $3 \times 4 = 12$
← Subtract: $12 - 12 = 0$

Step 6 Use multiplication to check the quotient.

$3 \times 24 = 72$ ← This matches the dividend.

The quotient is correct.

Solution **There will be 24 baseball cards in each case.**

When dividing greater numbers, first look at the digit in the greatest place of the dividend. Sometimes you will need to look at the first two places of the dividend.

Example 3

Divide.

$$6)\overline{456}$$

Strategy   **Divide each place from left to right.**

Step 1   Look at the digit in the greatest place of the dividend.

The digit is 4.

Because $4 < 6$, look at the digits in the first two places of the dividend.

$$6)\overline{45\,6}$$

Step 2   Divide 45 tens by 6.

$$
\begin{array}{r}
7 \\
6)\overline{456} \\
-42 \\
\hline
3
\end{array}
$$
← Multiply: $6 \times 7 = 42$
← Subtract: $45 - 42 = 3$

Step 3   Bring down the ones. Divide 36 ones by 6.

$$
\begin{array}{r}
76 \\
6)\overline{456} \\
-42\downarrow \\
\hline
36 \\
-36 \\
\hline
0
\end{array}
$$
← Multiply: $6 \times 6 = 36$
← Subtract: $36 - 36 = 0$

Step 4   Use multiplication to check the quotient.

$6 \times 76 = 456$ ← This matches the dividend.
The quotient is correct.

Solution   **$456 \div 6 = 76$**

Example 4

Will raised $648 and Dara raised $522 for their favorite charities. They combined their money and donated the same amount to each of 3 charities. How much did each charity receive?

Strategy   **Decide how to solve the problem. Find the total amount of money raised. Then divide the sum by 3.**

Step 1   Add to find the total amount of money raised.

$648 + $522 = $1,170

Step 2   Divide to find how much each charity received.

$1,170 ÷ 3 = ☐

Divide each place from left to right.

```
      390
3)1,170
   −9↓↓
     27 ↓
   −27 ↓
      00
    −00
       0
```

Step 3   Use multiplication to check the quotient.

3 × $390 = $1,170

Solution   **Each charity received $390.**

Coached Example

The circus has 8 equal sections of seats. There are 8,240 seats in all.

How many seats, s, are in each section?

Write a division sentence for the problem.

There are _____ seats in all.

There are _____ equal sections.

There are s seats in each section.

_____ ÷ _____ = _____

Write the problem another way.

Divide each place from left to right.

$$8\overline{)8,240}$$

So, 8,240 ÷ 8 = _____.

There are _____ seats in each section.

Lesson Practice • Part 1

Choose the correct answer.

1. Divide.

   $57 \div 3 = \boxed{}$

   A. 18
   B. 19
   C. 20
   D. 21

2. Gerald spent $81 on 3 tickets to a game. What is the cost of each ticket?

   A. $27
   B. $28
   C. $37
   D. $38

3. Divide.

   $65 \div 5 = \boxed{}$

   A. 10
   B. 11
   C. 12
   D. 13

4. An oak table cost $96. That is 8 times as much as a pine table costs. How much does a pine table cost?

   A. $12
   B. $11
   C. $10
   D. $9

5. Peter travels a total of 105 miles to and from work each week. He works 5 days each week. How many miles does Peter travel each day?

   A. 525 miles
   B. 210 miles
   C. 21 miles
   D. 15 miles

6. Divide.

   $264 \div 6 = \boxed{}$

   A. 44
   B. 46
   C. 47
   D. 48

7. Juanita bought a computer for $2,205. She will make 9 equal payments to pay off the computer. How much is each payment?

   A. $225

   B. $245

   C. $255

   D. $275

8. The workers paved 1,353 feet of a road today. That is 3 times as long as they paved yesterday. How much of the road did the workers pave yesterday?

   A.   450 feet

   B.   451 feet

   C.   551 feet

   D. 4,059 feet

9. Andrew, Nichole, and Sean are planning a canoe trip. They will split the cost of the supplies evenly. The table shows the supplies and the cost of each item.

Canoe Trip Supplies

Item	Cost
Canoe	$729
Life Jackets	$354
Paddles	$45

   A.   How much will the supplies cost in all? Show your work.

   B.   How much will each person pay for the canoe trip? Show your work.

Lesson Practice • Part 2

Choose the correct answer.

1. A room for 3 nights at the Memory Motel costs $252. What is the cost for each night?

   A. $84

   B. $86

   C. $94

   D. $96

2. Which explains the first step in this division problem?

   6)2,064

   A. divide 6 into 2

   B. divide 2 into 6

   C. divide 6 into 20

   D. divide 20 into 6

3. A total of 6,304 people attended the 8 performances of a play. Each performance had the same attendance. What was the attendance for each performance?

   A. 716

   B. 738

   C. 788

   D. 812

4. Movie Night tickets at The Strand cost $9 for adults and $7 for students. The box office received $2,025 in adult ticket sales and $1,904 for student ticket sales. How many tickets were sold?

   A. 501   C. 491

   B. 497   D. 436

5. Divide: $3,496 \div 8$

   A. 412   C. 432

   B. 417   D. 437

6. Logan was checking a friend's work of $632 \div 8 = 76$. Without performing the entire division, Logan said his friend was incorrect. Which explains whether or not Logan is correct in his assessment?

   A. Logan is incorrect because an estimate will show that the quotient is less than 80.

   B. Logan is correct because an estimate will show that the quotient is greater than 80.

   C. Logan is correct because the ones digit in the dividend must be an odd number.

   D. Logan is correct because the ones digit in the dividend must be 8 because $6 \times 8 = 48$.

7. The race that Hailey runs is 3,520 yards. That is 8 times as long as the race that Lillian runs. What is the length of the race that Lillian runs?

 A. 440 yards
 B. 3,512 yards
 C. 3,528 yards
 D. 28,160 yards

8. Divide: 8,308 ÷ 4

 A. 2,002
 B. 2,077
 C. 2,707
 D. 2,770

9. A gym has a 4-month membership for $224 and a 6-month membership for $312. Which sentence is true?

 A. The 4-month membership is $78 cheaper each month.
 B. The 4-month membership is $4 more each month.
 C. The 6-month membership is $39 more each month.
 D. The 6-month membership is $4 more each month.

10. Divide: 4,173 ÷ 3

 A. 1,391   C. 1,321
 B. 1,358   D. 1,059

11. The Bridges family drove 264 miles in 4 hours on the interstate highway and then drove 114 miles in 3 hours on the state highways.

 A. How many miles per hour faster did the Bridges family drive on the interstate highway than on the state highways? Show your work.

 _____

 _____

 B. How many miles per hour did the Bridges family drive for the entire trip? Show your work.

 _____

 _____

12. Circle the number that makes the sentences true.

$$4 \times \boxed{\begin{array}{c} 15 \\ 16 \\ 17 \end{array}} = 64 \qquad\qquad 64 \div 4 = \boxed{\begin{array}{c} 15 \\ 16 \\ 17 \end{array}}$$

13. Select True or False for each division sentence.

A. $72 \div 4 = 19$ ○ True   ○ False

B. $348 \div 6 = 58$ ○ True   ○ False

C. $177 \div 3 = 59$ ○ True   ○ False

D. $91 \div 7 = 13$ ○ True   ○ False

14. Draw a line from each division problem to the multiplication sentence that can be used to check the quotient.

A. $60 \div 4 = \square$ •   • $10 \times 6 = 60$

B. $72 \div 3 = \square$ •   • $4 \times 15 = 60$

C. $72 \div 4 = \square$ •   • $3 \times 24 = 72$

D. $72 \div 6 = \square$ •   • $4 \times 18 = 72$

E. $60 \div 6 = \square$ •   • $6 \times 12 = 72$

15. Use numbers from the box to complete the division sentences.

$78 \div 3 =$ _____

$654 \div 6 =$ _____

$1,345 \div 5 =$ _____

$5,697 \div 9 =$ _____

19	109
26	269
62	633

16. Which problem has an answer of 23? Circle all that apply.

A. Nam had 138 cans of vegetables to stack on grocery store shelves. If he put 6 cans on each shelf, how many shelves did Nam need?

B. A 161-minute movie is made up of 7 equal parts. What is the length, in minutes, of each part?

C. Jen's mother knitted a 72-inch-long scarf. The scarf is divided into 3 equal sections, each a different color. What is the length of each section?

D. Christine planted 180 flowers in 4 rows with an equal number of flowers in each row. How many flowers did Christine plant in each row?

E. Asa's recipe calls for 8 ounces of raisins for each batch of oatmeal cookies. Asa used 184 ounces of raisins. How many batches of cookies did he make?

17. Read each problem. Is the answer correct? Select Yes or No.

A. Danika hiked 4,569 feet yesterday. That is 3 times farther than she hiked today. She hiked 1,523 feet today. ○ Yes ○ No

B. Jorge paid $3,795 for a used car. He paid it off in 5 equal payments of $659. ○ Yes ○ No

C. Paul spent $92 on 4 theater tickets. Each ticket cost $24. ○ Yes ○ No

D. Workers packed 896 dishes into boxes of 8. They packed 112 boxes. ○ Yes ○ No

Division with Remainders

Getting the Idea

The **remainder** is a number that is left after division has been completed.

You can write the remainder with the letter R. A remainder must be less than the divisor.

To check an answer with a remainder, first multiply the divisor by the quotient.

Then add that product to the remainder.

Look at the following example.

$13 \div 3 = 4$ R1

The remainder 1 is less than the divisor 3.

To check the answer, multiply the divisor 3 by the quotient 4. $3 \times 4 = 12$

Then add the product 12 to the remainder 1. $12 + 1 = 13$

Example 1

Divide.

$61 \div 7 = \boxed{}$

Strategy   **Divide each place from left to right.**

Step 1   Write the problem another way. Divide.

$$
\begin{array}{r}
8 \\
7\overline{)61} \\
-56 \\
\hline
5
\end{array}
$$
  ← Multiply $7 \times 8 = 56$
  ← Subtract $61 - 56 = 5$

There are 5 left over. This is the remainder.

Step 2   Write the remainder.

$$
\begin{array}{r}
8 \textbf{ R5} \\
7\overline{)61} \\
-56 \\
\hline
5
\end{array}
$$

Step 3   Check the answer.

Multiply the divisor by the quotient. Then add the remainder.

$(7 \times 8) + 5 =$

$56 \quad + 5 = 61$ ← This matches the dividend.
The answer is correct.

Solution   **$61 \div 7 = 8$ R5**

Example 2

Divide.

$531 \div 4 = \boxed{}$

Strategy   **Divide each place from left to right.**

Step 1   Set up the division. Start by dividing 5 hundreds by 4.

$$\begin{array}{r} 1 \\ 4\overline{)531} \\ -4 \\ \hline 1 \end{array}$$ ← Multiply $4 \times 1 = 4$
← Subtract $5 - 4 = 1$

Step 2   Continue dividing and write the remainder.

$$\begin{array}{r} 132\ \textbf{R3} \\ 4\overline{)531} \\ -4 \\ \hline 13 \\ -12 \\ \hline 11 \\ -8 \\ \hline 3 \end{array}$$

Step 3   Check the quotient.

$(4 \times 132) + 3 =$

$528 \quad + 3 = 531$ ← This matches the dividend.
The answer is correct.

Solution   **$531 \div 4 = 132$ R3**

In a division word problem with remainders, you may need to interpret the remainder. There are three ways to interpret the remainder.

1. Drop the remainder.
2. The remainder is the answer.
3. Add 1 to the quotient.

Example 3

A group of 124 chorus members is going to a concert. A van can take 9 members. How many vans are needed to get all of the members to the concert?

Strategy   **Divide. Then interpret the remainder.**

Step 1   Write the division sentence for the problem.

There are 124 members. Each van can take 9 members.

Let v represent the number of vans needed.

$124 \div 9 = v$

Step 2   Divide each place from left to right. Write the remainder.

$$
\begin{array}{r}
13 \text{ R7} \\
9{\overline{)124}} \\
-9 \downarrow \\
\hline
34 \\
-27 \\
\hline
7
\end{array}
$$

Step 3   Check the answer.

$(9 \times 13) + 7 =$

$117 \quad + 7 = 124$ ← This matches the dividend.
The answer is correct.

Step 4   Interpret the remainder.

The answer, 13 R7, means 13 full vans with 7 members left over. Those 7 members remaining need to be driven. So one more van is needed. Add 1 to the quotient.

$13 + 1 = 14$

Solution   **To get all the members to the concert, 14 vans are needed.**

Example 4

A factory made 2,285 tea candles to be shipped to 8 different stores. Each store will receive the same number of candles with some left over. How many candles will each store receive?

Strategy   **Divide. Then interpret the remainder.**

Step 1   Write the division sentence for the problem.

There are 2,285 candles to be shipped to 8 stores.

Let c represent the number of candles each store will receive.

$2,285 \div 8 = c$

Step 2   Set up the division. Divide each place from left to right.

$$
\begin{array}{r}
285 \text{ R5} \\
8\overline{)2285} \\
-16 \\
\hline
68 \\
-64 \\
\hline
45 \\
-40 \\
\hline
5
\end{array}
$$

Step 3   Check the quotient.

$(8 \times 285) + 5 =$

$2,280 \ + 5 = 2,285$ ← This matches the dividend. The quotient is correct.

Step 4   Interpret the remainder.

The answer, 285 R5, means 285 candles for each store with 5 candles left over. Since the question asks for the number of candles each store will receive, drop the remainder.

Solution   **Each store will receive 285 candles.**

Coached Example

Nita has a 250-inch roll of ribbon. She needs to cut as many 9-inch pieces as she can from the roll. How many 9-inch pieces can Nita cut? What is the length of the ribbon left over?

Write the division sentence for the problem.

Nita has _____ inches of ribbon.

Each piece she will cut is _____ inches long.

Let p represent _____.

_____ ÷ _____ = p

Set up the division. Divide each place from left to right.

$9\overline{)250}$

Check the quotient.

Multiply the divisor by the quotient. Add that product to the remainder.

(9 × _____) + _____ = p

_____ + _____ = _____

Does that match the dividend? _____ Is your answer correct? _____

Interpret the remainder.

The answer, _____ R_____, means Nita can cut _____ 9-inch pieces with _____ inches left over.

Nita can cut _____ 9-inch pieces.

The length of the ribbon left over is _____ inches.

Lesson Practice • Part 1

Choose the correct answer.

1. Divide.

    $65 \div 3 = \square$

    A. 20 R4

    B. 21 R2

    C. 22 R1

    D. 22 R2

2. Which division sentence has a remainder?

    A. $99 \div 3 = \square$

    B. $38 \div 2 = \square$

    C. $77 \div 6 = \square$

    D. $65 \div 5 = \square$

3. The fourth-grade class collected 58 bottles to recycle. The students will pack 8 bottles in each box. The recycling depot only accepts full boxes. How many boxes will the class take to the recycling depot?

    A. 3

    B. 6

    C. 7

    D. 9

4. Divide.

    $267 \div 6 = \square$

    A. 44 R3

    B. 46 R1

    C. 47 R3

    D. 48 R7

5. Divide.

    $988 \div 7 = \square$

    A. 142 R6

    B. 142 R1

    C. 141 R6

    D. 141 R1

6. A total of 113 people signed up to take tennis lessons at the recreation center. Five people can have lessons every hour. How many hours are needed for everyone to have a lesson?

    A. 20 hours

    B. 22 hours

    C. 23 hours

    D. 25 hours

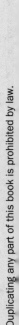

7. Divide.

$$2,603 \div 9 = \boxed{}$$

A. 289 R2

B. 289 R6

C. 290 R2

D. 291 R2

8. Nicole found that $3,429 \div 4 =$ 857 R1. Which can she use to check that her answer is correct?

A. $(1 \times 3,429) + 4$

B. $(4 \times 857) + 1$

C. $(4 \times 1) + 857$

D. $(4 \times 857) \times 1$

9. The school fair committee needs enough pizzas for 275 people. Each pizza has 8 slices. How many pizzas does the committee need to order so that each person can have 1 slice?

A. Write a number sentence for the problem. Use a variable to represent the number of pizzas.

_____

B. How many pizzas does the committee need to order so that each person can have 1 slice? Show your work. Explain your answer.

_____

_____

_____

Lesson Practice • Part 2

Choose the correct answer.

1. There are 62 students trying out for the cheerleading teams. Each team will have exactly 8 students. How many students will **not** make a team?

   A. 2

   B. 6

   C. 7

   D. 8

2. There are 172 people on line for a ride. Each ride can take 9 people at one time. How many rides are needed for everyone on line to get a turn?

   A. 17

   B. 18

   C. 19

   D. 20

3. Each baseball cap costs $7. Coach Calhoun has $120 to spend on baseball caps. How many baseball caps can she buy?

   A. 18

   B. 17

   C. 16

   D. 15

4. Divide: 8,174 ÷ 3

   A. 2,390 R2

   B. 2,391 R1

   C. 2,724 R2

   D. 2,725 R1

5. Bella was checking a friend's work of 1,244 ÷ 4 = 311 R1. Without performing the entire division, Bella said her friend was incorrect. Which explains whether or not Bella is correct in her assessment?

   A. Bella is correct because an estimate will show that the quotient is less than 300.

   B. Bella is incorrect because an estimate will show that the quotient is greater than 300.

   C. Bella is correct because if the divisor is 4 and the ones digit in the dividend is 4, then there can never be a remainder.

   D. Bella is correct because if the divisor is 4 and the ones digit in the dividend is even, then the remainder must be even.

6. Gavin has 175 rock CDs and 87 country CDs. He will put the CDs on 6 shelves that will each contain the same number of CDs. Any remaining CDs he will put inside his desk. How many CDs will Gavin put inside his desk?

A. 2 **C.** 4

B. 3 **D.** 5

7. Miguel has already put 36 sports cards each in 5 folders. He buys 372 more cards. He puts the same number of cards into the 5 folders with any extra cards going into the green folder. How many cards are now in the green folder?

A. 74 **C.** 110

B. 16 **D.** 112

8. A group has $478 to spend on play tickets that cost $9 each.

A. How many tickets can the group buy? Show your work.

_____

_____

B. How did you interpret the remainder? Explain your reasoning.

_____

_____

9. Which division sentence has a remainder? Circle all that apply.

A. $72 \div 6 = \boxed{}$

B. $65 \div 4 = \boxed{}$

C. $89 \div 7 = \boxed{}$

D. $48 \div 3 = \boxed{}$

E. $146 \div 5 = \boxed{}$

10. Read each problem situation. Are there any left over? Select Yes or No.

   A. 40 beads and 7 beads on each shirt   ○ Yes ○ No

   B. 127 strawberries for 9 people to share   ○ Yes ○ No

   C. 738 rice cakes and 6 rice cakes per box   ○ Yes ○ No

   D. 1,344 plants and 7 plants in each row   ○ Yes ○ No

   E. 110 eggs and 6 eggs in a carton   ○ Yes ○ No

11. Layla found that $2,687 \div 6 = 447$ R5. Can she use the expression to check that her answer is correct? Select Yes or No.

   A. $(6 \times 447) + 5$ ○ Yes ○ No

   B. $(5 \times 447) + 6$ ○ Yes ○ No

   C. $5 + (6 \times 447)$ ○ Yes ○ No

   D. $5 \times (6 \times 447)$ ○ Yes ○ No

   E. $(6 \times 5) + 447$ ○ Yes ○ No

12. Use numbers from the box to complete a sentence to check this division problem:
$5,654 \div 6 = 942$ R2.

(_____ $\times$ _____) + _____ = _____

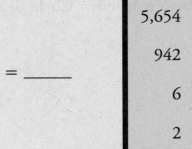

5,654

942

6

2

13. Decide whether or not each division sentence has a remainder. Write the division sentence in the correct box.

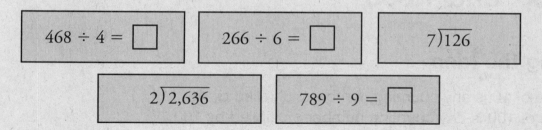

Remainder	No Remainder

14. Select a problem for which you must add 1 to the quotient to find the correct answer. Circle all that apply.

A. The school science club is going to the museum. There are 38 boys and 21 girls in the club. A van can take 8 students. How many vans are needed to take the science club members to the museum?

B. Tao and Lian packed 234 apple juice bottles and 330 orange juice bottles in bags for the end-of-school picnic. Each bag holds 9 bottles of juice. How many bags did Tao and Lian use?

C. Aretha made 144 cookies. She put 8 cookies on each plate. How many plates did Aretha use?

D. Miguel has a 160-inch piece of wood. He wants to cut it into smaller pieces that are each 7 inches long. How many 7-inch pieces can Miguel cut?

E. There are 236 people at a dinner party. Each dining table seats 9 people. How many dining tables are needed for the party?

Multiply and Divide by Multiples of 10, 100, and 1,000

Getting the Idea

A **multiple** of 10 is any counting number multiplied by 10.
A multiple of 100 is any counting number multiplied by 100.
A multiple of 1,000 is any counting number multiplied by 1,000.

To multiply a number by a multiple of 10, 100, or 1,000, multiply the number by the nonzero digit of the multiple of 10, and put one, two, or three zeros at the end of the product.

$$8 \times 20 = 16\mathbf{0}$$
$$8 \times 200 = 1,6\mathbf{00}$$
$$8 \times 2,000 = 16,\mathbf{000}$$

You can use mental math to multiply a number by multiples of 10, 100, and 1,000.

Example 1

What is 2×90?

Strategy   Use mental math.

Step 1   Multiply 2 by the nonzero digit of the multiple of 10.

9 is the nonzero digit of the multiple of 10. $2 \times 9 = 18$

Step 2   There is one zero in 90.

Put one zero at the end of the product: 18**0**

Solution $2 \times 90 = 180$

Example 2

A netbook computer costs $300. A desktop computer costs 5 times as much as the netbook computer. How much does the desktop computer cost?

Strategy   Use mental math.

Step 1   Write a multiplication sentence for the problem.

The netbook costs $300.

The desktop costs 5 times as much.

Let n represent the cost of the desktop.

$300 \times 5 = n$

Step 2 Multiply 5 by the nonzero digit of the multiple of 100.

3 is the nonzero digit of the multiple of 100. $5 \times 3 = 15$

Step 3 There are 2 zeros in 300.

Put two zeros at the end of the product: 15**00**

So, $5 \times 300 = 1,500$.

Solution **The desktop computer costs $1,500.**

Example 3

A store ordered 6 boxes of gumballs. Each box has 4,000 gumballs. How many gumballs in all did the store order?

Strategy **Use mental math.**

Step 1 Write the multiplication sentence for the problem.

There are 6 boxes.

Each box has 4,000 gumballs.

Let g represent the total number of gumballs.

$6 \times 4,000 = g$

Step 2 Multiply 6 by the nonzero digit of the multiple of 1,000.

$6 \times 4 = 24$

Step 3 There are 3 zeros in 4,000.

Put 3 zeros at the end of the product: 24,**000**

So, $6 \times 4,000 = 24,000$.

Solution **The store ordered 24,000 gumballs in all.**

Dividing a number by 10 is the opposite of multiplying by 10.

Instead of putting a zero at the end of a number, you take away a zero. For example, $140 \div 10 = 14$.

To divide a number by 100, take away two zeros from the dividend. For example, $1,400 \div 100 = 14$.

Example 4

Tanya has collected 90 dimes in a jar. She wrapped the dimes in rolls of 10 to bring to the bank. How many rolls of dimes did Tanya wrap?

Strategy   Use mental math.

Step 1   Write the division sentence for the problem.

There are 90 dimes.

There are 10 dimes in each roll.

Let r represent the number of rolls.

$90 \div 10 = r$

Step 2   Divide.

The divisor is 10, so take away a zero from the dividend.

$90 \div 10 = 9$

Solution   **Tanya wrapped 9 rolls of dimes.**

Coached Example

Mr. Cassidy typed 8,200 words in a report. He can type 100 words a minute. How many minutes did it take Mr. Cassidy to type his report?

Write the division sentence for the problem.

He typed _____ words in a report.

He can type _____ words a minute.

Let m represent the number of _____ it took to type the report.

_____ ÷ _____ = _____

Use mental math.

The divisor is _____, so take away _____ zeros from the dividend.

$8,200 \div 100 =$ _____

It took Mr. Cassidy _____ minutes to type his report.

Lesson Practice • Part 1

Choose the correct answer.

1. Multiply.

   $6 \times 30 = \square$

   A. 18

   B. 180

   C. 360

   D. 1,800

2. Jackie rides her bicycle 9 miles a day. If she does this for 10 days, how many miles will she ride in all?

   A. 9 miles

   B. 90 miles

   C. 900 miles

   D. 9,000 miles

3. Multiply.

   $2 \times 700 = \square$

   A. 14

   B. 140

   C. 1,400

   D. 14,000

4. Samuel is buying shirts for the soccer team. The shirts cost $8 each. He ordered 100 shirts. How much did Samuel pay in all for the shirts?

   A. $8

   B. $80

   C. $800

   D. $8,000

5. Multiply.

   $3 \times 8,000 = \square$

   A. 24

   B. 240

   C. 2,400

   D. 24,000

6. Divide.

   $1,000 \div 10 = \square$

   A. 1,000

   B. 100

   C. 10

   D. 1

7. There were 5,000 entries in a contest. One in every 100 entries will win a prize. How many prizes will be given?

   A. 5,000

   B.   500

   C.   50

   D.   5

8. Divide.

$$1,300 \div 100 = \boxed{}$$

   A. 1,300

   B.   130

   C.   13

   D.   3

9. A standard room at the Copperfield Hotel costs $100 a night.
A suite at the Copperfield Hotel costs $200 a night.

   A. The Browns stayed in a suite for 4 nights. How much did the Browns pay for their stay at the Copperfield Hotel? Explain how you solved the problem.

   _____

   _____

   _____

   B. Vicki paid $700 for her stay in a standard room. How many nights did Vicki stay at the Copperfield Hotel? Explain how you solved the problem.

   _____

   _____

   _____

Lesson Practice • Part 2

Choose the correct answer.

1. Which is a correct way to think about 400 ÷ 10?

   A. 40 tens divided 1 ten

   B. 40 tens divided 10 tens

   C. 400 tens divided by 1 ten

   D. 400 tens divided by 10 tens

2. There are 80 balloons in a bag. For a party, Ms. Podos bought 7 packs of balloons. How many balloons did Ms. Podos buy in all?

   A. 540

   B. 560

   C. 5,400

   D. 5,600

3. Divide.

   $$3,000 \div 10 = \boxed{}$$

   A. 3

   B. 30

   C. 300

   D. 3,000

4. Multiply.

   $$6 \times 9,000 = \boxed{}$$

   A. 540

   B. 5,400

   C. 54,000

   D. 540,000

5. A special event brought in $6,000 in ticket sales. Each ticket cost $100. How many tickets were sold?

   A. 60

   B. 600

   C. 60,000

   D. 600,000

6. Entrance into an amusement park is $40 per person. How much would it cost a family of 6 for everyone to enter?

   A. $200

   B. $240

   C. $2,000

   D. $2,400

7. Harmony is going to divide a 4-digit number by 10 and then divide the same 4-digit number by 100. Which sentence is true?

A. The first quotient will be 100 times less than the second quotient.

B. The first quotient will be 100 times as many as the second quotient.

C. The first quotient will be 10 times less than the second quotient.

D. The first quotient will be 10 times as many as the second quotient.

8. A bicycle vacation will include 60 miles of biking each day. How many miles will be biked in an 8-day vacation?

A. 420 miles

B. 480 miles

C. 4,200 miles

D. 4,800 miles

9. Parker was given $4,000 \times 7$ to multiply and $6,400 \div 100$ to divide.

A. What is the product of Parker's multiplication problem?

_____

B. What is the quotient of Parker's division problem? Explain how you solved the problem.

_____

_____

10. Circle the unknown number that makes the sentences true.

$5 \times \boxed{\begin{array}{c} 1 \\ 10 \\ 100 \end{array}} = 500$ $\qquad$ $500 \div \boxed{\begin{array}{c} 1 \\ 10 \\ 100 \end{array}} = 5$

11. Select True or False for each statement.

A. To divide 7,200 by 10, add one zero to the dividend.　　○ True　○ False

B. To multiply 500 by 3, add two zeros to the product of 5 and 3.　　○ True　○ False

C. To divide 8,000 by 100, take away two zeros from the dividend.　　○ True　○ False

D. To divide 6,400 by 10, take away two zeros from the dividend.　　○ True　○ False

E. To multiply 6,000 by 3, add two zeros to the product of 6 and 3.　　○ True　○ False

F. To divide 550 by 10, take away one zero from the dividend.　　○ True　○ False

12. Look at each division sentence. To find the quotient, will you take away one zero or two zeros from the dividend? Write the sentence in the correct box.

| $3,200 \div 10 = \square$ | $170 \div 10 = \square$ | $1,600 \div 100 = \square$ |
| $760 \div 10 = \square$ | $800 \div 100 = \square$ | $4,600 \div 100 = \square$ |

Take away 1 zero from the dividend	Take away 2 zeros from the dividend

13. Look at each number sentence. Will the answer have two zeros? Select Yes or No.

A. $5,000 \div 100 = \square$ ○ Yes   ○ No

B. $500 \times 5 = \square$ ○ Yes   ○ No

C. $1,700 \times 10 = \square$ ○ Yes   ○ No

D. $6,000 \div 10 = \square$ ○ Yes   ○ No

E. $2 \times 900 = \square$ ○ Yes   ○ No

14. Multiply or divide. Use numbers from the box to complete the sentences.

$9 \times 20 =$ _____

$9 \times 200 =$ _____

$18,000 \div 100 =$ _____

$1,800 \div 10 =$ _____

$9 \times 2,000 =$ _____

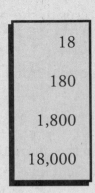

18

180

1,800

18,000

15. Which problem has an answer of 1,300? Circle all that apply.

A. There are 13,000 seats in the auditorium and 10 seats in each row. How many rows of seats are in the auditorium?

B. It cost Jeremy's family $130 per person to visit a theme park for 2 days. If there are 10 people in Jeremy's family, what was the total cost of the family's visit to the theme park?

C. Sahil rode his bike 10 miles a day for 13 days. How many miles in all did Sahil ride his bike?

D. Abbey bought plants to decorate tables for the school party. Each plant cost $13. How much did Abbey spend on 100 plants?

E. Don's recipe calls for 10 ounces of raisins for each loaf of zucchini bread. He used 1,300 ounces of raisins. How many loaves of zucchini bread did he make?

Domain 1: Cumulative Assessment for Lessons 1–10

1. Which sentence is true?

   A. $412,440 > 412,549$

   B. $416,543 < 415,811$

   C. $413,303 > 413,030$

   D. $411,312 < 411,231$

2. Which number has the digit 4 in the thousands place and the digit 8 in the hundreds place?

   A. 123,483

   B. 254,837

   C. 368,448

   D. 459,804

3. A green shirt costs $6. A yellow shirt costs 4 times as much as the green shirt. How much does the yellow shirt cost?

   A. $2

   B. $10

   C. $16

   D. $24

4. Multiply.

   $$3,652 \times 4 = \boxed{}$$

   A. 1,468

   B. 14,408

   C. 14,608

   D. 14,628

5. Which correctly shows the multiplicative identity property of 1?

   A. $32 \times 5 = 5 \times 32$

   B. $21 \times 1 = 21$

   C. $0 \times 22 = 0$

   D. $4 \times (31 \times 9) = (4 \times 31) \times 9$

6. Which shows another way to write this number sentence?

   $$23 \times 9 = \boxed{}$$

   A. $(20 + 9) \times (3 + 9)$

   B. $(20 + 9) + (3 + 9)$

   C. $(20 \times 9) + (3 \times 9)$

   D. $(20 \times 9) \times (3 \times 9)$

7. This week Doreen baked 48 muffins. That was 6 times as many muffins as she baked last week. How many muffins did Doreen bake last week?

A. 5

B. 6

C. 7

D. 8

8. Shelli is trading in 750 tickets that she won at the arcade for 6 toy bracelets. Each bracelet costs the same number of tickets. How many tickets does each bracelet cost?

A. 125

B. 744

C. 756

D. 4,500

9. Divide.

$$1,900 \div 100 = \boxed{}$$

_____

10. Willie has 394 trading cards. He wants to put the cards in 4 albums. Each album will have the same number of cards. He will give the extra cards to his brother. How many cards will be in each album?

A. Write a number sentence for the problem. Use a variable to represent the quotient.

_____

B. Solve the number sentence you wrote for Part A. Explain your answer.

_____

_____

Domain 2

Operations and Algebraic Thinking

Domain 2: Diagnostic Assessment for Lessons 11–17

1. Which is a factor pair of 36?

   A. {4, 8}

   B. {4, 12}

   C. {5, 7}

   D. {6, 6}

2. At a snow cone stand, 2,843 snow cones were made on Friday and 3,802 snow cones were made on Saturday. How many snow cones were made on Friday and Saturday in all?

   A. 6,645

   B. 6,641

   C. 5,645

   D. 959

3. Which number is **not** a multiple of 6?

   A. 18   C. 43

   B. 30   D. 54

4. Caroline is watching a movie that is 207 minutes long. To the nearest hundred minutes, what is the length of the movie?

   A. 200 minutes

   B. 210 minutes

   C. 220 minutes

   D. 310 minutes

5. A store's grand opening day had 5,382 customers. To the nearest thousand, about how many customers did the store have on its grand opening day?

   A. 5,400   C. 5,300

   B. 5,380   D. 5,000

6. Students read books for a fund-raiser. The table shows the number of books read by the students at four different schools.

   Books Read

School	Number of Books
Lincoln	5,130
Smith	3,205
Cherry Hill	6,089
Scotchtown	4,967

   To the nearest thousand, what is the total number of books read?

   A. 16,000   C. 19,000

   B. 18,000   D. 21,000

7. Which is the best way to estimate 37 × 41?

   A. 30 × 40

   B. 40 × 40

   C. 40 × 50

   D. 30 × 50

8. Jake has 87 model cars to display on 7 shelves. He will put about the same number of cars on each shelf. Which is the best estimate for the number of model cars on each shelf?

A. 10

B. 12

C. 14

D. 15

9. What is the next number of this pattern?

214   225   236   247   258   _?_

_____

10. The table shows the number of points that 4 players scored in a game.

Player Scores

Player	Number of Points
Jill	3,423
Manny	2,875
Eric	4,148
Karen	3,039

A. How many points did Jill and Karen score in all? Show your work.

B. How many more points did Eric score than Manny? Show your work.

Factors and Multiples

Getting the Idea

Factors are numbers that are multiplied together to get a product.
Every whole number greater than 1 has at least one pair of factors: 1 and itself.
For example, 1 and 10 is a factor pair of 10. Another factor pair of 10 is 2 and 5.
You can use an area model to find factor pairs.

Example 1

What are the factor pairs of 8?

Strategy   **Use area models.**

> **Step 1**   Draw an area model that has 8 squares.
>
> The area model shows 1 square by 8 squares.
> One factor pair is 1 and 8.
>
> **Step 2**   Draw another area model that has 8 squares.
>
> The area model shows 2 squares by 4 squares.
> Another factor pair is 2 and 4.
>
> **Step 3**   You cannot make a different area model that has 8 squares.
> List the factor pairs from the two area models.

Solution   **There are two factor pairs of 8: 1 and 8, 2 and 4.**

You can write a factor pair using braces. For example, one factor pair of 14 is {2, 7}.

Example 2

List the factor pairs of 24.

Strategy   **Use a multiplication table.**

Step 1   Write the first factor pair of 24.

Every whole number greater than 1 has 1 and itself as factors.

$1 \times 24 = 24$

So, 1 and 24 is one factor pair.

Step 2   Find all the 24s inside the multiplication table.

×	0	1	2	3	4	5	6	7	8	9	10	11	12
1	0	1	2	3	4	5	6	7	8	9	10	11	12
2	0	2	4	6	8	10	12	14	16	18	20	22	24
3	0	3	6	9	12	15	18	21	24	27	30	33	36
4	0	4	8	12	16	20	24	28	32	36	40	44	48
5	0	5	10	15	20	25	30	35	40	45	50	55	60
6	0	6	12	18	24	30	36	42	48	54	60	66	72
7	0	7	14	21	28	35	42	49	56	63	70	77	84
8	0	8	16	24	32	40	48	56	64	72	80	88	96
9	0	9	18	27	36	45	54	63	72	81	90	99	108
10	0	10	20	30	40	50	60	70	80	90	100	110	120
11	0	11	22	33	44	55	66	77	88	99	110	121	132
12	0	12	24	36	48	60	72	84	96	108	120	132	144

Step 3   Write a number sentence for each factor pair of 24.

$2 \times 12 = 24$

$3 \times 8 = 24$

$4 \times 6 = 24$

Some factors are used more than once.

You only need to list them once.

Step 4   List all the factor pairs of 24.

1 and 24

2 and 12

3 and 8

4 and 6

Solution   **The factor pairs of 24 are {1, 24}, {2, 12}, {3, 8}, and {4, 6}.**

A **multiple** is the product of two factors. Multiples form a skip-counting pattern. To find the first few multiples of a number, keep that number as one factor, and multiply by 1, then 2, then 3, and so on. Here are eight multiples of 5:

$5 \times 1 = \mathbf{5}$ $5 \times 2 = \mathbf{10}$ $5 \times 3 = \mathbf{15}$ $5 \times 4 = \mathbf{20}$

$5 \times 5 = \mathbf{25}$ $5 \times 6 = \mathbf{30}$ $5 \times 7 = \mathbf{35}$ $5 \times 8 = \mathbf{40}$

You can also use a multiplication table to find multiples of a number. Read down a column, or to the right along a row, to find multiples of a number.

You can use a square area model to show a multiple with two of the same factors, such as $5 \times 5 = 25$.

Example 3

Is 36 a multiple of 6?

Strategy   **List multiples of 6.**

$6 \times 1 = 6$
$6 \times 2 = 12$
$6 \times 3 = 18$
$6 \times 4 = 24$
$6 \times 5 = 30$
$6 \times 6 = 36$

Solution   **Yes, 36 is a multiple of 6.**

A **prime number** is a whole number that has exactly two factors, 1 and itself.
A **composite number** is a whole number that has more than one factor pair.
The number 1 is neither a prime number nor a composite number.

Example 4

Is 17 a prime number or a composite number?

Strategy   **Find the factors of 17.**

Step 1   Draw an area model that has 17 squares.

The area model shows 1 square by 17 squares.

Two factors of 17 are 1 and 17.

Step 2   Decide if you can make a different area model with 17 squares.

No, you cannot make another area model.

Because 17 has exactly two factors, it is a prime number.

Solution   **17 is a prime number.**

Example 5

Is 4 a prime number or a composite number?

Strategy   **Find the factors of 4.**

List the factors of 4.

The factors of 4 are 1, 2, and 4.

Solution   **Because 4 has more than two factors, it is a composite number.**

Coached Example

Paige has some dollar bills that she wants to exchange for quarters. She can exchange each dollar for 4 quarters. Can she get exactly 25 quarters by exchanging her dollar bills?

Decide whether 25 is a multiple of 4.

Use the pattern of multiples of 4.

$4 \times 1 =$ _____

$4 \times 2 =$ _____

$4 \times 3 =$ _____

$4 \times 4 =$ _____

$4 \times 5 =$ _____

$4 \times 6 =$ _____

$4 \times 7 =$ _____

The number 25 is between the products _____ and _____.

25 _____ a multiple of 4.

Paige _____ **get exactly 25 quarters by exchanging dollar bills.**

Lesson Practice • Part 1

Choose the correct answer.

1. Which are **not** factors of 36?

   A. 2 and 16

   B. 3 and 12

   C. 4 and 9

   D. 6 and 6

2. Which number has 3 and 9 as factors?

   A. 12

   B. 24

   C. 27

   D. 49

3. Which number is a multiple of 4?

   A. 9

   B. 10

   C. 11

   D. 12

4. Dustin had 28 grapes. He put the same number of grapes in each bag. Which group of bags did Dustin make?

   A. 2 bags of 12 grapes

   B. 3 bags of 11 grapes

   C. 4 bags of 7 grapes

   D. 6 bags of 8 grapes

5. Kate's street address is a number with only two factors. Which mailbox could be Kate's?

   A.

   B.

   C.

   D.

6. Which is a multiple of 8?

   A. 73

   B. 48

   C. 23

   D. 18

7. Which number is **not** a prime number?

   A. 2

   B. 5

   C. 7

   D. 16

8. Which number is a prime number and a factor of 18?

   A. 3

   B. 6

   C. 9

   D. 18

9. What number between 48 and 58 is a prime number?

   _____

10. Ms. Henley wrote these numbers on the board.

    14   29   32   47   55   64

    A. Which numbers are prime numbers? Explain your answer.

    _____

    _____

    B. Which numbers are **not** prime numbers? Prove your answer by making a list of all the factor pairs of each number.

    _____

    _____

    _____

    _____

    _____

Lesson Practice • Part 2

Choose the correct answer.

1. Which number is a multiple of 8 and has 6 as a factor?

   A. 24

   B. 32

   C. 40

   D. 56

2. Which is the greatest prime number less than 100?

   A. 96

   B. 97

   C. 98

   D. 99

3. Which sentence about the multiples of 3 and 6 is true?

   A. Every multiple of 3 is also a multiple of 6.

   B. Every multiple of 6 is also a multiple of 3.

   C. Only the odd multiples of 6 are also multiples of 3.

   D. Only the odd multiples of 3 are also multiples of 6.

4. Which is **not** a factor pair of 36?

   A. 2 and 18

   B. 3 and 12

   C. 4 and 9

   D. 5 and 7

5. How many prime numbers are greater than 20 and less than 30?

   A. 4

   B. 3

   C. 2

   D. 1

6. Which has an odd number of factors?

   A. 25

   B. 27

   C. 32

   D. 41

7. Which number is a multiple of 4 and 9?

   A. 18

   B. 54

   C. 72

   D. 84

8. A whole number greater than 1 has 0 in its ones place. Which sentence is true?

   A. It has 2 and 4 as factors.

   B. It has 2 and 5 as factors.

   C. It has 4 and 5 as factors.

   D. It has 2, 4, and 5 as factors.

9. Which is a prime number and a factor of 49?

   A. 3   C. 6

   B. 5   D. 7

10. A number cube has faces 1 through 6. How many of the numbers on the cube are composite?

   A. 1   C. 3

   B. 2   D. 4

11. Which number is a multiple of 9 and has 6 as a factor?

   A. 24

   B. 27

   C. 36

   D. 42

12. Which shows all of the correct factors for 64?

   A. 1, 2, 4, 8, 16, 32, 64

   B. 1, 2, 3, 4, 8, 16, 21, 32, 64

   C. 2, 4, 8, 16, 32

   D. 2, 3, 4, 8, 16, 21, 32

13. Marty is thinking of a number greater than 40 and less than 50. His number is a composite number that has more ones than tens and has 3 and 6 as factors.

   A. Name the composite numbers that are greater than 40 and less than 50.

   _____

   B. What is Marty's number?

   _____

   C. Write the factor pairs for Marty's number.

   _____

   _____

14. Which is a factor of 56? Circle all that apply.

    A.   1

    B.   5

    C.   4

    D.   6

    E.   7

    F.   8

    G. 14

    H. 18

    I.   56

15. Select True or False for each statement.

    A. {6, 4} and {2, 12} are factor pairs of 24.   ◯ True ◯ False

    B. {4, 10} and {5, 8} are factor pairs of 40.   ◯ True ◯ False

    C. {8, 8} and {7, 7} are factor pairs of 64.   ◯ True ◯ False

    D. {3, 7} and {1, 21} are factor pairs of 21.   ◯ True ◯ False

    E. {6, 6} and {3, 6} are factor pairs of 36.   ◯ True ◯ False

16. Write each factor pair in the correct box.

{3, 16}   {6, 12}   {6, 8}   {4, 18}   {4, 12}   {8, 9}

Factor Pairs of 48	Factor Pairs of 72

17. Select True or False for each statement.

    A. 32 is a multiple of 8.   ○ True   ○ False

    B. 48 is a multiple of 6.   ○ True   ○ False

    C. 100 is a multiple of 11.   ○ True   ○ False

    D. 54 is a multiple of 4.   ○ True   ○ False

    E. 15 is a multiple of 3.   ○ True   ○ False

18. Draw a line from each statement to the number it describes.

    A. This number is a prime number and a factor of 27.   •   • 31

    B. This number is **not** a prime number and is a factor of 45.   •   • 30

    C. This number has 4 and 7 as factors.   •   • 18

    D. This number is a multiple of 6 and 10.   •   • 9

    E. This number is a multiple of 2 and 9.   •   • 28

    F. This number is between 25 and 32 and is a prime number.   •   • 3

19. Write each number in the correct box.

| 11 | 29 | 32 | 59 | 76 | 81 |

Prime Numbers	Composite Numbers

Add Whole Numbers

Getting the Idea

You can **add** to find the total when two or more groups are joined.

Here are the parts in an addition sentence.

2,411 + 3,524 = 5,935

addend   **addend**   **sum**

When you use paper and pencil to add, line up the digits on the ones place. Add the digits from right to left. If the sum of the digits in a column is 10 or greater, you will need to **regroup**.

Example 1

The table shows the number of miles Ms. Davis flew on each flight one day.

Miles Flown

From	To	Number of Miles
Boston, MA	Houston, TX	1,868
Houston, TX	Los Angeles, CA	1,524

How many miles did Ms. Davis fly in all?

Strategy **Write an addition sentence, then solve.**

Step 1 Write the addition sentence for the problem.

Let m represent the total number of miles.

$1,868 + 1,524 = m$

Step 2 Line up the digits on the ones place. Add from right to left.

Add the ones: $8 + 4 = 12$.

Regroup 12 ones as 1 ten 2 ones.

$$\begin{array}{r} 1 \\ 1,868 \\ +\,1,524 \\ \hline 2 \end{array}$$

Step 3   Add the tens: $1 + 6 + 2 = 9$.

$$
\begin{array}{r}
1 \\
1{,}868 \\
+\ 1{,}524 \\
\hline
92
\end{array}
$$

Step 4   Add the hundreds: $8 + 5 = 13$.

Regroup 13 hundreds as 1 thousand 3 hundreds.

$$
\begin{array}{r}
1\ \ 1 \\
1{,}868 \\
+\ 1{,}524 \\
\hline
392
\end{array}
$$

Step 5   Add the thousands: $1 + 1 + 1 = 3$.

$$
\begin{array}{r}
1\ \ 1 \\
1{,}868 \\
+\ 1{,}524 \\
\hline
3{,}392
\end{array}
$$

Solution   **Ms. Davis flew 3,392 miles in all.**

Example 2
Add.

$$8{,}715 + 6{,}409 = \boxed{}$$

Strategy   **Line up the digits on the ones place. Add from right to left.**

$$
\begin{array}{r}
1\ \ 1 \\
8{,}715 \\
+\ 6{,}409 \\
\hline
15{,}124
\end{array}
$$

Solution   **$8{,}715 + 6{,}409 = 15{,}124$**

Example 3

The table shows the number of points needed to trade for prizes.

Prize Points Needed for Trade

Prize	Number of Points
$100 Gift Card	5,950
MP3 Player	10,135
DVD Player	5,885

Alex has 13,050 points. For which two prizes can Alex trade his points?

Strategy **Find the sum of the points for two prizes. Then compare the sum to Alex's points.**

Step 1   Find the sum for the $100 gift card and MP3 player.

$$
\begin{array}{r}
1 \\
5,950 \\
+\ 10,135 \\
\hline
16,085
\end{array}
$$

Alex does not have enough points because 16,085 > 13,050.

Step 2   Find the sum for the $100 gift card and DVD player.

$$
\begin{array}{r}
1\ 1 \\
5,950 \\
+\ 5,885 \\
\hline
11,835
\end{array}
$$

Alex does have enough points because 11,835 < 13,050.

Step 3   Find the sum for the MP3 player and DVD player.

$$
\begin{array}{r}
1\ 1\ 1 \\
10,135 \\
+\ 5,885 \\
\hline
16,020
\end{array}
$$

Alex does not have enough points because 16,020 > 13,050.

Solution **Alex can trade his points for the gift card and the DVD player.**

Coached Example

Last year, a club had 12,468 members. This year, the club has 8,271 more members. How many members are in the club this year?

Write the addition sentence for the problem.

The club had _____ members last year.

The club has _____ more members this year.

Let *m* represent the total number of members in the club this year.

_____ + _____ = _____

Set up the problem.

Line up the digits on the ones place.

Add each place from right to left. Regroup if necessary.

The sum is _____.

There are _____ members in the club this year.

Lesson Practice • Part 1

Choose the correct answer.

1. Add.

$$3,674$$
$$+\ 4,369$$

A. 7,933

B. 7,943

C. 8,033

D. 8,043

2. Add.

$6,000 + 3,173 =$ ☐

A. 2,827

B. 9,173

C. 9,827

D. 10,937

3. The High Bridge in Kentucky is 1,125 feet long. The Brooklyn Bridge in New York is 4,864 feet longer than the High Bridge. What is the length of the Brooklyn Bridge?

A. 3,739 feet

B. 5,864 feet

C. 5,989 feet

D. 6,989 feet

4. Add.

$5,215 + 3,107 =$ ☐

A. 8,302

B. 8,312

C. 8,321

D. 8,322

5. Add.

$$43,674$$
$$+\ 3,372$$

A. 46,046

B. 46,946

C. 47,046

D. 77,396

6. At a tire factory, 3,166 tires were made on Thursday and 2,941 tires were made on Friday. How many tires were made on Thursday and Friday in all?

A. 6,107

B. 6,557

C. 6,602

D. 6,972

7. Mr. Newton ate 2,245 calories yesterday. He ate 2,583 calories today. How many calories did Mr. Newton eat in all?

A. 4,742

B. 4,828

C. 4,928

D. 5,828

8. Two years ago, Ms. Bolton bought a used car that showed 14,854 miles on the odometer. Last year, she drove 8,240 miles. This year, she drove 9,273 miles. How many miles does the odometer show now?

A. 17,513 miles

B. 24,127 miles

C. 31,367 miles

D. 32,367 miles

9. A recycling center recycles plastic bottles, aluminum cans, and glass bottles. The table shows the number of each material the center recycled in one day.

Materials Recycled

Material	Number Recycled
Plastic bottles	12,847
Aluminum cans	9,659
Glass bottles	3,273

A. Did the center recycle more plastic bottles or more aluminum cans and glass bottles combined that day? Show your work.

B. How many materials in all did the center recycle that day? Show your work.

Lesson Practice • Part 2

Choose the correct answer.

1. Add.

   $5{,}198 + 874 =$ ☐

   A. 5,962

   B. 5,972

   C. 6,062

   D. 6,072

2. Add.

   $$\begin{array}{r} 47{,}248 \\ +\ 36{,}185 \\ \hline \end{array}$$

   A. 73,323

   B. 73,433

   C. 83,433

   D. 84,433

3. The San Francisco Giants hosted three games in the 2014 World Series. The attendance figures for those games were 43,020; 43,066; and 43,087. What was the total attendance for the three games?

   A. 129,353

   B. 129,173

   C. 129,155

   D. 129,153

4. Add.

   $26{,}446 + 68{,}752 =$ ☐

   A. 84,198

   B. 85,198

   C. 95,198

   D. 95,208

5. Add.

   $$\begin{array}{r} 27{,}046 \\ +\ \ 9{,}427 \\ \hline \end{array}$$

   A. 36,473

   B. 36,563

   C. 36,573

   D. 37,463

6. There was already 28,450 pounds of goods on a freight elevator when 8 crates weighing 2,000 pounds each were loaded. What is the total weight on the freight elevator?

   A. 30,450 pounds

   B. 30,458 pounds

   C. 36,450 pounds

   D. 44,450 pounds

7. Each person in a club is asked to contribute $12 yearly dues. The club treasury has $1,725 before the contributions are collected. If all 57 members of the club contribute, how much money will be in the treasury?

A. $2,309

B. $2,399

C. $2,409

D. $2,419

8. Abby played a computer game three times. Her scores were 2,495; 3,115; and 2,675. What was Abby's total score?

A. 8,285

B. 8,275

C. 8,185

D. 7,175

9. The mean radius of Uranus is 15,759 miles. The mean radius of Saturn is 20,425 miles greater than Uranus's mean radius. Jupiter's mean radius is 7,257 miles greater than Saturn's mean radius.

A. What is the mean radius, in miles, of Saturn? Show your work.

B. What is the mean radius, in miles, of Jupiter? Show your work.

10. The recycling center received 15,670 plastic bottles on Monday, 789 bottles on Tuesday, and 456 bottles on Wednesday. Look at each number sentence. Can it be used to find the total number of plastic bottles, p, at the recycling center? Select Yes or No.

A. $15,670 - 789 - 456 = p$ ○ Yes ○ No

B. $15,670 + 789 + 456 = p$ ○ Yes ○ No

C. $(789 + 456) - 15,670 = p$ ○ Yes ○ No

D. $15,670 - (789 + 456) = p$ ○ Yes ○ No

E. $15,670 + (789 + 456) = p$ ○ Yes ○ No

11. Select True or False for each addition sentence.

A. $8,000 + 2,574 = 5,426$ ○ True ○ False

B. $3,843 + 5,379 = 9,222$ ○ True ○ False

C. $37,682 + 3,285 = 40,967$ ○ True ○ False

D. $2,909 + 3,160 = 5,069$ ○ True ○ False

12. Decide what regrouping is needed to find each sum. Write the addition problem in the correct box.

| 1,567 | 4,562 | 5,991 | 2,543 | 1,235 |
| +1,534 | +3,348 | +3,169 | +7,367 | +6,815 |

Regroup 2 Place Values	Regroup 3 Place Values

13. Jackson and his friends counted birds in their neighborhood last week. Jackson counted 175 wrens. His friends counted 235 robins and 126 sparrows. Circle the number that makes the statement true.

Jackson and his friends counted

361
426
536

birds in all.

14. Which problem has an answer of 8,850? Circle all that apply.

A. The chess club has 134 members. The members attended a national chess tournament along with 8,165 students from different schools and 551 adults. How many people were at the chess tournament?

B. In March, 3,567 people traveled by bus. In April, 5,323 people traveled by tram. What was the total number of bus and tram travelers?

C. The government printing office made 4,565 copies of a state map on Thursday and another 4,285 copies of the map on Friday. How many copies of the map were made in all?

D. Mount Denali in Alaska is 6,194 meters high. Mount Everest in southern Asia is 2,656 meters higher than Mount Denali. What is the height of Mount Everest?

15. Use numbers from the box to complete the sentences.

$8,765 + 2,770 =$ _____

$7,039 + 4,561 =$ _____

$1,989 + 2,103 =$ _____

$1,004 + 3,561 =$ _____

4,092
4,565
11,535
11,600

Subtract Whole Numbers

Getting the Idea

You can **subtract** to find how many are left when you take something away.

Here are the parts in a subtraction sentence.

$$3,667 \quad - \quad 1,243 \quad = \quad 2,424$$

minuend   **subtrahend**   **difference**

When you use paper and pencil to subtract, remember to line up the digits on the ones place. Subtract each digit from right to left. If the digit in the minuend is less than the digit in the subtrahend, you have to regroup.

Example 1

Peter scored 5,189 points playing a video game. Jacob scored 1,778 points playing the same game. How many more points did Peter score than Jacob?

Strategy   **Write a subtraction sentence, then solve.**

Step 1   Write the subtraction sentence for the problem.

Peter scored 5,189 points.

Jacob scored 1,778 points.

Let p represent how many more points Peter scored than Jacob.

$5,189 - 1,778 = p$

Step 2   Line up the digits on the ones place. Subtract from right to left.

Subtract the ones: $9 - 8 = 1$

$$\begin{array}{r} 5,189 \\ -\ 1,778 \\ \hline 1 \end{array}$$

Step 3   Subtract the tens: $8 - 7 = 1$

$$\begin{array}{r} 5,189 \\ -\ 1,778 \\ \hline 11 \end{array}$$

Step 4   There are not enough hundreds to subtract.

Regroup 1 thousand as 10 hundreds. Now there are 11 hundreds.

```
    4 11
    5,1 8 9
  − 1,7 7 8
          1 1
```

Step 5   Subtract the hundreds: 11 − 7 = 4

```
    4 11
    5,1 8 9
  − 1,7 7 8
      4 1 1
```

Step 6   Subtract the thousands: 4 − 1 = 3

```
    4 11
    5,1 8 9
  − 1,7 7 8
    3,4 1 1
```

Solution   **Peter scored 3,411 more points than Jacob.**

When subtracting with zeros in the minuend, you may have to regroup from more than one place.

Example 2

Subtract.

4,007 − 1,526 = ☐

Strategy   **Line up the digits on the ones place. Subtract from right to left.**

Step 1   Line up the digits on the ones place.

Subtract the ones: 7 − 6 = 1

```
    4,007
  − 1,526
        1
```

Step 2   There are not enough tens to subtract and no hundreds to regroup.

Regroup 1 thousand as 10 hundreds.

Then regroup 1 hundred as 10 tens.

$$
\begin{array}{r}
9 \\
3 \;\; \cancel{10} \;\; 10 \\
\cancel{4},\cancel{0}\,\cancel{0}\,7 \\
-\,1,5\,2\,6 \\
\hline
1
\end{array}
$$

Step 3   Subtract the tens: $10 - 2 = 8$

$$
\begin{array}{r}
9 \\
3 \;\; \cancel{10} \;\; 10 \\
\cancel{4},\cancel{0}\,\cancel{0}\,7 \\
-\,1,5\,2\,6 \\
\hline
8\,1
\end{array}
$$

Step 4   Subtract the hundreds: $9 - 5 = 4$

$$
\begin{array}{r}
9 \\
3 \;\; \cancel{10} \;\; 10 \\
\cancel{4},\cancel{0}\,\cancel{0}\,7 \\
-\,1,5\,2\,6 \\
\hline
4\,8\,1
\end{array}
$$

Step 5   Subtract the thousands: $3 - 1 = 2$

$$
\begin{array}{r}
9 \\
3 \;\; \cancel{10} \;\; 10 \\
\cancel{4},\cancel{0}\,\cancel{0}\,7 \\
-\,1,5\,2\,6 \\
\hline
2,4\,8\,1
\end{array}
$$

Solution $4,007 - 1,526 = 2,481$

Addition is the inverse operation of subtraction.
You can check the answer to a subtraction problem using addition.

$$
\begin{array}{r}
2,481 \\
+\,1,526 \\
\hline
4,007
\end{array}
\qquad
\begin{array}{r}
4,007 \\
-\,1,526 \\
\hline
2,481
\end{array}
$$

The sum is 4,007, which matches the minuend. So, the answer is correct.

Example 3

In a survey about favorite movies, 4,893 male students and 5,203 female students gave a response. There were also responses from 1,572 adults. How many more students than adults responded to the survey?

Strategy   **Write number sentences to represent the problem. Then solve.**

Step 1   Write an addition sentence to find the total number of students.

There were 4,893 male students.

There were 5,203 female students.

Let s represent the total number of students.

$4{,}893 + 5{,}203 = s$

Step 2   Find the total number of students.

Add. Regroup if necessary.

$$
\begin{array}{r}
1 \\
4{,}893 \\
+\ 5{,}203 \\
\hline
10{,}096
\end{array}
$$

Step 3   Write a subtraction sentence to find how many more students than adults responded to the survey.

There were 10,096 students.

There were 1,572 adults.

Let n represent how many more students.

$10{,}096 - 1{,}572 = n$

Step 4   Find how many more students than adults responded to the survey.

Subtract. Regroup if necessary.

$$
\begin{array}{r}
9 \\
0\ 10\ 10 \\
\cancel{1}\cancel{0}{,}\ \cancel{0}\ 9\ 6 \\
-\ \ 1{,}5\ 7\ 2 \\
\hline
8{,}5\ 2\ 4
\end{array}
$$

Step 5   Use addition to check the subtraction.

$$
\begin{array}{r}
1 \\
8,524 \\
+\ 1,572 \\
\hline
10,096 \\
\end{array}
$$ ← This matches the minuend.

The answer is correct.

Solution   **8,524 more students than adults responded to the survey.**

Coached Example

Lynn had $2,812 in her checking account. She spent $1,150 on a television and $665 on a video camera. How much does Lynn have left in her checking account?

Decide how to solve the problem.

_____ to find the total amount Lynn spent on the television and the video camera.

Then _____ the sum from the amount Lynn had in her checking account.

Add to find the total amount Lynn spent.

Add from right to left. Regroup if necessary.

Subtract to find how much Lynn has left in her checking account.

Subtract from right to left. Regroup if necessary.

Use addition to check the subtraction.

Lynn has $_____ left in her checking account.

Lesson Practice • Part 1

Choose the correct answer.

1. Subtract.

   8,715
   − 5,923

   A. 2,792

   B. 2,802

   C. 2,892

   D. 3,792

2. Subtract.

   6,000 − 2,173 = ☐

   A. 8,173

   B. 3,937

   C. 3,927

   D. 3,827

3. Sara scored 2,293 points in a video game. That was 1,536 points more than Elvin's score on the same game. How many points did Elvin score?

   A. 757

   B. 1,757

   C. 1,767

   D. 3,829

4. Subtract.

   9,534
   − 4,085

   A. 4,449   **C.** 5,549

   B. 5,449   **D.** 5,551

5. Subtract.

   18,143
   − 5,923

   A. 12,220

   B. 12,320

   C. 12,820

   D. 41,113

6. The highest point of the Great Smoky Mountains in Tennessee is 6,643 feet. The highest point of the mountain Jordan has climbed is 1,870 feet. How much higher is the highest point of the Great Smoky Mountains than the highest point of the mountain Jordan climbed?

   A. 4,663 feet

   B. 4,773 feet

   C. 4,873 feet

   D. 5,233 feet

7. There are 11,510 seats in the basketball arena. For one game, 9,465 seats were filled. How many seats were empty?

A. 2,165

B. 2,155

C. 2,045

D. 1,045

8. Carol bought a car with a final price of $17,067. This price included an interior leather package for $1,258 and satellite radio for $359. What was the price of the car without these features?

A. $16,708

B. $16,450

C. $15,809

D. $15,450

9. A toy company made $27,358 from selling game consoles. It also made $3,725 from video games and $8,440 from board games.

A. How much more did the company make from board games than from video games? Show your work.

B. How much more did the company make from game consoles than from video and board games combined? Explain how you solved the problem.

_____

_____

_____

Lesson Practice • Part 2

Choose the correct answer.

1. Subtract: 7,208 − 2,654 = ☐

    A. 4,544

    B. 4,554

    C. 4,654

    D. 5,644

2. Subtract.

    $$\begin{array}{r} 47,008 \\ -\ 28,192 \\ \hline \end{array}$$

    A. 18,806

    B. 18,816

    C. 18,906

    D. 18,916

3. At 31,700 square miles, Lake Superior has the greatest area of the Great Lakes. Lake Ontario, at 7,340 square miles, has the least area of the Great Lakes. How much greater is the area of Lake Superior than Lake Ontario?

    A. 23,360 square miles

    B. 23,460 square miles

    C. 24,360 square miles

    D. 24,460 square miles

4. Subtract: 78,615 − 48,852 = ☐

    A. 29,763

    B. 29,863

    C. 30,243

    D. 30,853

5. Subtract.

    $$\begin{array}{r} 80,000 \\ -\ 13,684 \\ \hline \end{array}$$

    A. 66,316

    B. 67,326

    C. 76,316

    D. 77,426

6. Michigan has a total area of 96,714 square miles. Included in that area is 40,175 square miles of water. What is Michigan's land area?

    A. 55,539 square miles

    B. 55,649 square miles

    C. 56,539 square miles

    D. 56,639 square miles

7. Mr. Arnold has $4,172 in his checking account. He buys a computer for $1,379 and a printer for $244. He uses a check to pay for both items. What is the amount that is left in Mr. Arnold's checking account?

   A. $5,795

   B. $3,037

   C. $2,549

   D. $1,623

8. A team's goal was to have a total attendance of 45,000 in its 6 home games. The team had an attendance of 7,275 each game. Which sentence about the total attendance is true?

   A. It was short of the goal by 225.

   B. It was short of the goal by 1,350.

   C. It was short of the goal by 2,450.

   D. It was short of the goal by 37,725.

9. The table shows the number of days it takes some planets to revolve around the Sun.

Revolution Around the Sun

Planet	Number of Days
Jupiter	4,330
Saturn	10,752
Uranus	30,664

   A. How many more days does it take Saturn than Jupiter to revolve around the Sun? Show your work.

   B. How many more days does it take Uranus to revolve around the Sun than Jupiter and Saturn combined? Show your work.

10. Circle the number that makes the sentence true.

    $5,617 - 4,538 =$

    1,189

    1,121

    1,079

11. Select True or False for each subtraction sentence.

    A. $5,000 - 3,063 = 1,937$ ○ True   ○ False

    B. $8,923 - 6,106 = 2,807$ ○ True   ○ False

    C. $2,351 - 1,561 = 1,790$ ○ True   ○ False

    D. $11,251 - 6,441 = 4,810$ ○ True   ○ False

12. A tire factory makes bicycle, car, and truck tires. In one week, the factory made 98,900 tires. It made 57,567 car tires and 29,880 truck tires. How many bike tires were made that week? Use numbers from the box to write the number sentences to solve the problem. Then complete the statement.

_____ + _____ = _____

_____ − _____ = _____

The factory made _____ bike tires.

11,453
29,880
57,567
87,447
98,900

13. Draw a line from each subtraction problem to its difference.

    A. $3,490 - 1,207$ •   • 2,073

    B. $11,344 - 9,271$ •   • 2,283

    C. $6,891 - 4,678$ •   • 2,703

    D. $7,999 - 5,296$ •   • 2,213

14. Solve each problem. Is the difference 2,447? Select Yes or No.

   A. $4,586 - 2,139 = \boxed{}$ ○ Yes   ○ No

   B. $3,897 - 1,490 = \boxed{}$ ○ Yes   ○ No

   C. $11,401 - 8,954 = \boxed{}$ ○ Yes   ○ No

   D. $8,505 - 5,358 = \boxed{}$ ○ Yes   ○ No

15. Use the numbers to complete the subtraction problem. Write the correct digit in each box.

1	2	3	4	5	6

```
      6    4    5    4
  −   2    9    9  [   ]
  ─────────────────────
  [   ][   ][   ]   9
```

Round Whole Numbers

Getting the Idea

You can **round** a number to the nearest 10 or 100. When rounding, you replace a number with one that tells *about* how much or *about* how many. Rounding gives a number close to the exact amount.

You can use a number line to help you round numbers.

A number line can help you decide which 10 or 100 a number is closer to.

Example 1

What is 128 rounded to the nearest 10?

Strategy   **Use a number line.**

Step 1   Place 128 on a number line.

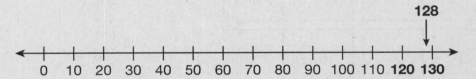

Step 2   Decide whether 128 is closer to 120 or 130.

128 is closer to 130 than to 120.

128 rounds up to 130.

Solution   **128 rounded to the nearest 10 is 130.**

You can also use rounding rules to round numbers.

Rounding Rules

1. Look at the digit to the right of the place you are rounding to.

2. If the digit is less than 5, round down.
   Leave the digit in the rounding place as is.

3. If the digit is greater than or equal to 5, round up.
   Increase the digit in the rounding place by 1.

4. Change the digits to the right of the rounding place to zeros.

Example 2

A chandelier has 1,723 crystal pieces. To the nearest hundred, about how many crystal pieces does the chandelier have?

Strategy **Use rounding rules to round to the nearest hundred.**

Step 1 Find the rounding place.

Underline the digit in the place you want to round to, the hundreds place.

1,<u>7</u>23

Step 2 Decide to round up or down.

Look at the digit to the right of the rounding place, in the tens place.

1,7<u>2</u>3

The digit is 2. It is less than 5, so round down.

Step 3 Round 1,723 down to the nearest hundred.

Leave the digit in the hundreds place.

Change the digits to the right of the hundreds place to 0.

1,723 → 1,700

Solution **To the nearest hundred, the chandelier has about 1,700 crystal pieces.**

Example 3

Quinn has 23,867 frequent flyer miles. To the nearest thousand, about how many frequent flyer miles does Quinn have?

Strategy   **Use rounding rules to round to the nearest thousand.**

Step 1   Find the place you want to round to. Look at the digit to the right.

You are rounding to the nearest thousand, so find the thousands digit.

Then look at the hundreds digit.

2<u>3</u>,**867**

Step 2   Decide to round up or down.

8 is greater than 5, so round up.

Step 3   Round 23,867 up to the nearest thousand.

Increase the thousands digit by 1.

Change the digits to the right of the thousands place to 0.

23,867 ⟶ 24,000

Solution   **To the nearest thousand, Quinn has about 24,000 frequent flyer miles.**

Example 4

Martin's Music Shop earned $12,445 in April, $15,125 in May, and $14,675 in June. During which two months did Martin's Music Shop earn about the same amount of money?

Strategy   **Round to the nearest thousand. Then compare.**

Step 1   Round each money amount to the nearest thousand.

April: $12,445 rounds down to $12,000.

May: $15,125 rounds down to $15,000.

June: $14,675 rounds up to $15,000.

Step 2   Compare the amounts.

The amounts for May and June both rounded to $15,000.

Solution   **Martin's Music Shop earned about the same amount of money in May and June.**

Coached Example

A game Web site received 129,354 hits in one day. To the nearest ten thousand, about how many hits did the game Web site receive that day?

The place to be rounded to is _____.

The digit in this place is _____.

The digit to the right of the rounding place is _____.

This digit is _____ than 5.

Since the digit to the right is greater than 5, round _____.

Change all the digits to the right of the rounding place to _____.

129,354 rounds to _____.

To the nearest ten thousand, the game Web site received about _____ hits that day.

Lesson Practice • Part 1

Choose the correct answer.

1. What is 33,719 rounded to the nearest thousand?

   A. 30,000

   B. 33,000

   C. 34,000

   D. 40,000

2. Which shows 144,683 rounded to the nearest ten thousand?

   A. 100,000

   B. 140,000

   C. 144,000

   D. 145,000

3. Which number does **not** round to 500?

   A. 459

   B. 486

   C. 521

   D. 550

4. Francesca has 281 marbles in her collection. To the nearest hundred, about how many marbles does Francesca have?

   A. 300

   B. 290

   C. 280

   D. 200

5. To the nearest ten, which number rounds to 320?

   A. 314

   B. 322

   C. 326

   D. 330

6. In the first week of August, 4,784 people visited a water park. To the nearest hundred, about how many people visited the water park in the first week?

   A. 4,800

   B. 4,700

   C. 4,600

   D. 4,000

7. A resort vacation for two people costs $1,577. To the nearest hundred dollars, about how much does the trip cost?

   A. $2,000

   B. $1,680

   C. $1,600

   D. $1,500

8. The table shows the number of books in each library.

Library	Number of Books
North Park	7,935
Central	8,162
Mountain View	7,493
Golden Hill	8,046

To the nearest thousand, which library has about 7,000 books?

   A. North Park

   B. Central

   C. Mountain View

   D. Golden Hill

9. For the county bake sale, the softball team baked 322 cookies, 295 brownies, and 248 muffins.

   A. Round each type of baked good to the nearest hundred.

_____

_____

_____

   B. The softball team baked about the same amount of two types of baked goods. What types were they? Explain your answer.

_____

_____

_____

Lesson Practice • Part 2

Choose the correct answer.

1. The longest land tunnel in the United States is 8,960 feet long. Layla said that 8,960 rounds to 9,000. To which place or places did Layla round?

   A. ten only

   B. hundred only

   C. thousand only

   D. hundred and thousand

2. Monaco is the world's most densely populated country with 39,508 people per square mile. To the nearest hundred, what is 39,508?

   A. 39,000

   B. 39,500

   C. 39,600

   D. 40,000

3. The leading truck had 713,960 sales in the United States in 2013. What is 713,960 rounded to the nearest thousand?

   A. 710,000

   B. 713,000

   C. 714,000

   D. 720,000

4. What is the greatest whole number that rounds to 5,000 to any place?

   A. 5,009

   B. 5,049

   C. 5,499

   D. 5,999

5. The table shows the number of cars that were imported into the United States from the United Kingdom during four years.

   Cars Imported from United Kingdom

Year	Number of Cars
2010	96,689
2011	95,742
2012	114,073
2013	115,326

   To the nearest ten thousand, in which years was the number of cars imported about 100,000?

   A. 2010 and 2011

   B. 2010 and 2013

   C. 2011 and 2012

   D. 2012 and 2013

6. The new car that Ms. Wise bought cost $23,975. Which sentence about the cost is **not** true?

   A. The cost was $20,000 to the nearest ten thousand dollars.

   B. The cost was $23,000 to the nearest thousand dollars.

   C. The cost was $24,000 to the nearest hundred dollars.

   D. The cost was $23,980 to the nearest ten dollars.

7. To which place or places does 769,600 round to 770,000?

   A. thousands and ten thousands

   B. hundreds and thousands

   C. hundreds and ten thousands

   D. hundreds, thousands, and ten thousands

8. The Kansas City Chiefs play in a stadium that seats 76,416 people for football. The Denver Broncos' stadium seats 76,125 for football. Which sentence is true?

   A. Both stadiums can seat 76,000 to the nearest thousand.

   B. Neither stadium can seat 76,000 to the nearest thousand.

   C. Only Kansas City's stadium can seat 76,000 to the nearest thousand.

   D. Only Denver's stadium can seat 76,000 to the nearest thousand.

9. Which number does **not** round to 60,000 to the nearest ten thousand?

   A. 57,293   **C.** 64,326

   B. 59,141   **D.** 65,043

10. The land area of Washington state is 66,456 square miles.

   A. What is 66,456 rounded to the nearest hundred?

   _____

   B. What is 66,456 rounded to the nearest ten thousand?

   _____

   C. Ann said that 66,456 rounds to 67,000 to the nearest thousand. Is she correct? Explain your reasoning.

   _____

   _____

   _____

11. To the nearest hundred, which number rounds to 600? Circle all that apply.

   A. 569

   B. 613

   C. 654

   D. 587

   E. 649

12. Roberto collected 456 bottles to recycle. Circle the number that completes each statement.

To the nearest ten, Roberto collected

400
450
460
500

bottles.

To the nearest hundred, Roberto collected

400
450
460
500

bottles.

13. Draw a line from each number to its nearest hundred.

   A. 347 •   • 500

   B. 209 •   • 400

   C. 350 •   • 300

   D. 456 •   • 200

14. Which number rounds to 2,000? Circle all that apply.

    A. 2,578 rounded to the nearest thousand

    B. 1,999 rounded to the nearest hundred

    C. 1,604 rounded to the nearest thousand

    D. 1,691 rounded to the nearest hundred

    E. 2,490 rounded to the nearest thousand

    F. 1,551 rounded to the nearest thousand

15. Mira rounded the number of photos on her computer to the nearest thousand and got 11,000. Look at each number. Could it be the number of photos Mira has? Select Yes or No.

    A. 11,559   ○ Yes ○ No

    B. 11,168   ○ Yes ○ No

    C. 10,890   ○ Yes ○ No

    D. 11,090   ○ Yes ○ No

    E. 10,489   ○ Yes ○ No

16. To round each number to the nearest hundred, should you round down or round up? Write the number in the correct box.

| 12,758 | 5,578 | 817 | 761 | 29,319 | 2,748 |

Round Down	Round Up

Estimate Sums and Differences

Getting the Idea

You can use rounded numbers to **estimate** sums and differences.
Your estimates will vary depending on what place you round to.

Rounding to tens	**Rounding to hundreds**	**Rounding to thousands**
4,252 → 4,250	4,252 → 4,300	4,252 → 4,000
+1,607 → +1,610	+1,607 → +1,600	+1,607 → +2,000
5,860	5,900	6,000

Example 1

Kendra scored 9,235 points in the first round of a computer game. She scored 8,790 points in the second round. About how many points did she score in all?

Strategy   **Round each number to its greatest place and then solve.**

> Step 1   Round each number to its greatest place: thousands.
>
> The number 9,235 rounds down to 9,000 because 2 < 5.
>
> The number 8,790 rounds up to 9,000 because 7 > 5.

> Step 2   Add the rounded numbers.
>
> 9,000 + 9,000 = 18,000

Solution   **Kendra scored about 18,000 points in all.**

Example 2

Lee has 4,837 building blocks. He gave 1,175 building blocks to Sarah. To the nearest thousand, about how many blocks does Lee have left?

Strategy   **Round each number to the thousands place and then solve.**

Step 1   Round each number to the thousands place.

4,837 rounds up to 5,000 because 8 > 5.

1,175 rounds down to 1,000 because 1 < 5.

Step 2   Subtract the rounded numbers.

$5,000 - 1,000 = 4,000$

Solution   **To the nearest thousand, Lee has about 4,000 building blocks left.**

When you need an exact answer, estimating before you add or subtract is a good way to see if your answer is reasonable. You can quickly tell if you made an error when adding or subtracting the numbers.

Example 3

Pam said that $37,249 + 46,867$ is equal to 74,126. Is her answer reasonable?

Strategy   **Estimate to check whether an answer is reasonable.**

Step 1   Estimate by rounding to thousands.

37,249 rounds down to 37,000 because 2 < 5.

46,867 rounds up to 47,000 because 8 > 5.

Step 2   Add the rounded numbers.

$37,000 + 47,000 = 84,000$

Step 3   Compare the estimate to the answer.

84,000 is not close to 74,216.

Solution   **Pam's answer is not reasonable.**

Coached Example

A theme park had 74,868 visitors last month. This month, the park had 79,967 visitors. About how many more visitors did the theme park have this month than last month?

Estimate by rounding to thousands.

The number 74,868 rounds to _____.

The number 79,967 rounds to _____.

Subtract the rounded numbers.

_____ − _____ = _____

About _____ more people visited the theme park this month than last month.

Lesson Practice • Part 1

Choose the correct answer.

1. Which is the best way to estimate 68 + 71?

    A. 60 + 70

    B. 60 + 80

    C. 70 + 70

    D. 80 + 70

2. Which is the best way to estimate 278 − 127?

    A. 200 − 100

    B. 300 − 100

    C. 200 − 200

    D. 300 − 200

3. Janelle cut 4 pieces of rope that measured 43 inches, 82 inches, 53 inches, and 27 inches. Which is the best estimate of the total length of all 4 pieces of rope?

    A. 100 inches

    B. 150 inches

    C. 200 inches

    D. 300 inches

4. A store had 135 customers in the morning and 884 customers in the afternoon. About how many more customers did the store have in the afternoon than in the morning?

    A.   600

    B.   800

    C.   900

    D. 1,000

5. A movie theater sold 23,874 tickets in August. It sold 15,345 tickets in September. About how many more tickets were sold in August than in September?

    A. 2,000

    B. 3,000

    C. 5,000

    D. 9,000

6. Reggie scored 3,219 points in the first round of a game. He scored 5,199 points in the second round. How many points did he score in all, to the nearest thousand?

    A. 2,000

    B. 4,000

    C. 8,000

    D. 9,000

Use the table for questions 7 and 8.

Distances Craig Biked

Year	Distance (in miles)
2013	1,287
2014	1,365
2015	2,082

7. To the nearest thousand, how much farther did Craig bike in 2015 than in 2014?

   A. 1,000 miles

   B. 2,000 miles

   C. 3,000 miles

   D. 4,000 miles

8. To the nearest hundred, how many miles did Craig bike in all?

   A. 4,000 miles

   B. 4,300 miles

   C. 4,600 miles

   D. 4,800 miles

9. Last month, Ms. Barkley spent $378 on food, $925 on rent, and $272 on utilities.

   A. What is the total amount Ms. Barkley spent on those three things last month? Show your work.

   B. Find the estimated total amount Ms. Barkley spent on those three things. Compare the estimate to the exact amount. Is your answer reasonable? Explain your answer.

   _____

   _____

   _____

Lesson Practice • Part 2

Choose the correct answer.

1. Florida has 3,331 miles of shoreline. Georgia has 2,344 miles of shoreline. To the nearest hundred, how much more shoreline does Florida have than Georgia?

   A. 900 miles

   B. 1,000 miles

   C. 1,100 miles

   D. 1,200 miles

2. Austin is going to estimate the difference of 32,551 − 32,549. To which place should Austin **not** use to round for the estimate?

   A. tens

   B. hundreds

   C. thousands

   D. ten thousands

3. Charlotte jogged 128 miles in April, 142 miles in May, 175 miles in June, and 157 miles in July. Which is the best estimate for the distance she jogged during those four months?

   A. 800 miles

   B. 620 miles

   C. 610 miles

   D. 580 miles

4. The greatest elevation in Oregon is Mount Hood at 11,240 feet. The greatest elevation in North Carolina is Mount Mitchell at 6,684 feet. To the nearest hundred, how much greater is the elevation of Mount Hood than Mount Mitchell?

   A. 4,500 feet

   B. 4,600 feet

   C. 4,700 feet

   D. 5,000 feet

5. Pennsylvania has two Major League Baseball teams. The Phillies' stadium seats 43,651 and the Pirates' stadium seats 38,362. Which is the best estimate for the number of seats that the stadiums have combined?

   A. 80,000

   B. 81,000

   C. 82,000

   D. 83,000

6. Caleb is going to estimate the sum of 692 + 204. He said that he should round to the nearest ten instead of the nearest hundred because rounding to a lesser place always gives the better estimate. Which sentence is true?

   A. Caleb is correct because rounding to the lesser place always gives a better estimate.

   B. Caleb is incorrect because both places will give the same estimate.

   C. Caleb is incorrect because rounding to the greater place always gives a better estimate.

   D. Caleb is incorrect because rounding to the nearest hundred gives a better estimate.

7. Tony scored 78,295 points on a computer game. Brayden scored 92,755 points playing the same game. Which is the best estimate for how many more points Brayden scored than Tony?

   A. 10,000   C. 30,000

   B. 20,000   D. 40,000

8. Mrs. Forman's monthly budget includes $2,435 for mortgage, $1,159 for healthcare, and $520 for power. Which is the best estimate for the amount Mrs. Forman budgets for these items each month?

   A. $4,600   C. $4,100

   B. $4,300   D. $4,000

9. The table shows the daily attendance for a festival.

Festival Attendance

Day	Attendance
Friday	6,792
Saturday	15,347
Sunday	12,628

   A. The organizers of the festival hoped to have 30,000 total attendance. Will an estimate tell if the organizers achieved their goal? Explain your answer.

   _____

   _____

   B. About how many more people attended on Saturday than on Friday? Show your work.

   _____

10. Use numbers from the box to estimate the sum of 239 + 588.

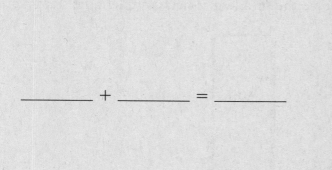

_____ + _____ = _____

| 200 |
| 300 |
| 500 |
| 600 |
| 700 |
| 800 |

11. Select True or False for each statement.

   A. To the nearest hundred, 2,340 − 1,103 is 1,200.   ○ True   ○ False

   B. To the nearest thousand, 6,740 − 3,103 is 3,000.   ○ True   ○ False

   C. To the nearest hundred, 1,459 + 8,399 is 9,700.   ○ True   ○ False

   D. To the nearest thousand, 5,240 + 6,703 is 12,000.   ○ True   ○ False

12. Which number sentence has an estimated sum or difference of 800? Circle all that apply.

   A. 4,730 − 3,925 = ☐

   B. 689 + 150 = ☐

   C. 1,005 − 259 = ☐

   D. 507 + 332 = ☐

   E. 1,473 − 668 = ☐

13. Fourth-grade students at Hill Elementary School made colored fliers for their class play. They made 215 green fliers and 463 yellow fliers. They handed out 413 fliers. To the nearest hundred, about how many fliers did they have left? Use numbers from the box to write number sentences to solve the problem. Then complete the statement.

_____ + _____ = _____

_____ − _____ = _____

They had about _____ fliers left.

200
300
400
500
600
700

14. Many loggerhead sea turtles make their nests each year on Florida beaches. The table shows the number of sea turtle nests found at a Florida wildlife refuge over a four-year period. Which statement is true? Circle all that apply.

Number of Loggerhead Turtle Nests

Year	Number of Nests
2009	10,374
2010	14,468
2011	11,841
2012	18,809

A. To the nearest thousand, 31,000 nests were found in 2011 and 2012.

B. To the nearest hundred, 24,800 nests were found in 2009 and 2010.

C. To the nearest thousand, there were 9,000 more nests found in 2012 than in 2009.

D. To the nearest thousand, a total of 55,000 nests were found in the four-year period.

Estimate Products and Quotients

Getting the Idea

As with addition and subtraction problems, sometimes you do not need an exact answer to solve multiplication and division problems.

To estimate a product, round the numbers given in the problem. Then use mental math to find the estimated answer.

Example 1

Phil delivers 38 newspapers each Sunday. About how many Sunday newspapers does he deliver in a year? There are about 52 weeks in a year.

Strategy   **Round each number. Use mental math to multiply.**

Step 1   Decide how to solve the problem.

He delivers 38 newspapers each Sunday.

There are 52 weeks in a year.

Estimate 52 × 38.

Step 2   Round each number to the nearest 10.

52   ×   38   =   ☐

↓   ↓

50   ×   40   =   ☐

Step 3   Use mental math to multiply the rounded numbers.

Think: 5 × 4 = 20

50 × 40 = 2,000

Solution   **Phil delivers about 2,000 Sunday newspapers a year.**

You can use estimation to decide if an answer is reasonable. Before you find the exact answer, find the estimated product. Then compare the estimate to the exact answer to see if the answer makes sense.

Example 2

Ms. Barrows pays $479 to rent a car for a month. How much will Ms. Barrows pay to rent a car for 3 months?

Strategy   **Find the estimated answer. Then compare it to the exact answer.**

Step 1   Write the multiplication sentence for the problem.

She pays $479 for 1 month.

She rents the car for 3 months.

Let n represent the total amount she will pay for 3 months.

$3 \times \$479 = n$

Step 2   Estimate the answer.

$479 rounds up to $500.

$3 \times \$500 = \$1,500$

The answer should be about $1,500.

Step 3   Find the exact answer.

$$\begin{array}{r} 22 \\ \$479 \\ \times\ \ \ \ 3 \\ \hline \$1,437 \end{array}$$

Step 4   Compare the exact answer to the estimated answer.

$1,437 is close to $1,500.

The answer is reasonable.

Solution   **Ms. Barrows will pay $1,437 to rent a car for 3 months.**

You can use **compatible numbers** and mental math to estimate quotients. Compatible numbers are close to the exact numbers and are easy to compute with. To estimate $55 \div 7$, think of a number close to 55 that can be evenly divided by 7. 56 is close to 55 and $56 \div 7 = 8$. So, $55 \div 7$ is about 8.

Example 3

A basketball team scored 143 points in 3 games. If the team scored the same number of points in each game, about how many points did the team score in one game?

Strategy   **Use compatible numbers to estimate the quotient.**

Step 1   Decide how to solve the problem.

The team scored 143 points in 3 games.

Estimate $143 \div 3 = \boxed{}$.

Step 2   Find a number close to 143 that is compatible with 3.

150 is close to 143 and can be evenly divided by 3.

Step 3   Estimate the quotient.

$15 \div 3 = 5$, so $150 \div 3 = 50$.

Solution   **The basketball team scored about 50 points a game.**

Sometimes you may need to change both numbers to find compatible numbers.

Example 4

Adele orders 135 roses for a reception. She wants to put the same number of roses in each vase. If she has 9 vases, how many roses will Adele put in each vase?

Strategy   **Use compatible numbers to find the estimated answer.**
Then compare it to the exact answer.

Step 1   Write the division sentence for the problem.

She has 135 roses and 9 vases.

Find $135 \div 9 = \boxed{}$.

Step 2   Use compatible numbers to estimate the answer.

135 is close to 140. 9 is close to 10.

$140 \div 10 = 14$

The answer should be about 14.

Step 3   Find the exact answer.

$135 \div 9 = 15$

Step 4   Compare the exact answer to the estimated answer.

15 is close to 14. The answer is reasonable.

Solution   **Adele will put 15 roses in each vase.**

Coached Example

A T-shirt factory shipped 7 boxes of shirts. Each box had 275 shirts. How many shirts did the factory ship in all?

Write the number sentence for the problem.

Find _____ × _____ = ☐.

Estimate the answer.

Round 275 to the nearest 100.

275 rounds to _____.

Multiply the rounded numbers.

_____ × _____ = _____

The answer should be about _____.

Find the exact answer.

Is the exact answer close to the estimated answer? _____

Is the answer reasonable? _____

The factory shipped _____ shirts in all.

Lesson 16: Estimate Products and Quotients

Lesson Practice • Part 1

Choose the correct answer.

1. Which is the best estimate for
1,589 × 4?

   A. 5,600

   B. 6,000

   C. 6,400

   D. 8,000

2. The local bakery makes 7 trays of
oatmeal cookies each morning. Each
tray holds 22 cookies. About how
many cookies does the bakery make
each morning?

   A. 140

   B. 180

   C. 210

   D. 300

3. Which is the best way to estimate
258 ÷ 5?

   A. 350 ÷ 5

   B. 300 ÷ 5

   C. 250 ÷ 5

   D. 200 ÷ 5

4. Which is the best way to estimate
314 ÷ 9?

   A. 270 ÷ 9

   B. 300 ÷ 9

   C. 314 ÷ 10

   D. 310 ÷ 10

5. Yesterday morning, a museum exhibit
was open for 3 hours. There were
2,378 visitors each hour. Which is the
best estimate for how many visitors in
all 3 hours?

   A. 7,000

   B. 7,200

   C. 7,500

   D. 8,000

6. Which is the best estimate for
1,639 ÷ 4?

   A. 100

   B. 200

   C. 300

   D. 400

Duplicating any part of this book is prohibited by law.

173

7. There are 6 bins of aluminum cans to be recycled. Each bin has 858 cans. Which is the best estimate for the number of cans in all 6 bins?

A. 4,800

B. 5,400

C. 6,000

D. 8,000

8. Crystal has taken 8 quizzes with a total score of 619. She received about the same score for each quiz. Which is the best estimate of the score for each quiz?

A. 72

B. 75

C. 78

D. 82

9. The fourth-grade class performed 4 shows for a total of 788 people.

A. If each show had the same number of people, how many people attended each show? Show your work.

B. Find the estimated quotient. Compare the estimate to the exact answer in Part A. Is your answer reasonable? Explain.

_____

_____

_____

Lesson Practice • Part 2

Choose the correct answer.

1. Which is the best estimate for 77 × 52?

   A. 3,500

   B. 4,000

   C. 4,200

   D. 4,800

2. There are 184 green marbles and 379 red marbles. The marbles will be put into 8 jars. About how many marbles will go into each jar?

   A. 50

   B. 60

   C. 70

   D. 80

3. It costs $32 per hour to reserve a dining room at the Silvertown Inn. A party had a food bill of $575 and used the dining room for 6 hours. Which shows how to get the best estimate for the total cost?

   A. 30 × 6 + 580

   B. 30 × 10 + 600

   C. 40 × 6 + 580

   D. 40 × 10 + 600

4. Why is it better to use compatible numbers than rounding to find an estimate for division?

   A. Using compatible numbers will always give a closer estimate for the quotient.

   B. Using compatible numbers always gives an estimate that is less than the exact quotient.

   C. Using compatible numbers always gives an estimate that is greater than the exact quotient.

   D. Using compatible numbers allows for basic facts and a pattern to be used for the quotient.

5. Felix has 5 photo albums. Each album has 72 pages and there are 4 photos on each page. Which is the best estimate for the number of photos that Felix has in albums?

   A. 140

   B. 160

   C. 1,400

   D. 1,600

6. Amusement park tickets cost $48 for adults and $32 for students. Some families from a neighborhood went together and bought 6 adult tickets and 9 student tickets. Which is the best estimate for the total cost of the tickets?

A. $510

B. $570

C. $600

D. $630

7. Which pair of compatible numbers will give the closest estimate to 7,420 ÷ 8?

A. 7,200 ÷ 8

B. 7,400 ÷ 10

C. 8,000 ÷ 8

D. 8,000 ÷ 10

8. Aria keeps the cards she receives. She has 132 postcards, 76 birthday cards, and 45 holiday cards. She mixes the cards and puts them into 5 folders. About how many cards are in each folder?

A. 70

B. 60

C. 50

D. 40

9. Which is the best estimate for 376 × 9?

A. 4,000

B. 3,600

C. 3,000

D. 2,700

10. There are 365 days in a year. Isaac turned 8 years old today. Isaac has lived through 2 leap years, which are 366 days.

A. Isaac has visited his grandparents every 7 days of his life. About how many times has Isaac visited his grandparents?

_____

B. Explain how you determined your estimate in Part A.

_____

_____

_____

11. Circle the number that makes the statement true.

The best estimate for 68 × 42 is

2,400
2,800
3,000
3,500

12. Which is the best way to estimate 159 × 83? Use numbers from the box to complete the number sentence.

_____ × _____ = _____

80	12,000
90	12,800
150	13,500
160	14,400

13. Draw a line from each division problem to its estimated quotient.

A. 305 ÷ 9   • 300

B. 2,418 ÷ 3   • 70

C. 382 ÷ 5   • 80

D. 635 ÷ 9   • 30

E. 1,838 ÷ 6   • 800

14. Kim drove 212 miles in 5 hours. What is the best estimate of her speed? Use numbers from the box to write and solve a division sentence for the estimate. Then complete the statement.

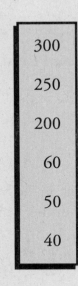

300
250
200
60
50
40

_____ ÷ 5 = _____

The best estimate of Kim's speed is _____ miles per hour.

15. Which problem has an estimated answer of either 500 or 700? Circle all that apply.

A. There are 215 blueberries in a basket. There are 4 baskets. About how many blueberries are there in all?

B. Janelle has a box with 4,890 beads. She wants to use 7 beads to make each bracelet. About how many bracelets can she make?

C. There are 4,926 seats in the auditorium and 9 seats in each row. About how many rows of seats are in the auditorium?

D. One bushel of onions weighs 72 pounds. About how many pounds are in 7 bushels of onions?

E. The Sweet Shop Bakery makes 400 blueberry muffins and 2,104 cranberry muffins in 5 days. About how many muffins are made each day?

Patterns

Getting the Idea

A **pattern** is a series of numbers or figures that follows a **rule**. In a number pattern, the numbers are the **terms**. The rule describes how each term is related to the next term.

This number pattern has 5 terms. The rule of the pattern is "add 4."

27   31   35   39   43

You can find the next term in a number pattern by finding the rule.
Some patterns increase, so try adding or multiplying by the same number.
Some patterns decrease, so try subtracting or dividing by the same number.

Example 1

What is the next term of this pattern?

15   22   29   36   ___?___

Strategy   **Find the rule of the pattern.**

Step 1   Decide if the terms increase or decrease.

The numbers increase.

Step 2   Find how many are between each term.

Since the numbers increase, use addition or multiplication.

Try addition.

15 + ? = 22   →   15 + **7** = 22

22 + ? = 29   →   22 + **7** = 29

29 + ? = 36   →   29 + **7** = 36

Each number is 7 more than the previous number.

Step 3   Find a rule.

A rule is "add 7."

Step 4   Use the rule to find the next term.

Add 7 to the last number.

36 + 7 = 43

Solution   **The next term of this pattern is 43.**

Notice another pattern of the numbers in Example 1.

15	22	29	36	42
odd	even	odd	even	odd

The terms in the pattern alternate between odd and even numbers.

The rule of the pattern is "add 7" and 7 is an odd number.

This rule will create alternating odd and even numbers because:

odd number + odd number = even number

even number + odd number = odd number

Example 2

The table shows how much money Martin had in his school lunch account at the end of each week for four weeks.

Week 1	Week 2	Week 3	Week 4	Week 5
$150	$135	$120	$105	?

If the pattern continues, how much money will Martin have in his account at the end of Week 5?

Strategy **Find the rule of the pattern.**

Step 1 Decide if the terms increase or decrease.

The numbers decrease.

Step 2 Find the rule.

Since the numbers decrease, use subtraction or division.

Try subtraction.

150 − ? = 135 → 150 − **15** = 135

135 − ? = 120 → 135 − **15** = 120

120 − ? = 105 → 120 − **15** = 105

The rule is "subtract 15."

Step 3 Use the rule to find the next term.

Subtract 15 from the last number.

105 − 15 = 90

Solution **If the pattern continues, Martin will have $90 in his account at the end of Week 5.**

Notice that the terms in the pattern in Example 2 also alternate between even and odd numbers. Remember that:

even number − odd number = odd number

odd number − odd number = even number

Example 3

Jenny is making a number pattern with 6 terms. The first term is 2.
The rule of the pattern is "multiply by 2." What are the six terms in Jenny's pattern?

Strategy   **Use the rule.**

Step 1   Identify the information given in the problem.

The pattern has 6 terms.

The pattern starts with 2.

The rule is "multiply by 2."

2   <u>?</u>   <u>?</u>   <u>?</u>   <u>?</u>   <u>?</u>

Step 2   Use the rule to find the next term of the pattern.

Multiply the first term, 2, by 2.

$2 \times 2 = 4$ ←   second term

Step 3   Use the rule to find the rest of the terms in the pattern.

$4 \times 2 = $ **8**   ←   third term

$8 \times 2 = $ **16**   ←   fourth term

$16 \times 2 = $ **32**   ←   fifth term

$32 \times 2 = $ **64**   ←   sixth term

Notice that the terms are all even numbers.

The rule of the pattern is multiply by 2, so each term doubles the previous term.

Solution   **The six terms in Jenny's pattern are 2, 4, 8, 16, 32, and 64.**

A pattern made up of figures also uses a rule. Use the rule to continue the pattern. You can use a table to help you.

Example 4

What is the 17th figure in this pattern?

Strategy   **Use a table.**

Step 1   Find the rule of the pattern.

This is a repeating pattern.

1 triangle, 1 rectangle, 2 circles

Step 2   Use the table to extend the pattern.

You know the first 8 figures.

Make a table for figures 9 through 17.

Figure	9	10	11	12	13	14	15	16	17
Shape	△	▯	◯	◯	△	▯	◯	◯	△

Solution   **The 17th figure is a triangle.**

Example 5

How many dots are in the 5th figure?

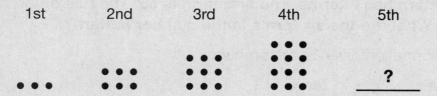

1st	2nd	3rd	4th	5th
				?

Strategy   **Find the rule of the pattern. Use a table.**

Step 1   Count the number of dots in each figure.

Figure	1st	2nd	3rd	4th
Number of Dots	3	6	9	12

Step 2   Find the rule.

Each figure has 1 row of 3 dots more than the previous figure.

Figure	1st	2nd	3rd	4th
Number of Dots	3	6	9	12
	1×3	2×3	3×3	4×3

Step 3   Use the rule to find the number of dots in the next figure.

The next figure will have 3 more dots than the 4th figure.

It will have 5 rows of 3 dots. $5 \times 3 = 15$

Solution   **There will be 15 dots in the 5th figure.**

Coached Example

A number pattern has 6 terms. The first term is 55. The rule of the pattern is "subtract 9." What are the six terms in the number pattern?

Identify the information given in the problem.

The pattern has _____ terms.

The pattern starts with _____ .

The rule is _____ .

Use the rule to find the rest of the terms.

Subtract _____ from 55.

_____ – _____ = _____	←	second term
_____ – _____ = _____	←	third term
_____ – _____ = _____	←	fourth term
_____ – _____ = _____	←	fifth term
_____ – _____ = _____	←	sixth term

The six terms in the number pattern are _____, _____, _____, _____, _____, and _____.

Lesson Practice • Part 1

Choose the correct answer.

1. What is the rule of this pattern?

22 28 34 40 46 52

A. add 4

B. multiply by 4

C. add 6

D. multiply by 6

2. Which follows the rule "subtract 7"?

A. 72 65 59 53 46

B. 81 74 67 60 53

C. 76 69 64 58 52

D. 71 78 85 92 99

3. What is the next number in this pattern?

6 14 22 30 38 ?

A. 42

B. 46

C. 48

D. 51

4. What is the missing number in this pattern?

95 89 83 77 ? 65

A. 79

B. 73

C. 71

D. 68

5. A number pattern has 5 terms. The pattern starts with 27. The rule of the pattern is "add 4." Which could be the pattern?

A. 27 31 39 51 67

B. 27 23 19 15 11

C. 27 31 35 39 43

D. 27 28 30 33 37

6. What is the next number in this pattern?

1 3 9 27 81 ?

A. 97

B. 99

C. 135

D. 243

7. If the pattern continues, how many dots will be in the next figure?

	1st	2nd	3rd	4th	5th
	• •	••	• • • •	(4x4 dots)	?

A. 32

B. 24

C. 20

D. 16

8. Which is the 14th figure in this pattern?

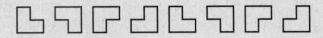

A. ⌐ (figure)

B. ⌐ (figure)

C. ⌐ (figure)

D. ⌐ (figure)

9. Nelson wrote two number patterns. Each pattern has six terms. The first term in both patterns is 115.

   A. Nelson used the rule "add 13" in the first pattern. What are the six terms in this pattern?

   _____

   B. Nelson used the rule "subtract 4" in the second pattern. What are the six terms in this pattern?

   _____

Lesson Practice • Part 2

Choose the correct answer.

1. Which pattern follows the rule "add 9"?

   A. 37   46   55   64   73

   B. 42   51   62   71   80

   C. 54   63   71   78   84

   D. 66   75   83   93   102

2. Which pattern follows the rule "subtract 7"?

   A. 53   46   38   29   19

   B. 55   49   43   37   31

   C. 62   55   48   41   34

   D. 66   58   50   42   34

3. Nora is beginning a pattern using a rule of "add 4" starting with 7. Which is true about Nora's pattern?

   A. All of the numbers in Nora's pattern will be even.

   B. All of the numbers in Nora's pattern will be odd.

   C. The numbers in Nora's pattern will alternate between odd and even starting with odd.

   D. The numbers in Nora's pattern will alternate between odd and even starting with even.

4. Gabe wrote a pattern using the rule "add 12." The first two terms of his pattern are 17 and 29. Which number will be part of Gabe's pattern?

   A. 46

   B. 55

   C. 73

   D. 89

5. Olivia made this shape pattern.

   1st   2nd   3rd   4th

   If Olivia's pattern continues, how many dots will be in the next figure?

   A. 20

   B. 24

   C. 25

   D. 32

6. The first term in a pattern is 96. The rule is "divide by 2." What is the last whole number in the pattern?

   A. 3

   B. 5

   C. 7

   D. 9

7. If this pattern continues, how many sides will the next figure have?

    A. 5

    B. 6

    C. 7

    D. 8

8. Which is the missing number in this pattern?

    32, 45, 58, _____, 84, 97

    A. 69

    B. 70

    C. 71

    D. 72

9. Tara is beginning a pattern using a rule of "subtract 6" starting with 51. Which is true about Nora's pattern?

    A. All of the numbers in Tara's pattern will be even.

    B. All of the numbers in Tara's pattern will be odd.

    C. The numbers in Tara's pattern will alternate between odd and even starting with odd.

    D. The numbers in Tara's pattern will alternate between odd and even starting with even.

10. Penny wrote a pattern using the rule "subtract 9." The first two terms of her pattern are 94 and 85. Which number will be part of Penny's pattern?

    A. 70   **C.** 44

    B. 61   **D.** 22

11. Mason wrote the following pattern on the board for his classmates.

    6, 30, 150, 750, …

    A. What is the rule of Mason's pattern?

    _____

    B. What are the next two terms in Mason's pattern?

    _____

    C. Create a pattern that uses the same rule as Mason's starting with 4. Include the first 5 terms.

    _____

    _____

12. Draw a line from each pattern to the next term in the pattern.

   A. 4 8 16 32 64 ___?___ ●   ● 18

   B. 2 7 12 17 22 ___?___ ●   ● 27

   C. 3 6 9 12 15 ___?___ ●   ● 66

   D. 16 26 36 46 56 ___?___ ●   ● 128

13. Which pattern follows the rule "add 6?" Circle all that apply.

   A. 4 10 16 22 28

   B. 3 18 108 648 3,888

   C. 7 13 19 25 31

   D. 5 65 125 185 245

14. Find the rule of each pattern. Write the pattern in the correct box.

2 10 18 26 34	7 21 63 189 567	4 12 36 108 324
3 9 27 81 243	6 14 22 30 38	13 21 29 37 45

Add 8	**Multiply by 3**

15. Look at the pattern below. Is the figure for the term correct? Select Yes or No.

△ ▢ ◯ △ ▢ ◯

A. 10th term: △   ◯ Yes   ◯ No

B. 12th term: ◯   ◯ Yes   ◯ No

C. 16th term: ▢   ◯ Yes   ◯ No

D. 19th term: △   ◯ Yes   ◯ No

16. Select True or False for each statement.

A. The 5th term in the pattern has 11 dots.   ◯ True   ◯ False
B. The 6th term in the pattern has 12 dots.   ◯ True   ◯ False
C. The 11th term in the pattern has 22 dots.   ◯ True   ◯ False
D. The 15th term in the pattern has 28 dots.   ◯ True   ◯ False

Domain 2: Cumulative Assessment for Lessons 11–17

1. Which is **not** a factor pair of 56?

   A. {1, 56}

   B. {2, 28}

   C. {7, 8}

   D. {4, 13}

2. A TV show had 16,982 viewers last Tuesday. This Tuesday, the show had 3,472 more viewers than last Tuesday. How many viewers did the show have this Tuesday?

   A. 51,702

   B. 20,454

   C. 19,354

   D. 13,510

3. Which is a multiple of 9?

   A. 19

   B. 28

   C. 64

   D. 72

4. Marvin spent $827 on a computer. To the nearest hundred, what is the cost of the computer?

   A. $800   C. $830

   B. $820   D. $900

5. The tallest building in the world is 2,716 feet high. To the nearest thousand, what is the height of the tallest building?

   A. 2,700 feet

   B. 2,720 feet

   C. 2,800 feet

   D. 3,000 feet

6. The table shows the distances traveled by 3 students during the summer months.

   Distances Traveled

Student	Distance Traveled (in miles)
Hank	2,683
Nina	5,893
Ruby	453

   Which is the best estimate of how many more miles Nina traveled than Ruby?

   A. 2,000 miles

   B. 5,000 miles

   C. 5,500 miles

   D. 6,000 miles

7. Franklin typed for a total of 88 minutes. He can type 38 words in one minute. To find how many words he typed in all, which rounded numbers can you use to check the answer?

A. 80×30

B. 80×40

C. 90×30

D. 90×40

8. Cheryl's car traveled 226 miles on 8 gallons of gas. She traveled about the same number of miles with each gallon. Which is the best estimate for the number of miles she traveled with each gallon of gas?

A. 20 miles

B. 30 miles

C. 40 miles

D. 60 miles

9. A number pattern has 5 terms. The first term is 13. The rule of the pattern is "add 9." What are the 5 terms of the pattern?

10. The table shows the number of species of some animal groups.

Number of Species

Animal Group	Number of Species
Birds	9,956
Mammals	5,416
Amphibians	6,199
Reptiles	8,240

A. How many species of mammals and amphibians are there?

B. How many more species of birds than reptiles are there?

Domain 3

Number and Operations–Fractions

Domain 3: Diagnostic Assessment for Lessons 18–27

Domain 3: Cumulative Assessment for Lessons 18–27

Domain 3: Diagnostic Assessment for Lessons 18–27

1. Vienna drew this rectangle.

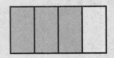

Which fraction is equivalent to the shaded part of Vienna's rectangle?

A. $\frac{3}{6}$ **C.** $\frac{6}{8}$

B. $\frac{7}{10}$ **D.** $\frac{8}{12}$

2. Karim walked $\frac{3}{10}$ mile to Fred's apartment. Then he walked $\frac{4}{10}$ mile to the park. How far did Karim walk in all?

A. $\frac{1}{10}$ mile

B. $\frac{7}{10}$ mile

C. $\frac{12}{10}$ mile

D. $\frac{7}{20}$ mile

3. Anthony has a piece of paper that is $\frac{11}{12}$ inch long. He cuts $\frac{1}{4}$ inch off the length of it. How long is the paper now?

A. $\frac{1}{2}$ inch   **C.** $\frac{8}{12}$ inch

B. $\frac{5}{8}$ inch   **D.** $\frac{9}{12}$ inch

4. Multiply.

$$3 \times \frac{3}{5} = \square$$

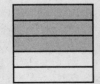 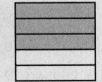

A. $\frac{6}{5}$

B. $\frac{9}{5}$

C. $\frac{5}{9}$

D. $\frac{9}{15}$

5. Which symbol makes this sentence true?

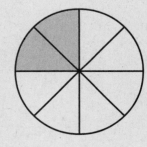 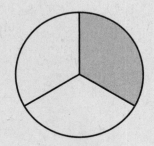

A. >

B. <

C. =

D. +

6. Which decimal represents the shaded parts of the grids?

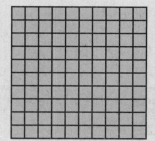 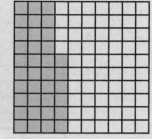

A. 0.36   **C.** 1.36

B. 1.30   **D.** 1.40

7. It rained 0.7 of the days of Omar's vacation. What fraction of the days did it rain?

A. $\frac{3}{100}$ **C.** $\frac{3}{10}$

B. $\frac{7}{100}$ **D.** $\frac{7}{10}$

8. Which lists the decimals from least to greatest?

A. 0.50   0.58   0.80

B. 0.50   0.80   0.58

C. 0.58   0.80   0.50

D. 0.80   0.58   0.50

9. What mixed number goes in the box to make the sentence true?

$$\square - 3\frac{4}{10} = 5\frac{3}{10}$$

_____

10. Shelly bought $\frac{6}{8}$ pound of potato salad and $\frac{4}{8}$ pound of macaroni salad.

A. How many pounds of salad did she buy in all? Show your work.

_____

_____

_____

B. Shelly also bought $2\frac{2}{8}$ pound of tuna salad. How many more pounds of tuna salad did she buy than macaroni salad? Show your work.

_____

_____

_____

Equivalent Fractions

Getting the Idea

A **fraction** names parts of a whole or part of a group.

The **denominator**, the bottom number, tells how many equal parts in the whole or group.

The **numerator**, the top number, tells how many equal parts are being considered.

The diagram below shows 6 equal parts in the whole. Each part is $\frac{1}{6}$ of the whole. The figure is $\frac{4}{6}$ shaded. You read the fraction $\frac{4}{6}$ as four sixths.

$\frac{1}{6}$	$\frac{1}{6}$	$\frac{1}{6}$	$\frac{1}{6}$	$\frac{1}{6}$	$\frac{1}{6}$

Example 1

What fraction of the circle is shaded?

Strategy   **Find the denominator and the numerator.**

Step 1   Count the number of equal parts in the circle.

There are 5 equal parts. The denominator is 5.

Step 2   Count the number of shaded parts in the circle.

There are 3 shaded parts. The numerator is 3.

Step 3   Write the fraction.

$$\frac{\text{numerator}}{\text{denominator}} = \frac{3}{5}$$

Solution   **Three-fifths, or $\frac{3}{5}$, of the circle is shaded.**

Equivalent fractions are fractions that name the same value, but have different numerators and denominators. The models below show that $\frac{1}{2}$ and $\frac{2}{4}$ are equivalent fractions.

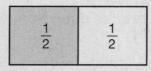

$$\frac{1}{2} = \frac{2}{4}$$

Example 2

What fraction with 12 as a denominator is equivalent to $\frac{2}{3}$?

$$\frac{2}{3} = \frac{\Box}{12}$$

Strategy   **Use fraction strips.**

Step 1   Use $\frac{1}{3}$ fraction strips.

Show $\frac{2}{3}$.

| $\frac{1}{3}$ | $\frac{1}{3}$ | |

Step 2   Use $\frac{1}{12}$ fraction strips.

Use as many strips as needed to make the same length as $\frac{2}{3}$.

| $\frac{1}{3}$ | $\frac{1}{3}$ | |

| $\frac{1}{12}$ | $\frac{1}{12}$ | $\frac{1}{12}$ | $\frac{1}{12}$ | $\frac{1}{12}$ | $\frac{1}{12}$ | $\frac{1}{12}$ | $\frac{1}{12}$ | |

Step 3   Count the number of $\frac{1}{12}$ strips.

There are 8 strips of $\frac{1}{12}$.

So, $\frac{8}{12}$ is equal to $\frac{2}{3}$.

Solution $\frac{2}{3} = \frac{8}{12}$

You can use number lines to find equivalent fractions.

Example 3

What fraction with 5 as a denominator is equivalent to $\frac{6}{10}$?

Strategy   **Use number lines.**

Step 1   Make a number line in tenths and another one in fifths.
Find $\frac{6}{10}$.

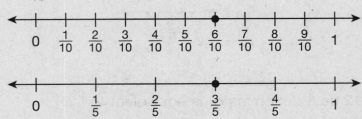

Step 2   Find the fraction on the number line in fifths that lines up with $\frac{6}{10}$.

$\frac{3}{5}$ lines up with $\frac{6}{10}$.

Solution $\frac{3}{5}$ is equivalent to $\frac{6}{10}$.

Another way to find equivalent fractions is to multiply the numerator and the denominator by the same number. For example:

$$\frac{3}{5} = \frac{3 \times 2}{5 \times 2} = \frac{6}{10}$$

Example 4

What is an equivalent fraction of $\frac{3}{4}$?

Strategy   **Multiply the numerator and denominator by the same number.**

> **Step 1**   Multiply both the numerator and denominator by 2.
>
> $$\frac{3}{4} \times \frac{2}{2} = \frac{6}{8}$$

> **Step 2**   Use models to check.
>
> The models for $\frac{3}{4}$ and $\frac{6}{8}$ have the same size.

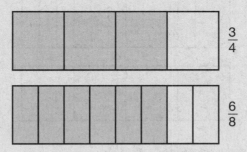

Solution $\frac{6}{8}$ **is an equivalent fraction of** $\frac{3}{4}$**.**

A fraction is in **simplest form** if its numerator and denominator have only 1 as a common factor. A fraction and its simplest form are equivalent fractions.

You can simplify a fraction by dividing the numerator and denominator by the greatest common factor. The **greatest common factor (GCF)** is the greatest factor that is common to two or more numbers.

For example, simplify $\frac{6}{8}$.

2 is the GCF of 6 and 8.

So, divide the numerator and the denominator by 2.

$$\frac{6}{8} = \frac{6 \div 2}{8 \div 2} = \frac{3}{4}$$

$\frac{3}{4}$ is the simplest form of $\frac{6}{8}$.

Example 5

Simplify the fraction $\frac{9}{12}$.

Strategy **Divide the numerator and denominator by the GCF.**

> **Step 1** Find the GCF of 9 and 12.
>
> The GCF is 3.

> **Step 2** Divide both the numerator and denominator by 3.
>
> $$\frac{9}{12} = \frac{9 \div 3}{12 \div 3} = \frac{3}{4}$$

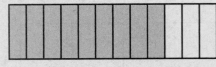

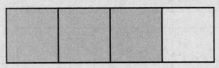

Solution $\frac{9}{12}$ in simplest form is $\frac{3}{4}$.

Coached Example

What fraction with 12 as a denominator is equivalent to $\frac{3}{6}$?

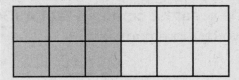

What is the denominator of $\frac{3}{6}$? _____

What is the denominator of the equivalent fraction? _____

By what number can you multiply 6 to get 12? _____

To find the equivalent fraction, multiply the numerator and denominator by

_____.

$$\frac{3 \times \text{_____}}{6 \times \text{_____}} = \text{_____}$$

_____ is a fraction with 12 as a denominator that is equivalent to $\frac{3}{6}$.

Lesson Practice • Part 1

Choose the correct answer.

1. Which shows $\frac{3}{4}$ of the figure shaded?

   A.

   B.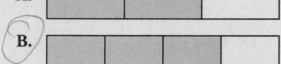

   C.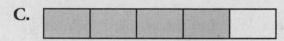

   D.

2. The fraction strips show $\frac{10}{12}$.

   Which fraction is equivalent to $\frac{10}{12}$?

   A. $\frac{1}{6}$

   B. $\frac{1}{3}$

   C. $\frac{2}{3}$

   D. $\frac{5}{6}$

3. The model is shaded to represent a fraction.

   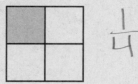

   Which model shows an equivalent fraction?

   A.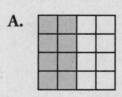

   B.

   C.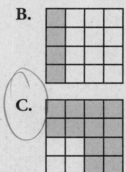

   D.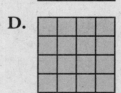

4. What fraction with 9 as a denominator is equivalent to $\frac{2}{3}$?

   A. $\frac{1}{9}$ C. $\frac{4}{9}$

   B. $\frac{2}{9}$ D. $\frac{6}{9}$

5. What fraction with 3 as a denominator is equivalent to $\frac{8}{12}$?

A. $\frac{1}{3}$

B. $\frac{2}{3}$

C. $\frac{3}{3}$

D. $\frac{4}{3}$

$\frac{8 \times 3}{12 \times 3} = \frac{12}{36}$

6. Which fraction is **not** equivalent to $\frac{1}{2}$?

A. $\frac{5}{10}$

B. $\frac{4}{8}$

C. $\frac{3}{12}$

D. $\frac{2}{4}$

7. Which fraction is written in simplest form?

A. $\frac{1}{5}$

B. $\frac{6}{8}$

C. $\frac{3}{9}$

D. $\frac{4}{12}$

8. Which is the simplest form of $\frac{2}{8}$?

A. $\frac{1}{4}$

B. $\frac{1}{8}$

C. $\frac{2}{4}$

D. $\frac{4}{16}$

9. Jonah made the figure below.

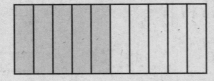

A. What fraction of the figure is shaded?

$\frac{5}{10}$

B. Write two equivalent fractions to the fraction in Part A.

$\frac{5 \times 5}{10 \times 5} = \frac{1}{2}$ $\frac{5 \times 5}{5 \quad 10} = \frac{1}{2}$

Mixed Numbers and Improper Fractions

Getting the Idea

You can write equivalent fractions for **improper fractions**.

Example 1

When simplified, what improper fraction is equivalent to the model?

| $\frac{1}{4}$ | $\frac{1}{4}$ | $\frac{1}{4}$ | $\frac{1}{4}$ | | $\frac{1}{4}$ | $\frac{1}{4}$ | $\frac{1}{4}$ | $\frac{1}{4}$ |

Strategy   **Write the fraction in the model. Then simplify the fraction.**

Step 1   Write the denominator for the improper fraction.

Each bar shows fourths. The denominator is 4.

Step 2   Count the number of shaded parts.

There are 6 shaded parts. The numerator is 6.

Step 3   Write the fraction.

The fraction is $\frac{6}{4}$.

Step 4   Divide the numerator and denominator by 2.

$$\frac{6}{4} \div \frac{2}{2} = \frac{3}{2}$$

Solution   **The improper fraction $\frac{3}{2}$ is equivalent to the model.**

A **mixed number** has a whole number part and a fraction part. You use a mixed number when you say your age is $9\frac{1}{2}$ or your shoe size is $5\frac{1}{2}$.

Example 2

What mixed number does this model represent?

$\frac{1}{5}$	$\frac{1}{5}$	$\frac{1}{5}$	$\frac{1}{5}$	$\frac{1}{5}$

$\frac{1}{5}$	$\frac{1}{5}$	$\frac{1}{5}$	$\frac{1}{5}$	$\frac{1}{5}$

$\frac{1}{5}$	$\frac{1}{5}$	$\frac{1}{5}$	$\frac{1}{5}$	$\frac{1}{5}$

Strategy **Decompose the fraction.**

Step 1 Write the improper fraction as the sum of each part.

There are 2 fractions bars that are completely shaded.

$\frac{13}{5} = \frac{5}{5} + \frac{5}{5} + \frac{3}{5}$

Remember that $\frac{5}{5} = 1$.

The whole number part is 2.

Step 2 Find the fraction part.

The third fraction bar has 3 shaded parts out of 5 parts.

The fraction part is $\frac{3}{5}$.

Step 3 Write the mixed number.

The whole number part is on the left.

The fraction part is on the right.

$2\frac{3}{5}$

Solution **The model represents the mixed number $2\frac{3}{5}$.**

Example 3

Where is point C located on the number line? Write the answer as an improper fraction and as a mixed number.

Strategy   **Decide what each tick mark represents. Then count.**

   Step 1   What does each tick mark represent?

            Each tick mark shows $\frac{1}{4}$.

   Step 2   To find the improper fraction, count the number of tick marks past 0.

            Point C is 10 tick marks to the right of 0.

            The improper fraction is $\frac{10}{4}$.

   Step 3   To find the mixed number, count the number of tick marks past the whole number.

            Point C is two marks to the right of 2.

            The mixed number $2\frac{2}{4}$.

Solution   **Point C is located at $\frac{10}{4}$ or $2\frac{2}{4}$ or $2\frac{1}{2}$ on the number line.**

You can change an improper fraction to a mixed number and a mixed number to an improper fraction. To change a mixed number to an improper fraction, multiply the whole number part by the denominator. Then add the numerator to that product. The denominator stays the same.

Example 4

Jamie brought a batch of pies to a potluck dinner. Each pie was cut into 6 equal pieces. After dinner, there were $3\frac{5}{6}$ pies left over. What is $3\frac{5}{6}$ as an improper fraction?

Strategy   **Use multiplication and addition.**

Step 1   Multiply the whole number part by the denominator of the fraction part.
$$3 \times 6 = 18$$

Step 2   Add that product to the numerator of the fraction part.
$$18 + 5 = 23$$

Step 3   The denominator stays the same. Write the improper fraction.
$$\frac{23}{6}$$

Solution $3\frac{5}{6} = \frac{23}{6}$

To change an improper fraction to a mixed number, divide the numerator by the denominator. The quotient is the whole number; the remainder is the numerator of the fraction. The denominator stays the same.

Example 5

Flora made placemats using $\frac{13}{3}$ yards of fabric. What is $\frac{13}{3}$ as a mixed number?

Strategy   **Divide the numerator by the denominator.**

Step 1   Divide the numerator by the denominator.
$$13 \div 3 = 4 \text{ R1}$$

Step 2   Write the mixed number.

The quotient, 4, is the whole number part.

The remainder, 1, is the numerator of the fraction part.

The denominator, 3, stays the same.

Solution $\frac{13}{3} = 4\frac{1}{3}$

Coached Example

Write an improper fraction and a mixed number to represent this model.

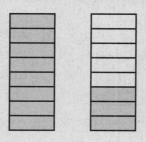

First, write an improper fraction.

Each figure is divided into _____ parts.

The denominator of the improper fraction is _____.

There are _____ shaded parts.

The improper fraction is _____.

Now write the mixed number.

How many figures are completely shaded? _____

The whole number part of the mixed number is _____.

The second figure has _____ parts in all and _____ shaded parts.

The fraction part of the mixed number is _____.

The mixed number is _____.

The model represents _____ or _____.

Lesson Practice • Part 1

Choose the correct answer.

1. Look at the model below.

| $\frac{1}{6}$ | $\frac{1}{6}$ | $\frac{1}{6}$ | $\frac{1}{6}$ | $\frac{1}{6}$ | $\frac{1}{6}$ | | $\frac{1}{6}$ | $\frac{1}{6}$ | $\frac{1}{6}$ | $\frac{1}{6}$ | $\frac{1}{6}$ | $\frac{1}{6}$ |

| $\frac{1}{6}$ | $\frac{1}{6}$ | $\frac{1}{6}$ | $\frac{1}{6}$ | $\frac{1}{6}$ | $\frac{1}{6}$ | | $\frac{1}{6}$ | $\frac{1}{6}$ | $\frac{1}{6}$ | $\frac{1}{6}$ | $\frac{1}{6}$ | $\frac{1}{6}$ |

What improper fraction does the model represent?

A. $\frac{4}{20}$

B. $\frac{20}{6}$

C. $\frac{22}{6}$

D. $\frac{24}{6}$

2. Which improper fraction is equal to $3\frac{1}{2}$?

A. $\frac{6}{3}$

B. $\frac{7}{3}$

C. $\frac{6}{2}$

D. $\frac{7}{2}$

3. Hayley ordered several pizzas for a party. The picture below shows the amount of pizza that is left after the party.

How much pizza is left after the party?

A. $1\frac{1}{5}$

B. $1\frac{5}{8}$

C. $8\frac{3}{8}$

D. $8\frac{5}{8}$

4. Which improper fraction can be written as a whole number?

A. $\frac{10}{6}$ 0.6

B. $\frac{12}{6}$ 0.5

C. $\frac{14}{6}$ 2.3

D. $\frac{16}{6}$ 0.375

5. Look at the number line below.

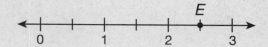

What mixed number is shown by point E on the number line?

A. $1\frac{1}{2}$

B. $2\frac{1}{4}$

C. $2\frac{1}{2}$

D. $2\frac{3}{4}$

6. Look at the number line below.

What mixed number is shown by point F on the number line?

A. $\frac{9}{4}$

B. $\frac{11}{4}$

C. $\frac{12}{4}$

D. $\frac{13}{4}$

7. Look at the model below.

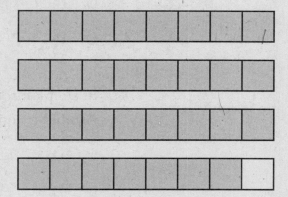

A. Write an improper fraction to represent the model.

_____

B. Write a mixed number to represent the model.

_____

Lesson Practice • Part 2

Choose the correct answer.

1. Look at the model below.

In simplest form, what mixed number does the model represent?

A. $2\frac{1}{4}$

B. $2\frac{1}{2}$

C. $3\frac{1}{4}$

D. $3\frac{1}{2}$

2. Which improper fraction is equivalent to $4\frac{3}{4}$?

A. $\frac{15}{4}$

B. $\frac{17}{4}$

C. $\frac{19}{4}$

D. $\frac{23}{4}$

3. Look at the number line below.

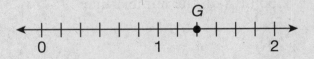

In simplest form, what mixed number is represented by point G on the number line?

A. $1\frac{1}{6}$

B. $1\frac{1}{3}$

C. $1\frac{1}{2}$

D. $1\frac{2}{3}$

4. In simplest form, which mixed number is equivalent to $\frac{22}{8}$?

A. $2\frac{1}{4}$

B. $2\frac{1}{2}$

C. $2\frac{3}{4}$

D. $3\frac{1}{4}$

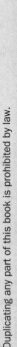

5. Which does **not** have the same value as the others?

   A. $5\frac{1}{2}$

   B. $\frac{11}{2}$

   C. $\frac{22}{4}$

   D. $\frac{30}{6}$

6. Which improper fraction can be written as a whole number?

   A. $\frac{7}{2}$

   B. $\frac{9}{3}$

   C. $\frac{11}{5}$

   D. $\frac{15}{6}$

7. Which describes how to rename a mixed number as an improper fraction?

   A. Multiply the whole number times the numerator. Then add the product to the numerator of the fraction, which is the numerator of the improper fraction.

   B. Multiply the whole number times the denominator. Then add the product to the denominator of the fraction, which is the denominator of the improper fraction.

   C. Multiply the whole number times the numerator. Then add the product to the denominator of the fraction, which is the denominator of the improper fraction.

   D. Multiply the whole number times the denominator. Then add the product to the numerator of the fraction, which is the numerator of the improper fraction.

8. Look at the model below.

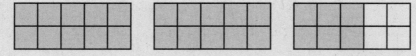

   A. Write an improper fraction to represent the model.

   _____

   B. Write a mixed number in simplest form to represent the model.

   _____

9. Draw a line from each model to the mixed number it represents.

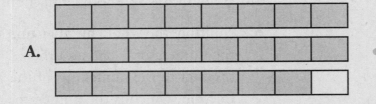

A. • • $1\dfrac{5}{8}$

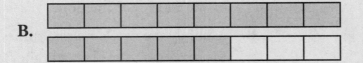

B. • • $1\dfrac{7}{8}$

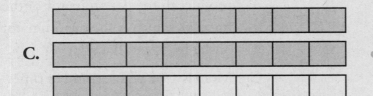

C. • • $2\dfrac{3}{8}$

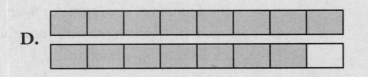

D. • • $2\dfrac{7}{8}$

10. What improper fraction or mixed number is shown by point A on the number line? Circle all that apply.

A. $2\dfrac{3}{4}$

B. $3\dfrac{1}{4}$

C. $\dfrac{14}{4}$

D. $8\dfrac{3}{4}$

E. $\dfrac{11}{4}$

11. Can the improper fraction be written as a whole number? Select Yes or No.

    A. $\frac{12}{3}$ ○ Yes ○ No

    B. $\frac{14}{4}$ ○ Yes ○ No

    C. $\frac{48}{12}$ ○ Yes ○ No

    D. $\frac{25}{5}$ ○ Yes ○ No

    E. $\frac{17}{2}$ ○ Yes ○ No

12. Select True or False for each number sentence.

    A. $1\frac{5}{8} = \frac{15}{8}$ ○ True ○ False

    B. $2\frac{2}{5} = \frac{12}{5}$ ○ True ○ False

    C. $4\frac{2}{9} = \frac{22}{9}$ ○ True ○ False

    D. $\frac{13}{8} = 1\frac{5}{8}$ ○ True ○ False

    E. $\frac{27}{8} = 3\frac{3}{8}$ ○ True ○ False

13. Barton brought several loaves of banana bread to a potluck brunch. The picture shows how much banana bread was left after the brunch. How much banana bread was left? Circle all that apply.

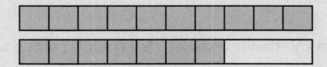

    A. $\frac{17}{10}$

    B. $1\frac{3}{10}$

    C. $10\frac{7}{10}$

    D. $1\frac{7}{10}$

Compare Fractions

Getting the Idea

Remember to refer to the same whole, when comparing fractions.
For example,

$\frac{1}{2}$ of a square is equal to $\frac{1}{2}$ of the same size square.

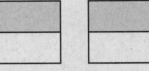

$\frac{1}{2}$ of a square is not equal to $\frac{1}{2}$ of a circle.

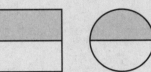

To compare fractions with the same denominators,
look at the numerators.

The greater fraction has the greater numerator.

For example, $\frac{2}{3} > \frac{1}{3}$.

To compare fractions with the same numerator, look at the denominators.

The greater fraction has the lesser denominator.

For example, $\frac{2}{3} > \frac{2}{5}$.

Example 1

Which symbol makes the sentence true? Write >, <, or =.

$\frac{1}{8} \bigcirc \frac{1}{4}$

Strategy   **Look at the denominators. Use fraction strips to check.**

Step 1   Both fractions have the same numerator, 1.

Compare the denominators. $8 > 4$

Since 8 is the greater denominator, $\frac{1}{8}$ is the lesser fraction.

Step 2   Use fraction strips to check.

The $\frac{1}{8}$ fraction strip is shorter than $\frac{1}{4}$ fraction strip.

$\frac{1}{8}$							

$\frac{1}{4}$			

Step 3   Use the correct symbol.

$<$ means is less than.

Solution $\frac{1}{8} \, \textcircled{<} \, \frac{1}{4}$

You can use number lines to help, when comparing fractions.
The fraction farther to the right is the greater fraction.

Example 2

Which symbol makes the sentence true? Write $>$, $<$, or $=$.

$\frac{2}{3} \bigcirc \frac{7}{12}$

Strategy   **Use number lines.**

Step 1   Draw two number lines from 0 to 1.

Make one number line in thirds. Find $\frac{2}{3}$.

Make another number line in twelfths. Find $\frac{7}{12}$.

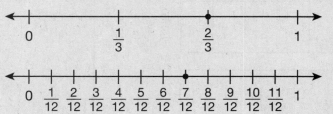

Step 2   Compare the fractions.

$\frac{2}{3}$ is farther to the right than $\frac{7}{12}$.

So, $\frac{2}{3}$ is the greater fraction.

Solution $\frac{2}{3} \, \textcircled{>} \, \frac{7}{12}$

For Example 2, you can also use a common denominator to compare $\frac{2}{3}$ and $\frac{7}{12}$.
A **common denominator** is a common multiple of the denominators.

The **least common multiple (LCM)** of 3 and 12 is 12.

Change $\frac{2}{3}$ to an equivalent fraction with 12 as the denominator.

$$\frac{2}{3} = \frac{2 \times 4}{3 \times 4} = \frac{8}{12}$$

Now compare the numerators.

Since 8 is greater, $\frac{8}{12} > \frac{7}{12}$. So, $\frac{2}{3} > \frac{7}{12}$.

Example 3

Shari and Billy each bought the same candy bar. Shari ate $\frac{2}{5}$ of her candy bar.

Billy ate $\frac{1}{2}$ of his candy bar. Who ate more of their candy bar?

Strategy   **Use a common denominator.**

Step 1   Find a common denominator for $\frac{2}{5}$ and $\frac{1}{2}$.
The LCM of 5 and 2 is 10.

Step 2   Change $\frac{2}{5}$ and $\frac{1}{2}$ to equivalent fractions with 10 as the denominator.

$$\frac{2}{5} = \frac{2 \times 2}{5 \times 2} = \frac{4}{10} \qquad \frac{1}{2} = \frac{1 \times 5}{2 \times 5} = \frac{5}{10}$$

Step 3   Compare the numerators.

Since 4 is the lesser numerator, $\frac{4}{10} < \frac{5}{10}$. So $\frac{2}{5} < \frac{1}{2}$.

Step 4   Use models to check.

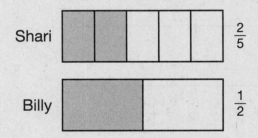

Solution   **Billy ate more of his candy bar.**

You can also use common numerators to compare fractions.

A common numerator is a common multiple of the numerators.

Example 4

Lilly needs $\frac{3}{8}$ cup of milk and $\frac{1}{3}$ cup of heavy cream to make pancakes.

Does she need more milk or more heavy cream to make the pancakes?

Strategy   **Use a common numerator.**

Step 1   Find a common numerator for $\frac{3}{8}$ and $\frac{1}{3}$.

   The LCM of 3 and 1 is 3.

Step 2   Change $\frac{1}{3}$ to an equivalent fraction with 3 as the numerator.

   $$\frac{1}{3} = \frac{1 \times 3}{3 \times 3} = \frac{3}{9}$$

   $\frac{3}{8}$ already has a 3 as the numerator.

Step 3   Compare the denominators.

   The fraction with the lesser denominator is the greater fraction.

   Since 8 is the lesser denominator, $\frac{3}{8} > \frac{3}{9}$.

   So $\frac{3}{8} > \frac{1}{3}$.

Step 4   Use models to check.

| $\frac{1}{8}$ | $\frac{1}{8}$ | $\frac{1}{8}$ | | | | | | $\frac{3}{8}$ |

| $\frac{1}{3}$ | | $\frac{1}{3}$ |

Solution   **Lilly needs more milk to make the pancakes.**

Fractions can be compared using **benchmarks**. A benchmark is a common number that can be compared to another number. Three benchmarks are 0, $\frac{1}{2}$, and 1. You can think of a number line when using a benchmark.

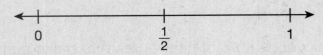

Example 5

What symbol makes this sentence true? Write >, <, or =.

$\frac{4}{10}$ ◯ $\frac{5}{6}$.

Strategy Use $\frac{1}{2}$ as a benchmark.

Step 1 Find $\frac{4}{10}$ on a number line.

Compare $\frac{4}{10}$ to $\frac{1}{2}$.

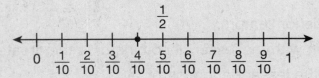

$\frac{4}{10}$ is less than $\frac{1}{2}$.

Step 2 Find $\frac{5}{6}$ on a number line.

Compare $\frac{5}{6}$ to $\frac{1}{2}$.

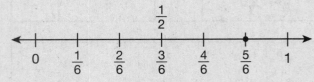

$\frac{5}{6}$ is greater than $\frac{1}{2}$.

Step 3 Compare $\frac{5}{6}$ to $\frac{4}{10}$.

Since $\frac{4}{10}$ is less than $\frac{1}{2}$ and $\frac{5}{6}$ is greater than $\frac{1}{2}$,

$\frac{4}{10}$ is less than $\frac{5}{6}$.

Solution $\frac{4}{10}$ ◯< $\frac{5}{6}$

Coached Example

What symbol makes this sentence true?
Use benchmarks 0, $\frac{1}{2}$, and 1 to compare.

Write >, <, or =.

$\frac{4}{5}$ ◯ $\frac{1}{6}$

Find $\frac{4}{5}$ on a number line.

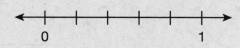

Compare to 0, $\frac{1}{2}$, and 1 on a number line.

$\frac{4}{5}$ is closest to the benchmark _____.

Find $\frac{1}{6}$ on a number line.

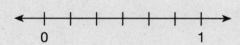

Compare to 0, $\frac{1}{2}$, and 1 on the number line.

$\frac{1}{6}$ is closest to the benchmark _____.

Since $\frac{4}{5}$ is closest to the benchmark _____, and $\frac{1}{6}$ is closest to the benchmark

_____, $\frac{4}{5}$ is _____ than $\frac{1}{6}$.

$\frac{4}{5}$ ◯ $\frac{1}{6}$

Lesson Practice • Part 1

Choose the correct answer.

1. Which symbol makes this sentence true?

$$\frac{2}{6} \bigcirc \frac{1}{5}$$

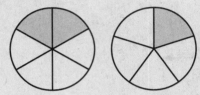

A. >

B. <

C. =

D. +

2. Which symbol makes this sentence true?

$$\frac{3}{4} \bigcirc \frac{3}{8}$$

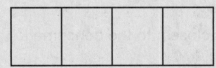

A. >

B. <

C. =

D. +

3. Which sentence is true?

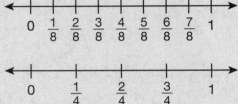

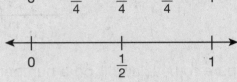

A. $\frac{1}{8} > \frac{1}{4}$

B. $\frac{1}{2} < \frac{2}{4}$

C. $\frac{3}{8} > \frac{1}{2}$

D. $\frac{5}{8} < \frac{3}{4}$

4. Which symbol makes this sentence true?

$$\frac{7}{12} \bigcirc \frac{3}{4}$$

A. >   C. =

B. <   D. +

5. Which sentence is **not** true?

A. $\frac{1}{5} > \frac{1}{8}$ C. $\frac{1}{7} < \frac{1}{2}$

B. $\frac{1}{3} > \frac{1}{6}$ D. $\frac{1}{4} < \frac{1}{9}$

6. Which fraction makes this sentence true?

$$\frac{3}{4} < \underline{\quad\quad}$$

A. $\frac{1}{2}$

B. $\frac{7}{8}$

C. $\frac{5}{10}$

D. $\frac{7}{12}$

7. Which fraction is closest to 1?

A. $\frac{2}{3}$ **C.** $\frac{7}{8}$

B. $\frac{3}{4}$ **D.** $\frac{7}{10}$

8. Which symbol makes this sentence true?

$$\frac{3}{10} \bigcirc \frac{25}{100}$$

A. $>$ **C.** $=$

B. $<$ **D.** $+$

---

9. Marjorie used $\frac{2}{5}$ cup of flour, $\frac{1}{4}$ cup of baking soda, and $\frac{1}{3}$ cup of sugar for a recipe.

A. Did Marjorie use more baking soda or more sugar? Show your work.

_____

B. Did Marjorie use more flour or more sugar for the recipe? Show your work.

_____

Lesson Practice • Part 2

Choose the correct answer.

1. Which symbol makes this sentence true?

   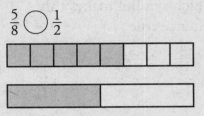

   $\frac{5}{8} \bigcirc \frac{1}{2}$

   A. >

   B. <

   C. =

   D. +

2. Which fraction is greater than $\frac{2}{3}$?

   A. $\frac{1}{2}$

   B. $\frac{3}{4}$

   C. $\frac{3}{5}$

   D. $\frac{5}{8}$

3. Which of these fractions is closest to 0 on a number line?

   A. $\frac{5}{12}$

   B. $\frac{3}{10}$

   C. $\frac{2}{5}$

   D. $\frac{1}{8}$

4. How can you tell if a fraction is greater than $\frac{1}{2}$?

   A. Divide the denominator by the numerator. If the quotient is greater than 2, the fraction is greater than $\frac{1}{2}$.

   B. Divide the denominator by the numerator. If the quotient is less than 2, the fraction is greater than $\frac{1}{2}$.

   C. Divide the numerator by the denominator. If the quotient is greater than 2, the fraction is greater than $\frac{1}{2}$.

   D. Divide the numerator by the denominator. If the quotient is less than 2, the fraction is greater than $\frac{1}{2}$.

5. Which symbol makes this sentence true?

   $\frac{3}{10} \bigcirc \frac{5}{12}$

   A. <   **C.** =

   B. >   **D.** +

6. Which fraction is greater than $\frac{3}{4}$?

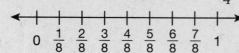

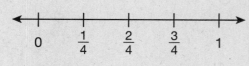

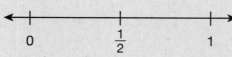

A. $\frac{7}{8}$ **C.** $\frac{1}{2}$

B. $\frac{5}{8}$ **D.** $\frac{1}{4}$

7. Which fraction makes this sentence true?

$$\frac{7}{12} < \underline{\hspace{2cm}}$$

A. $\frac{1}{2}$

B. $\frac{2}{5}$

C. $\frac{5}{8}$

D. $\frac{54}{100}$

8. Three friends are saving for a class trip. They all need to save the same amount of money. Adam saved $\frac{2}{5}$ of the money he needs. Nolan saved $\frac{1}{4}$ and Eli saved $\frac{3}{10}$.

A. Did Adam or Nolan save more money? Show your work.

_____

B. Did Adam or Eli save more money? Show your work.

_____

C. Did Nolan or Eli save more money? Show your work.

_____

9. Circle the symbol that makes the sentence true.

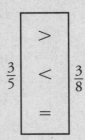

$$\frac{3}{5} \quad \boxed{\begin{array}{c} > \\ < \\ = \end{array}} \quad \frac{3}{8}$$

10. Is the sentence true? Select Yes or No.

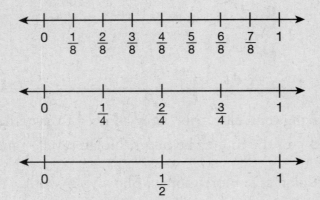

A. $\frac{1}{8} < \frac{1}{2}$ ○ Yes   ○ No

B. $\frac{3}{4} > \frac{3}{8}$ ○ Yes   ○ No

C. $\frac{1}{2} < \frac{4}{8}$ ○ Yes   ○ No

D. $\frac{7}{8} > \frac{3}{4}$ ○ Yes   ○ No

11. Select True or False for each sentence.

A. $\frac{1}{6} < \frac{1}{2}$ ○ True   ○ False

B. $\frac{1}{4} > \frac{1}{7}$ ○ True   ○ False

C. $\frac{1}{9} > \frac{1}{8}$ ○ True   ○ False

D. $\frac{1}{5} < \frac{1}{3}$ ○ True   ○ False

12. Which fraction is greater than $\frac{4}{6}$? Circle all that apply.

A. $\frac{4}{5}$ **C.** $\frac{5}{6}$

B. $\frac{4}{7}$ **D.** $\frac{9}{12}$

13. Compare each fraction to $\frac{1}{2}$. Write the fraction in the correct box.

| $\frac{2}{3}$ | $\frac{2}{5}$ | $\frac{4}{10}$ | $\frac{7}{12}$ | $\frac{5}{8}$ | $\frac{6}{9}$ |

Less than $\frac{1}{2}$	Greater than $\frac{1}{2}$

14. Circle the symbol that makes the sentence true.

$\frac{3}{7}$ $\begin{array}{c} > \\ < \\ = \end{array}$ $\frac{5}{9}$

15. Which fraction is less than $\frac{7}{9}$? Circle all that apply.

A. $\frac{2}{3}$ **C.** $\frac{7}{8}$

B. $\frac{7}{12}$ **D.** $\frac{5}{6}$

Add Fractions

Getting the Idea

You can show a fraction as the sum of smaller fractions including unit fractions.
A **unit fraction** is a fraction that has a numerator of 1.

$$\frac{3}{4} = \frac{1}{4} + \frac{1}{4} + \frac{1}{4}$$

Example 1

Show $\frac{3}{10}$ as $\frac{1}{10} + $ _____.

Strategy   **Break the fraction into unit fractions.**

Step 1   Show the fraction as unit fractions.

$$\frac{3}{10} = \frac{1}{10} + \frac{1}{10} + \frac{1}{10}$$

Step 2   Group the unit fractions.

$$\frac{3}{10} = \frac{1}{10} + \left(\frac{1}{10} + \frac{1}{10}\right)$$

Solution $\frac{3}{10} = \frac{1}{10} + \frac{2}{10}$

You can add fractions that have the same denominators, which are called **like denominators**. If fractions have like denominators, add the numerators. The denominator stays the same. If the sum is an improper fraction, rewrite it as a mixed number.

Example 2

Allison bought a pizza divided into 10 equal slices. Allison's friends ate $\frac{7}{10}$ of the pizza and she ate $\frac{2}{10}$ of the pizza. What fraction of the pizza was eaten in all?

Strategy   **Use fraction strips to model the problem.**

Step 1   Write an addition sentence for the problem.

Let p represent the total pizza eaten.

$\frac{7}{10} + \frac{2}{10} = p$

Step 2   Show $\frac{7}{10}$ with fraction pieces.

| $\frac{1}{10}$ | $\frac{1}{10}$ | $\frac{1}{10}$ | $\frac{1}{10}$ | $\frac{1}{10}$ | $\frac{1}{10}$ | $\frac{1}{10}$ |

Step 3   Add on $\frac{2}{10}$ with fraction pieces.

| $\frac{1}{10}$ | $\frac{1}{10}$ | $\frac{1}{10}$ | $\frac{1}{10}$ | $\frac{1}{10}$ | $\frac{1}{10}$ | $\frac{1}{10}$ | $\frac{1}{10}$ | $\frac{1}{10}$ |

Step 4   Count the numbers of $\frac{1}{10}$ fraction pieces.

There are nine $\frac{1}{10}$ fraction pieces in all.

Step 5   Write the sum.

$\frac{7}{10} + \frac{2}{10} = \frac{9}{10}$

Solution   **Allison and her friends ate $\frac{9}{10}$ of the pizza in all.**

Example 3

Add.

$$\frac{4}{6} + \frac{1}{6} = \square$$

Strategy   **Add like fractions.**

Step 1   Do the fractions have a like denominator?

Yes, both fractions have a denominator of 6.

Step 2   Add the numerators.

$4 + 1 = 5$

Step 3   The denominator stays the same.

$$\frac{4}{6} + \frac{1}{6} = \frac{5}{6}$$

Step 4   Use area models to check the sum.

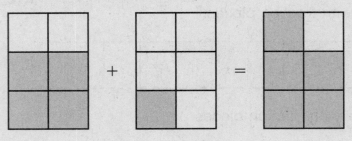

Solution $\frac{4}{6} + \frac{1}{6} = \frac{5}{6}$

You can write a sum in simplest form.

Example 4

Find the sum.

$$\frac{5}{8} + \frac{7}{8} = \square$$

Strategy   **Add the numerators.**

Step 1   Add the numerators. The denominator stays the same.

$$\frac{5}{8} + \frac{7}{8} = \frac{5+7}{8} = \frac{12}{8}$$

Step 2   Write the sum as a mixed number.

$$\frac{12}{8} = \frac{8}{8} + \frac{4}{8}$$

$$\frac{8}{8} = 1$$

So, $\frac{12}{8} = 1\frac{4}{8}$

Step 3   Write the fraction part in simplest form.

$$\frac{4}{8} \div \frac{4}{4} = \frac{1}{2}$$

So, $1\frac{4}{8} = 1\frac{1}{2}$

Solution $\frac{5}{8} + \frac{7}{8} = 1\frac{1}{2}$

Coached Example

Sam walked $\frac{1}{12}$ mile to Toni's house. Then Toni and Sam walked $\frac{4}{12}$ mile to school. How far did Sam walk in all?

Write the addition sentence for the problem.

Sam walked _____ mile to Toni's house.

Then Sam walked _____ mile to school.

Let m represent the total miles Sam walked.

_____ + _____ = _____

Find the sum.

Do the fractions have a like denominator?

_____, both fractions have a denominator of _____.

Add the numerators.

1 + 4 = _____

The denominator stays the same.

$\frac{1}{12} + \frac{4}{12} = \frac{\boxed{}}{\boxed{}}$

Sam walked _____ mile in all.

Lesson Practice • Part 1

Choose the correct answer.

1. Add.

   $$\frac{2}{5} + \frac{1}{5} = \boxed{}$$

$\frac{1}{5}$	$\frac{1}{5}$	$\frac{1}{5}$	$\frac{1}{5}$	$\frac{1}{5}$

   A. $\frac{3}{10}$ **C.** $\frac{3}{5}$

   B. $\frac{6}{7}$ **D.** $\frac{1}{5}$

2. Add.

   $$\frac{4}{8} + \frac{3}{8} = \boxed{\frac{7}{8}}$$

   A. $\frac{1}{7}$

   B. $\frac{1}{2}$

   C. $\frac{3}{4}$

   D. $\frac{7}{8}$

3. Add.

   $$\frac{3}{10} + \frac{5}{10} = \boxed{} \quad \frac{8}{10}$$

   A. $\frac{1}{5}$

   B. $\frac{3}{5}$ No answer

   C. $\frac{4}{5}$

   D. $\frac{9}{10}$

4. Natalie ate $\frac{3}{8}$ of the carrot sticks in a bag. Later she ate another $\frac{3}{8}$ of the carrot sticks. What fraction of the carrot sticks did she eat in all?

   A. $\frac{1}{8}$

   B. $\frac{3}{4}$ $\frac{3}{8} + \frac{3}{8} = \frac{6}{8}$

   C. $\frac{3}{8}$

   D. $\frac{7}{8}$ No answer

5. Find the sum.

   $$\frac{3}{12} + \frac{1}{12} = \boxed{}$$

   A. $\frac{1}{6}$ No answer

   B. $\frac{1}{4}$

   C. $\frac{1}{3}$ $\frac{3}{12} + \frac{1}{12} = \frac{4}{12}$

   D. $\frac{5}{12}$

6. Find the sum.

   $$\frac{7}{12} + \frac{4}{12} = \boxed{}$$

   A. $\frac{1}{4}$

   B. $\frac{11}{24}$

   C. $\frac{11}{12}$

   D. 1

7. Manny spent $\frac{2}{6}$ hour reading and $\frac{3}{6}$ hour studying for his math quiz. How long did Manny spend reading and studying for the quiz?

A. $\frac{5}{6}$ hour

B. $\frac{4}{9}$ hour

C. $\frac{4}{6}$ hour

D. $\frac{2}{3}$ hour

8. Jamal did $\frac{2}{8}$ of his chores before lunch. He did another $\frac{3}{8}$ of his chores after lunch. What fraction of his chores did he finish?

A. $\frac{4}{8}$

B. $\frac{5}{8}$

C. $\frac{4}{12}$

D. $\frac{5}{16}$

9. The drive from Collin's house to pick up Anderson took $\frac{4}{10}$ tank of gas. Another $\frac{3}{10}$ tank of gas was used to drive from Anderson's house to the water park. $\frac{4}{10} + \frac{3}{10} =$

A. How much gas was used to drive from Collin's house to the water park? Show your work.

It is $\frac{7}{10}$ gas used for drive

B. At the water park, Collin ate $\frac{1}{8}$ pound of fudge and brought $\frac{5}{8}$ pound home with him. In simplest form, how many pounds of fudge did Collin buy? Show your work.

$\frac{1}{8} + \frac{5}{8} = \frac{6}{8}$

Lesson Practice • Part 2

Choose the correct answer.

1. Which addition sentence is equivalent to $\frac{7}{8}$?

   A. $\frac{1}{8} + \frac{2}{8} + \frac{2}{8} + \frac{2}{8}$

   B. $\frac{1}{8} + \frac{2}{8} + \frac{3}{8}$

   C. $\frac{2}{8} + \frac{2}{8} + \frac{2}{8} + \frac{2}{8}$

   D. $\frac{2}{8} + \frac{3}{8} + \frac{3}{8}$

2. Carolyn pitched $\frac{4}{6}$ of the game for the Tigers. Monique pitched $\frac{1}{6}$ of the same game for the Tigers. What fraction of the game did they pitch in all?

   A. $\frac{1}{2}$

   B. $\frac{1}{4}$

   C. $\frac{5}{6}$

   D. $\frac{5}{12}$

3. Michele walked $\frac{5}{8}$ mile from her house to Stacey's house. They then walked another $\frac{5}{8}$ to the park. How far did Michele walk to the park?

   A. $1\frac{5}{8}$ miles

   B. $1\frac{1}{4}$ miles

   C. $\frac{4}{5}$ mile

   D. $\frac{5}{16}$ mile

   $\frac{5}{8} + \frac{5}{8} = \frac{10}{8}$

4. Which explains how to add fractions with like denominators?

   A. Subtract the numerators. Then add the denominators.

   B. Add the numerators. Then add the denominators.

   C. Add the denominators. The numerator stays as is.

   D. Add the numerators. The denominator stays as is.

5. Of the books in Harper's cloud, $\frac{5}{12}$ are novels. Another $\frac{3}{12}$ of her books are biographies. What fraction of the books in Harper's cloud are novels or biographies?

   A. $\frac{1}{12}$

   B. $\frac{1}{6}$

   C. $\frac{1}{3}$

   D. $\frac{2}{3}$

   $\frac{5}{12} + \frac{3}{12} = \frac{8}{12}$ no answer

6. Which is **not** equivalent to $\frac{7}{10}$?

   A. $\frac{1}{10} + \frac{1}{10} + \frac{2}{10} + \frac{3}{10}$

   B. $\frac{1}{10} + \frac{2}{10} + \frac{2}{10} + \frac{2}{10}$

   C. $\frac{1}{10} + \frac{2}{10} + \frac{4}{10}$

   D. $\frac{1}{10} + \frac{3}{10} + \frac{4}{10}$

7. Of the songs on the CD that Bentley is listening to, $\frac{4}{10}$ are instrumentals. Another $\frac{5}{10}$ of the songs are sung by female vocalists. What fraction of the songs is either instrumentals or sung by female vocalists?

   A. $\frac{9}{20}$ C. $\frac{1}{10}$

   B. $\frac{9}{10}$ D. $\frac{1}{20}$

8. Find the sum.

   $$\frac{3}{5} + \frac{4}{5} = \boxed{} \quad \frac{7}{5}$$

   A. $\frac{7}{10}$ C. $1\frac{1}{5}$

   B. $\frac{8}{10}$ D. $1\frac{2}{5}$

9. Hannah spoke on the phone with her grandmother for $\frac{3}{4}$ hour. Then she spoke with her grandfather for another $\frac{3}{4}$ hour. How long was Hannah on the phone with her grandparents?

   A. $1\frac{3}{4}$ hours   C. $\frac{3}{4}$ hour

   B. $1\frac{1}{2}$ hours   D. $\frac{3}{8}$ hour

10. Find the sum.

   $$\frac{24}{100} + \frac{42}{100} = \boxed{}$$

   A. $\frac{66}{100}$

   B. $\frac{66}{200}$

   C. $\frac{76}{100}$

   D. $\frac{76}{200}$

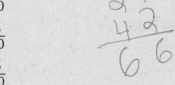

11. In this week's recycling, $\frac{4}{10}$ of the bottles are green, $\frac{2}{10}$ are brown, and $\frac{3}{10}$ are clear. The rest are blue. *I do not get it.*

   A. What fraction of the bottles are green or brown?

   _____

   B. What fraction of the bottles are brown or clear?

   _____

   C. What fraction of the bottles are green, brown, or clear?

   _____

12. Use numbers from the box to complete the sentence.

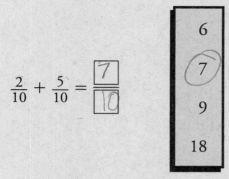

$$\frac{2}{10} + \frac{5}{10} = \frac{7}{10}$$

6

7

9

18

13. Select True or False for each sentence.

A. $\frac{1}{4} + \frac{2}{4} = \frac{3}{8}$ ○ True   ● False

B. $\frac{3}{6} + \frac{2}{6} = \frac{5}{6}$ ● True   ○ False

C. $\frac{5}{10} + \frac{4}{10} = \frac{1}{10}$ ○ True   ● False

D. $\frac{4}{10} + \frac{1}{10} = \frac{1}{2}$ ○ True   ● False

14. Draw a line from each addition problem to its sum.

A. $\frac{1}{10} + \frac{6}{10}$ $\frac{1}{2}$

B. $\frac{3}{10} + \frac{3}{10}$ $\frac{3}{5}$

C. $\frac{4}{10} + \frac{1}{10}$ $\frac{7}{10}$

D. $\frac{7}{10} + \frac{1}{10}$ $\frac{4}{5}$

15. Who exerciesed for $\frac{3}{4}$ hour? Circle all that apply.

A. Maria jogged for $\frac{3}{12}$ hour and biked for $\frac{6}{12}$ hour.

B. Bill swam for $\frac{8}{12}$ hour and jogged for $\frac{3}{12}$ hour.

C. Mavis ran for $\frac{10}{12}$ hour and stretched for $\frac{1}{12}$ hour.

D. Jenny biked for $\frac{5}{12}$ hour and jumped rope for $\frac{4}{12}$ hour.

16. Use numbers from the box to complete the sentence.

$$\frac{4}{12} + \frac{2}{12} = \frac{\boxed{6}}{\boxed{12}}$$

1

2

4

6

17. Does the trail mix have exactly $\frac{3}{4}$ cup of nuts? Select Yes or No.

A. $\frac{2}{8}$ cup peanuts and $\frac{3}{8}$ cup almonds ○ Yes ● No

B. $\frac{5}{8}$ cup cashews and $\frac{2}{8}$ cup almonds ○ Yes ● No

C. $\frac{1}{8}$ cup peanuts and $\frac{5}{8}$ cup pistachios ○ Yes ● No

D. $\frac{3}{8}$ cup almonds and $\frac{3}{8}$ cup walnuts ○ Yes ● No

Subtract Fractions

Getting the Idea

When you subtract fractions with like denominators, subtract only the numerators. The denominator stays the same.

Example 1

Subtract.

$$\frac{7}{8} - \frac{5}{8} = \boxed{}$$

Strategy   **Use fraction strips to model the problem.**

Step 1   Show $\frac{7}{8}$ with fraction pieces.

$\frac{1}{8}$	$\frac{1}{8}$	$\frac{1}{8}$	$\frac{1}{8}$	$\frac{1}{8}$	$\frac{1}{8}$	$\frac{1}{8}$

Step 2   Subtract or cross out $\frac{5}{8}$.

$$\frac{5}{8} = \frac{1}{8} + \frac{1}{8} + \frac{1}{8} + \frac{1}{8} + \frac{1}{8}$$

$\frac{1}{8}$	$\frac{1}{8}$	$\frac{1}{8}$	$\frac{1}{8}$	$\frac{1}{8}$	$\frac{1}{8}$	$\frac{1}{8}$

Step 3   Count the number of $\frac{1}{8}$ fraction pieces left.

There are two $\frac{1}{8}$ pieces left.

The numerator is 2.

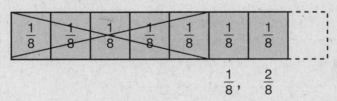

$$\frac{1}{8}, \quad \frac{2}{8}$$

Step 4   The denominator is the same.

The denominator is 8.

Solution $\frac{7}{8} - \frac{5}{8} = \frac{2}{8}$

Sometimes the answer may not be in simplest form. Remember to simplify the fraction using the greatest common factor (GCF).

For example, for the fraction $\frac{3}{12}$, 3 is the greatest common factor of 3 and 12.

$$\frac{3}{12} = \frac{3 \div 3}{12 \div 3} = \frac{1}{4}$$

Example 2

Rachel used $\frac{5}{8}$ can of blue paint. She also used $\frac{3}{8}$ can of yellow paint.

How much more blue paint than yellow paint did Rachel use?

Strategy   **Subtract the numerators. Keep the same denominator.**

Step 1   Write the subtraction sentence for the problem.

She used $\frac{5}{8}$ can of blue paint.

She used $\frac{3}{8}$ can of yellow paint.

Let b represent how much more blue paint she used.

$$\frac{5}{8} - \frac{3}{8} = b$$

Step 2   The denominators are the same, so subtract the numerators.

$$\frac{5}{8} - \frac{3}{8} = \frac{5-3}{8} = \frac{2}{8}$$

Step 3   Use fraction strips to check.

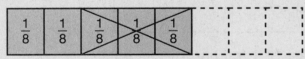

Step 4   Simplify the fraction $\frac{2}{8}$.

2 is the GCF of 2 and 8.

$$\frac{2}{8} = \frac{2 \div 2}{8 \div 2} = \frac{1}{4}$$

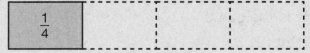

Solution   **Rachel used $\frac{2}{8}$ or $\frac{1}{4}$ can more blue paint than yellow paint.**

Example 3

Tim had $\frac{10}{12}$ roll of green streamer for a bulletin board. He used $\frac{7}{12}$ roll for the border. What fraction of the roll of green streamer does Tim have left?

Strategy   **Subtract the numerators. Keep the same denominator.**

Step 1   Write the subtraction sentence for the problem.

He had $\frac{10}{12}$ roll of streamer.

He used $\frac{7}{12}$ roll of streamer.

Let s represent how much is left over.

$$\frac{10}{12} - \frac{7}{12} = s$$

Step 2   The denominators are the same, so subtract the numerators.

$$\frac{10}{12} - \frac{7}{12} = \frac{10 - 7}{12} = \frac{3}{12}$$

Step 3   Simplify the fraction $\frac{3}{12}$.

3 is the GCF of 3 and 12.

$$\frac{3}{12} = \frac{3 \div 3}{12 \div 3} = \frac{1}{4}$$

Solution   **Tim has $\frac{3}{12}$ or $\frac{1}{4}$ roll of green streamer left.**

Remember, you can check the answer to a subtraction problem using addition.

$$\frac{3}{12} + \frac{7}{12} = \frac{10}{12}$$

The sum is $\frac{10}{12}$, which matches the minuend. So, the answer is correct.

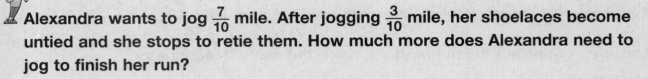

Coached Example

Alexandra wants to jog $\frac{7}{10}$ mile. After jogging $\frac{3}{10}$ mile, her shoelaces become untied and she stops to retie them. How much more does Alexandra need to jog to finish her run?

Write the subtraction sentence for the problem.

The words "how much more" tell you to _____.

Alexandra wants to jog _____ mile.

She ties her shoelaces after _____ mile.

Let *m* represent how much more she needs to jog to finish her run.

_____ − _____ = _____

Find the difference.

Do the fractions have a like denominator?

_____, both fractions have a denominator of _____.

Subtract the numerators.

7 − 3 = _____

The denominator stays the same.

$\frac{7}{10} - \frac{3}{10} = \frac{\boxed{}}{\boxed{}}$

Simplify the fraction. _____

Alexandra has _____ mile more to jog to finish her run.

Lesson Practice • Part 1

Choose the correct answer.

1. Subtract.

$$\frac{7}{8} - \frac{2}{8} = \boxed{}$$

$\frac{1}{8}$	$\frac{1}{8}$	$\frac{1}{8}$	$\frac{1}{8}$	$\frac{1}{8}$	$\frac{1}{8}$	$\frac{1}{8}$	$\frac{1}{8}$

A. $\frac{4}{8}$ C. $\frac{0}{5}$

B. $\frac{5}{8}$ D. $\frac{1}{6}$

2. Subtract.

$$\frac{9}{10} - \frac{3}{10} = \boxed{}$$

A. $\frac{6}{20}$

B. $\frac{7}{10}$

C. $\frac{6}{10}$

D. $\frac{12}{20}$

3. Mary Ellen drew a rectangle with a length of $\frac{11}{12}$ inch. The height of the rectangle is $\frac{6}{12}$ inch shorter than the length. What is the height of the rectangle?

A. $\frac{0}{6}$ inch C. $\frac{1}{7}$ inch

B. $\frac{5}{12}$ inch D. $\frac{16}{12}$ inch

4. There was $\frac{3}{4}$ of a pad of paper on the counter. Greta used $\frac{1}{4}$ of the pad to write thank-you letters. What fraction of the pad of paper is left?

A. $\frac{1}{4}$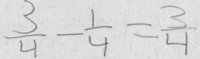

B. $\frac{1}{2}$

C. $\frac{3}{4}$

D. 1

5. Find the difference.

$$\frac{1}{2} - \frac{1}{2} = \boxed{}$$

A. 0

B. $\frac{1}{4}$

C. $\frac{1}{2}$

D. $\frac{2}{4}$

6. Find the difference.

$$\frac{65}{100} - \frac{34}{100} = \boxed{}$$

A. $\frac{21}{100}$

B. $\frac{31}{100}$

C. $\frac{41}{100}$

D. $\frac{99}{100}$

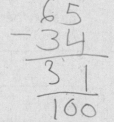

7. Jasmine ordered $\frac{3}{6}$ pound of American cheese and $\frac{5}{6}$ pound of cheddar cheese. How much more cheddar cheese than American cheese did Jasmine order?

A. $\frac{1}{3}$ pound

B. $\frac{1}{2}$ pound

C. $\frac{3}{4}$ pound

D. 1 pound

$\frac{3}{6} - \frac{5}{6} =$

8. Kyle planted vegetables in $\frac{3}{8}$ of the space in his garden. He planted flowers in $\frac{2}{8}$ of the space in his garden. How much more of the garden space did Kyle plant with vegetables than with flowers?

A. $\frac{0}{8}$ C. $\frac{1}{4}$

B. $\frac{1}{8}$ D. $\frac{3}{8}$

9. The table shows the amount of fruit that Keisha put in a fruit salad.

Keisha's Fruit Salad

Fruit	Amount (in pounds)
Grapes	$\frac{3}{10}$
Blueberries	$\frac{2}{10}$
Watermelon	$\frac{8}{10}$

$\frac{8}{10} - \frac{3}{10} = \frac{5}{10}$

A. How many more pounds of watermelon than pounds of grapes are in the fruit salad? Show your work.

It is $\frac{5}{10}$ in the fruit salad

B. Keisha added $\frac{7}{10}$ pound strawberries to the fruit salad. How many more pounds of strawberries than pounds of blueberries are in the salad? Show your work.

$\frac{5}{10}$ are in the fruit salad

Lesson Practice • Part 2

Choose the correct answer.

1. Billy lives $\frac{9}{10}$ mile from school. Elijah lives $\frac{3}{10}$ mile from school. How much closer to school does Elijah live than Billy?

   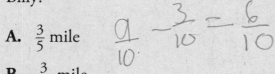

   A. $\frac{3}{5}$ mile

   B. $\frac{3}{10}$ mile

   C. $\frac{1}{2}$ mile

   D. $1\frac{1}{5}$ miles

2. The Knights scored at least 15 points in $\frac{3}{4}$ of the quarters in their last game. In what fraction of the quarters did the Knights score less than 15 points?

   A. $\frac{1}{4}$

   B. $\frac{1}{2}$

   C. $\frac{3}{4}$

   D. 1

3. Of the students playing volleyball, $\frac{7}{12}$ are girls and $\frac{5}{12}$ are boys. What fraction more of the players are girls?

   A. $\frac{1}{3}$ C. $\frac{1}{6}$

   B. $\frac{1}{4}$ D. $\frac{1}{12}$

4. Which explains how to subtract fractions with like denominators?

   A. Subtract the numerators. Then add the denominators.

   B. Subtract the numerators. Then subtract the denominators.

   C. Subtract the denominators. The numerator stays as is.

   D. Subtract the numerators. The denominator stays as is.

5. Of the songs in Aiden's cloud, $\frac{37}{100}$ are rock and $\frac{18}{100}$ are country. What fraction more of the songs on Aiden's cloud are rock songs?

   A. $\frac{19}{200}$ C. $\frac{11}{40}$

   B. $\frac{19}{100}$ D. $\frac{11}{20}$

6. A bulletin board is $\frac{7}{8}$ filled. What fraction greater is the part of the bulletin board that is filled than empty?

   A. $\frac{1}{8}$

   B. $\frac{1}{2}$

   C. $\frac{3}{4}$

   D. $\frac{7}{8}$

7. The Fillmore School tennis team has $\frac{5}{12}$ fourth-grade students and $\frac{3}{12}$ fifth-grade students. The rest of the team members are in sixth grade. What fraction of the team are sixth-grade students?

A. $\frac{1}{4}$

B. $\frac{1}{3}$

C. $\frac{2}{3}$

D. $\frac{3}{4}$

8. In a rose garden, $\frac{2}{8}$ of the roses are yellow and $\frac{3}{8}$ are white. The rest are red. What fraction of the roses in the garden is red?

A. $\frac{3}{4}$

B. $\frac{5}{8}$

C. $\frac{3}{8}$

D. $\frac{1}{8}$

9. The table shows the primary positions that the players play on a travel softball team.

Softball Primary Positions

Position Type	Fraction
Pitchers	$\frac{1}{8}$
Catchers	$\frac{1}{8}$
Infielders	$\frac{4}{8}$
Outfielders	?

A. What fraction more of the players are infielders than catchers?

_____

B. What fraction of the players are outfielders? Show your work?

_____

_____

C. What fraction more of the players are outfielders than pitchers? Show your work.

_____

10. Select True or False for each sentence.

A. $\frac{6}{8} - \frac{3}{8} = \frac{3}{5}$ ○ True   ○ False

B. $\frac{5}{12} - \frac{4}{12} = \frac{1}{12}$ ○ True   ○ False

C. $\frac{4}{5} - \frac{2}{5} = \frac{2}{5}$ ○ True   ○ False

D. $\frac{6}{10} - \frac{2}{10} = \frac{1}{2}$ ○ True   ○ False

11. Draw a line from each subtraction problem to its difference.

A. $\frac{7}{12} - \frac{3}{12}$ •   • $\frac{1}{2}$

B. $\frac{9}{10} - \frac{4}{10}$ •   • $\frac{1}{3}$

C. $\frac{11}{12} - \frac{8}{12}$ •   • $\frac{1}{4}$

D. $\frac{6}{10} - \frac{4}{10}$ •   • $\frac{1}{5}$

12. Find each difference. Write the problem in the correct box.

| $\frac{3}{4} - \frac{1}{4}$ | $\frac{3}{4} - \frac{2}{4}$ | $\frac{9}{12} - \frac{3}{12}$ | $\frac{7}{8} - \frac{3}{8}$ | $\frac{5}{8} - \frac{3}{8}$ | $\frac{8}{12} - \frac{5}{12}$ |

$\frac{1}{4}$	$\frac{1}{2}$

13. The table shows the volumes of four different colors of paint. Select True or False for each statement about the table.

Paint Volumes

Paint	Volume (in gallons)
Red	$\frac{4}{10}$
Blue	$\frac{3}{10}$
Green	$\frac{8}{10}$
Yellow	$\frac{6}{10}$

A. There is $\frac{1}{5}$ gallon more green paint than yellow paint. ○ True ○ False

B. There is $\frac{3}{10}$ gallon more yellow paint than blue paint. ○ True ○ False

C. There is $\frac{1}{2}$ gallon more green paint than red paint. ○ True ○ False

D. There is $\frac{2}{10}$ gallon more yellow paint than red paint. ○ True ○ False

14. Is the sentence correct? Select Yes or No.

A. $\frac{7}{8} - \frac{5}{8} = \frac{2}{8}$ ○ Yes ○ No

B. $\frac{26}{100} - \frac{21}{100} = \frac{5}{100}$ ○ Yes ○ No

C. $\frac{5}{6} - \frac{3}{6} = \frac{1}{6}$ ○ Yes ○ No

D. $\frac{2}{10} - \frac{2}{10} = \frac{1}{10}$ ○ Yes ○ No

Domain 3 • Lesson 23

Add and Subtract Mixed Numbers

Getting the Idea

You can show a mixed number as a sum of smaller numbers.

$$2\frac{1}{4} = 1 + 1 + \frac{1}{4}$$

$$2\frac{1}{4} = \frac{4}{4} + \frac{4}{4} + \frac{1}{4}$$

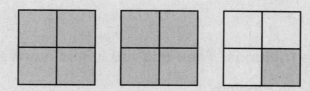

Example 1

Show the mixed number $1\frac{2}{5}$ as a sum of fractions.

Make a model to show the equation.

Strategy **Break the mixed number into whole numbers and fractions.**

   Step 1 Show the mixed number as whole numbers and fractions.

   $$1\frac{2}{5} = 1 + \frac{2}{5}$$

   Step 2 Show the 1 whole as a fraction with 5 as a denominator.

   $$1 = \frac{5}{5}$$

   $$1\frac{2}{5} = \frac{5}{5} + \frac{2}{5}$$

   Step 3 Make a model.

   Draw rectangles. Show each rectangle in fifths.

   $$1\frac{2}{5} = \frac{5}{5} + \frac{2}{5}$$

Solution $1\frac{2}{5} = \frac{5}{5} + \frac{2}{5}$

251

Remember that a unit fraction has a 1 in the numerator.

In Example 1, you could also use all unit fractions.

$$1\frac{2}{5} = \frac{1}{5} + \frac{1}{5} + \frac{1}{5} + \frac{1}{5} + \frac{1}{5} + \frac{1}{5} + \frac{1}{5}$$

When you add mixed numbers, first add the fraction parts, then add the whole number parts.

Example 2

Add.

$$1\frac{1}{4} + 2\frac{1}{4} = \boxed{}$$

Strategy   **Add the fractions. Then add the whole numbers.**

Step 1   Rewrite the problem.

Line up the whole numbers and fractions.

$$\begin{array}{r} 1\frac{1}{4} \\ + 2\frac{1}{4} \\ \hline \end{array}$$

Step 2   Add the fraction parts: $\frac{1}{4} + \frac{1}{4}$.

$$\begin{array}{r} 1\frac{1}{4} \\ + 2\frac{1}{4} \\ \hline \frac{2}{4} \end{array}$$

Step 3   Add the whole number parts: $1 + 2$.

$$\begin{array}{r} 1\frac{1}{4} \\ + 2\frac{1}{4} \\ \hline 3\frac{2}{4} \end{array}$$

Step 4   Simplify the fraction part.

$$\frac{2}{4} = \frac{2 \div 2}{4 \div 2} = \frac{1}{2}$$

So, $3\frac{2}{4} = 3\frac{1}{2}$.

Solution $1\frac{1}{4} + 2\frac{1}{4} = 3\frac{1}{2}$

Another way to add mixed numbers is to write each mixed number as an equivalent improper fraction. Then add the improper fractions. Show the answer as a mixed number.

Example 3

Kelsey drank $1\frac{2}{3}$ cups of water in the morning and $2\frac{2}{3}$ cups of water in the afternoon.

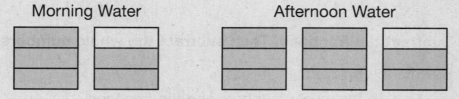

Morning Water   Afternoon Water

How much water did Kelsey drink in all?

Strategy   **Write each mixed number as an improper fraction. Then add.**

Step 1   Write a number sentence for the problem.

Let w represent the amount of water Kelsey drank in all.

$1\frac{2}{3} + 2\frac{2}{3} = w$

Step 2   Write $1\frac{2}{3}$ as an equivalent improper fraction.

$1\frac{2}{3} = 1 + \frac{2}{3}$

$1 = \frac{3}{3}$, because $\frac{1}{3} + \frac{1}{3} + \frac{1}{3} = \frac{3}{3}$.

$1\frac{2}{3} = \frac{3}{3} + \frac{2}{3} = \frac{5}{3}$

Step 3   Write $2\frac{2}{3}$ as an equivalent improper fraction.

$2\frac{2}{3} = 2 + \frac{2}{3}$

$2 = \frac{6}{3}$, because $\frac{3}{3} + \frac{3}{3} = \frac{6}{3}$.

$2\frac{2}{3} = \frac{6}{3} + \frac{2}{3} = \frac{8}{3}$

Step 4   Add the improper fractions.

$\frac{5}{3} + \frac{8}{3} = \frac{13}{3}$

Step 5   Change the sum to a mixed number.

Divide the numerator by the denominator.

$13 \div 3 = 4\ R1$

So, $\frac{13}{3} = 4\frac{1}{3}$.

Solution   **Kelsey drank $4\frac{1}{3}$ cups of water in all.**

When you subtract mixed numbers, first subtract the fraction parts, then subtract the whole number parts.

Example 4

Subtract.

$$3\frac{5}{8} - 1\frac{3}{8} = \boxed{}$$

Strategy **Subtract the fractions. Then subtract the whole numbers.**

Step 1 Rewrite the problem.

Line up the whole numbers and the fractions.

$$\begin{array}{r} 3\frac{5}{8} \\ -\ 1\frac{3}{8} \\ \hline \end{array}$$

Step 2 Subtract the fraction parts: $\frac{5}{8} - \frac{3}{8}$.

$$\begin{array}{r} 3\frac{5}{8} \\ -\ 1\frac{3}{8} \\ \hline \frac{2}{8} \end{array}$$

Step 3 Subtract the whole number parts: $3 - 1$.

$$\begin{array}{r} 3\frac{5}{8} \\ -\ 1\frac{3}{8} \\ \hline 2\frac{2}{8} \end{array}$$

Step 4 Simplify the fraction part.

$$\frac{2}{8} = \frac{2 \div 2}{8 \div 2} = \frac{1}{4}$$

So, $2\frac{2}{8} = 2\frac{1}{4}$.

Solution $3\frac{5}{8} - 1\frac{3}{8} = 2\frac{1}{4}$

You can use the relationship between addition and subtraction to find a missing number.

Example 5

What mixed number goes in the box to make the sentence true?

$$\square - 2\frac{1}{3} = 3\frac{1}{3}$$

Strategy **Use the relationship between addition and subtraction.**

Step 1 Addition and subtraction are inverse operations.

To find $\square$, add $2\frac{1}{3} + 3\frac{1}{3}$.

Step 2 Add $2\frac{1}{3}$ and $3\frac{1}{3}$.

Add the fraction parts.

Then add the whole number parts.

$$\begin{array}{r} 2\frac{1}{3} \\ + 3\frac{1}{3} \\ \hline 5\frac{2}{3} \end{array}$$

Step 3 Subtract to check your answer.

$$\begin{array}{r} 5\frac{2}{3} \\ - 2\frac{1}{3} \\ \hline 3\frac{1}{3} \end{array}$$

Solution $5\frac{2}{3} - 2\frac{1}{3} = 3\frac{1}{3}$

Coached Example

Mr. Lee bought a $4\frac{1}{4}$-feet-long wooden board. He wants to cut a piece that is $2\frac{3}{4}$ feet from the board. How long will the board be that Mr. Lee has left?

Write a number sentence for the problem.

The board is _____ feet long.

He will cut a _____ feet piece.

Let b represent the length of board left.

_____ − _____ = _____

Write $4\frac{1}{4}$ as an equivalent improper fraction.

Write the whole number part as a fraction with a denominator of 4.

$4 = \frac{4}{4} +$ _____ $+$ _____ $+$ _____

Add the fractions.

$4\frac{1}{4} = \frac{4}{4} + \frac{4}{4} + \frac{4}{4} + \frac{4}{4} + \frac{1}{4} =$ _____

So, $4\frac{1}{4} =$ _____ .

Write $2\frac{3}{4}$ as an equivalent improper fraction.

Write the whole number part as a fraction with a denominator of 4.

$2 =$ _____ $+$ _____

Add the fractions.

$2\frac{3}{4} =$ _____ $+$ _____ $+$ _____ $=$ _____

So, $2\frac{3}{4} =$ _____ .

Subtract the improper fractions.

_____ − _____ = _____

Change the improper fraction to mixed number.

Divide the numerator by the denominator.

_____ ÷ _____ = _____

The mixed number is _____ .

Simplify the fraction part of the mixed number. _____

Mr. Lee has _____ feet of the board left.

Lesson Practice • Part 1

Choose the correct answer.

1. Which mixed number does this show?

$$\frac{3}{3} + \frac{3}{3} + \frac{1}{3} + \frac{1}{3} = \frac{8}{3}$$

A. $2\frac{1}{3}$

B. $1\frac{2}{3}$

C. $2\frac{2}{3}$ ⟵ circled

D. $3\frac{1}{3}$

$2\frac{2}{3}$

2. Which equation is true?

A. $2\frac{1}{12} = \frac{12}{12} + \frac{12}{12} + \frac{12}{12}$

B. $2\frac{1}{12} = \frac{12}{12} + \frac{12}{12} + \frac{10}{12}$

C. $2\frac{1}{12} = \frac{12}{12} + \frac{12}{12} + \frac{1}{12}$

D. $2\frac{1}{12} = \frac{1}{12} + \frac{1}{12} + \frac{1}{12}$

3. Add.

$$3\frac{2}{5} + 3\frac{2}{5} = \square$$

A. $4\frac{5}{6}$

B. $5\frac{2}{5}$

C. $6\frac{2}{5}$

D. $6\frac{4}{5}$ ⟵ circled

$3\frac{2}{5} + 3\frac{2}{5} = 6\frac{4}{5}$

4. Subtract.

$$4\frac{3}{4} - 2\frac{1}{4} = \square$$

A. $2\frac{1}{2}$

B. $2\frac{1}{4}$ ⟵ circled

C. $6\frac{1}{2}$

D. $7\frac{1}{4}$

$4\frac{3}{4} - 2\frac{1}{4} = 2\frac{2}{4}$

5. Connor watched $13\frac{1}{3}$ hours of TV this week and $7\frac{1}{3}$ hours last week. How many hours of TV did Connor watch in all in 2 weeks?

A. $6\frac{1}{3}$ hours

B. $19\frac{1}{3}$ hours

C. $20\frac{2}{3}$ hours ⟵ circled

D. $11\frac{2}{3}$ hours

$13\frac{1}{3} + 7\frac{1}{3} = 20\frac{2}{3}$

6. Nora has a red ribbon that is $3\frac{1}{8}$ feet long. She also has a purple ribbon that is $1\frac{5}{8}$ feet long. How many feet longer is the red ribbon than the purple ribbon?

$\frac{0 \times 5/0}{8}$

$3\frac{1}{8} - 1\frac{5}{8}$

A. $1\frac{1}{4}$ feet   C. $2\frac{1}{8}$ feet

B. $1\frac{1}{2}$ feet   D. $3\frac{2}{3}$ feet ⟵ circled

$2\frac{0}{0}$

7. Which number goes in the box to make the sentence true?

$$5\frac{7}{10} - \boxed{} = 2\frac{3}{10}$$

A. $7\frac{2}{5}$

B. $3\frac{4}{5}$

C. $3\frac{2}{5}$

D. $3\frac{1}{4}$

8. Which number goes in the box to make the sentence true?

$$\boxed{} - 1\frac{1}{8} = 2\frac{5}{8}$$

A. $4\frac{3}{4}$

B. $3\frac{3}{4}$

C. $3\frac{1}{2}$

D. $1\frac{1}{2}$

9. Gordon bought $6\frac{1}{4}$ pounds of ground beef to make food for a party. He used $2\frac{1}{4}$ pounds of beef to make lasagna and another $2\frac{1}{4}$ pounds to make hamburgers.

A. How many pounds of beef did Gordon use in all to make lasagna and hamburgers? Show your work.

_____

_____

B. How much ground beef does Gordon have left? Show your work.

_____

_____

Lesson Practice • Part 2

Choose the correct answer.

1. Which mixed number makes both number sentences true?

$$2\frac{3}{5} + \boxed{1\frac{1}{5}} = 3\frac{4}{5}$$

$$3\frac{4}{5} - \boxed{} = 2\frac{3}{5}$$

   A. $\frac{2}{5}$

   B. $\frac{4}{5}$

   C. $1\frac{1}{10}$

   D. $1\frac{1}{5}$

2. A board was $7\frac{1}{4}$ inches long before Hazel cut $2\frac{3}{4}$ inches off of it. What is the length of the larger piece?

   A. $4\frac{1}{2}$ inches

   B. $4\frac{3}{4}$ inches

   C. $5\frac{1}{4}$ inches

   D. $5\frac{1}{2}$ inches

3. Which is equivalent to $2\frac{5}{8}$?

   A. $\frac{8}{8} + \frac{2}{8} + \frac{3}{8}$

   B. $\frac{8}{8} + \frac{8}{8} + \frac{2}{8} + \frac{2}{8}$

   C. $1 + 1 + \frac{1}{8} + \frac{2}{8} + \frac{2}{8}$

   D. $1 + 1 + \frac{2}{8} + \frac{2}{8} + \frac{2}{8}$

4. Which explains how to add mixed numbers with like denominators?

   A. Add the numerators of the fractions and then add the whole numbers. Finally, add the denominators.

   B. Add the denominators of the fractions and then add the whole numbers. The numerators stay as is.

   C. Add the numerators of the fractions and then add the whole numbers. The denominator stays as is.

   D. Add the numerators of the fractions and the whole numbers together. The denominator stays as is.

5. Which number sentence requires renaming the minuend?

   A. $2\frac{7}{8} - 1\frac{5}{8} = \boxed{}$

   B. $4\frac{1}{4} - 1\frac{3}{4} = \boxed{}$

   C. $5\frac{1}{2} - 2\frac{1}{2} = \boxed{}$

   D. $6\frac{5}{6} - 4\frac{1}{6} = \boxed{}$

6. Kimber jogged $3\frac{7}{10}$ miles on Monday and $4\frac{9}{10}$ miles on Tuesday. How many miles did Kimber jog altogether?

A. $7\frac{2}{5}$ miles

B. $7\frac{3}{5}$ miles

C. $8\frac{2}{5}$ miles

D. $8\frac{3}{5}$ miles

7. Jameson made a poster that has a length of $3\frac{5}{12}$ feet and a width of $2\frac{7}{12}$ feet. How much longer is the length than the width?

A. $\frac{5}{6}$ foot

C. $1\frac{1}{12}$ feet

B. $\frac{11}{12}$ foot

D. $1\frac{1}{6}$ feet

8. Scarlett sold $5\frac{3}{5}$ books of raffle tickets in 3 days. She sold $2\frac{2}{5}$ books on the first day and $1\frac{4}{5}$ books on the second day.

A. How many books of raffle tickets did Scarlett sell during the first two days? Show your work.

_____

_____

B. How many books of raffle tickets did Scarlett sell on the third day? Show your work.

_____

_____

9. Use numbers from the box to write the sum as a mixed number in simplest form.

$2\frac{3}{8} + 3\frac{6}{8} = \boxed{5}\,\dfrac{\boxed{9}}{\boxed{8}}$

1

5

6

8

9

10. Select True or False for each sentence.

A. $4\frac{4}{5} - 1\frac{1}{5} = 3\frac{3}{5}$ ⊘ True   ○ False

B. $3\frac{4}{8} - 2\frac{5}{8} = \frac{1}{8}$ ○ True   ⊘ False

C. $12\frac{8}{12} - 5\frac{4}{12} = 7\frac{1}{3}$ ○ True   ⊘ False

D. $8\frac{6}{10} - 2\frac{3}{10} = 6\frac{3}{10}$ ⊘ True   ○ False

11. Draw a line from each addition problem to its sum.

A. $1\frac{5}{8} + 5\frac{2}{8}$ $6\frac{3}{8}$

B. $5\frac{1}{8} + 2\frac{4}{8}$ $6\frac{7}{8}$

C. $3\frac{2}{8} + 3\frac{1}{8}$ $7\frac{5}{8}$

D. $4\frac{4}{8} + 3\frac{3}{8}$ $7\frac{7}{8}$

12. Find the equivalent mixed number. Write the expression in the correct box.

$\frac{8}{8} + \frac{8}{8} + \frac{1}{8} + \frac{1}{8}$	$\frac{4}{4} + \frac{4}{4} + \frac{1}{4}$	$\frac{18}{8}$
$\frac{8}{8} + \frac{8}{8} + \frac{1}{8} + \frac{1}{8} + \frac{1}{8}$	$\frac{19}{8}$	$\frac{9}{4}$

$2\frac{1}{4}$	$2\frac{3}{8}$
$\frac{8}{8} + \frac{8}{8} + \frac{1}{8} + \frac{1}{8} + \frac{1}{8}$ $\frac{4}{4} + \frac{4}{4} + \frac{1}{4}$ $\frac{9}{4}$	$\frac{8}{8} + \frac{8}{8} + \frac{8}{8} + \frac{1}{8} + \frac{1}{8}$ $\frac{11}{8}$ $\frac{18}{8}$

13. Which has a value of $3\frac{3}{5}$? Circle all that apply.

A. $\frac{1}{5} + \frac{1}{5} + \frac{1}{5} + \frac{3}{5}$

B. $\frac{10}{10} + \frac{10}{10} + \frac{10}{10} + \frac{1}{10} + \frac{1}{10} + \frac{1}{10} + \frac{1}{10} + \frac{1}{10} + \frac{1}{10}$

C. $\frac{1}{10} + \frac{1}{10} + \frac{1}{10} + \frac{6}{10}$

D. $\frac{5}{5} + \frac{5}{5} + \frac{5}{5} + \frac{1}{5} + \frac{1}{5} + \frac{1}{5}$

14. Use numbers from the box to write the difference as a mixed number in simplest form.

$$9\frac{8}{10} - 8\frac{4}{10} = \boxed{}\frac{\boxed{}}{\boxed{}}$$

1
2
4
5
10

15. Draw a line from each subtraction sentence to the missing number that makes it true.

A. $\boxed{} - 1\frac{1}{8} = 2\frac{3}{8}$ •   • $3\frac{1}{2}$

B. $\boxed{} - 5\frac{1}{8} = 1\frac{5}{8}$ •   • $4\frac{1}{4}$

C. $7\frac{7}{8} - \boxed{} = 2\frac{5}{8}$ •   • $5\frac{1}{4}$

D. $7\frac{3}{8} - \boxed{} = 3\frac{1}{8}$ •   • $6\frac{3}{4}$

Multiply Fractions with Whole Numbers

Getting the Idea

You can use models to help you multiply a fraction by a whole number.

Example 1

Multiply.

$4 \times \frac{1}{2} = \square$

Strategy   **Use models.**

Step 1   Show 4 groups of $\frac{1}{2}$.

$\frac{1}{2}$	$\frac{1}{2}$	$\frac{1}{2}$	$\frac{1}{2}$	=		$\frac{4}{2} = 2$

Step 2   Find the product.

There are 4 halves, or 2 wholes, in all.

Solution $4 \times \frac{1}{2} = \frac{4}{2} = 2$

Multiplication is the same as repeated addition. You can use repeated addition to multiply a fraction by a whole number.

For example, to multiply $5 \times \frac{1}{4}$, add $\frac{1}{4}$ five times.

$$\frac{1}{4} + \frac{1}{4} + \frac{1}{4} + \frac{1}{4} + \frac{1}{4} = \frac{5}{4}$$

So, $5 \times \frac{1}{4} = \frac{5}{4}$.

Since $\frac{5}{4}$ is the product of 5 and $\frac{1}{4}$, $\frac{5}{4}$ is a multiple of $\frac{1}{4}$.

Example 2

Multiply.

$$3 \times \frac{2}{3} = \boxed{}$$

Strategy **Use repeated addition.**

Step 1 Write the multiplication as repeated addition.

$$3 \times \frac{2}{3} = \frac{2}{3} + \frac{2}{3} + \frac{2}{3}$$

Step 2 Add the numerators. The denominator stays the same.

$$\frac{2}{3} + \frac{2}{3} + \frac{2}{3} = \frac{2 + 2 + 2}{3} = \frac{6}{3}$$

Step 3 Simplify.

$$\frac{6}{3} = 2$$

Step 4 Use models to check.

Show 3 groups of $\frac{2}{3}$.

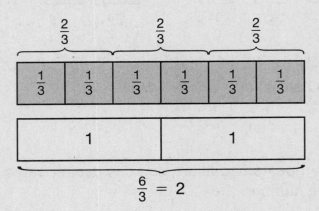

$$\frac{6}{3} = 2$$

There are 2 groups of $\frac{3}{3}$.

$$\frac{3}{3} + \frac{3}{3} = 1 + 1$$

$$1 + 1 = 2$$

Solution $3 \times \frac{2}{3} = 2$

In Example 2, the product is $\frac{6}{3}$ or 2. So, 2 is a multiple of $\frac{2}{3}$.

You can also show $3 \times \frac{2}{3}$ as $6 \times \frac{1}{3}$. Both give the same product.

So, 2 is also a multiple of $\frac{1}{3}$.

$$3 \times \frac{2}{3} = \frac{6}{3} = 2 \qquad\qquad 6 \times \frac{1}{3} = \frac{6}{3} = 2$$

| $\frac{1}{3}$ | $\frac{1}{3}$ | $\frac{1}{3}$ | $\frac{1}{3}$ | $\frac{1}{3}$ | $\frac{1}{3}$ | | $\frac{1}{3}$ | $\frac{1}{3}$ | $\frac{1}{3}$ | $\frac{1}{3}$ | $\frac{1}{3}$ | $\frac{1}{3}$ |

When you multiply a fraction and a whole number, you can rename the whole number as a fraction. Then multiply the numerators and the denominators.

Example 3

Carrie and Eddie each ordered $\frac{3}{4}$ pound of chocolate. How much chocolate did they order in all? Between what two whole numbers does the answer lie?

Strategy   **Write the whole number as a fraction. Multiply.**

Step 1   Write the multiplication sentence for the problem.

Each person ordered $\frac{3}{4}$ pound.

Let t represent the total number of pounds of chocolate ordered.

$2 \times \frac{3}{4} = t$

Step 2   Write the whole number as a fraction.

$2 = \frac{2}{1}$

Step 3   Multiply the numerators and denominators.

$\frac{2}{1} \times \frac{3}{4} = \frac{2 \times 3}{1 \times 4} = \frac{6}{4}$

Step 4   Use models to check.

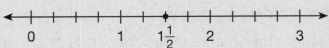

$$\frac{3}{4} \quad + \quad \frac{3}{4} \quad = \quad \frac{6}{4}$$

Step 5   Change the improper fraction to a mixed number.

$$\frac{6}{4} = \frac{4}{4} + \frac{2}{4}$$

$$\frac{4}{4} + \frac{2}{4} = 1 + \frac{2}{4}$$

$$1 + \frac{2}{4} = 1\frac{2}{4}$$

Step 6   Simplify the mixed number.

$$\frac{2}{4} = \frac{2 \div 2}{4 \div 2} = \frac{1}{2}$$

So $1\frac{2}{4} = 1\frac{1}{2}$.

Step 7   Use a number line to find the two whole numbers the sum lies between.
Put a point at $1\frac{1}{2}$.

```
◄──┼──┼──┼──┼──┼──●──┼──┼──┼──┼──┼──►
   0        1   1½   2           3
```

The sum is between 1 and 2.

Solution   They ordered $1\frac{1}{2}$ pounds of chocolate in all.
The answer lies between 1 and 2.

Coached Example

Multiply.

$4 \times \frac{3}{5} = \square$

Write the multiplication as repeated addition.

$4 \times \frac{3}{5} =$ _____ + _____ + _____ + _____

Look at the denominators.

Are the denominators the same? _____

Add the numerators.

_____ + _____ + _____ + _____ = _____

Write the sum over the denominator. _____

Change the sum to a mixed number.

Divide the numerator by the denominator.

$\frac{12}{5} =$ _____

Make a model of the problem to check your answer.

$4 \times \frac{3}{5} =$ _____

Lesson Practice • Part 1

Choose the correct answer.

1. Multiply.

$$5 \times \frac{1}{6} = \boxed{}$$

- **A.** $\frac{1}{3}$
- **B.** $\frac{1}{2}$
- **C.** $\frac{2}{3}$
- **D.** $\frac{5}{6}$

2. Multiply.

$$3 \times \frac{2}{10} = \boxed{}$$

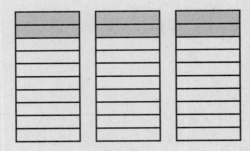

- **A.** $\frac{5}{10}$
- **B.** $\frac{6}{10}$
- **C.** $\frac{8}{7}$
- **D.** 1

3. Which will have the same product as $4 \times \frac{2}{5}$?

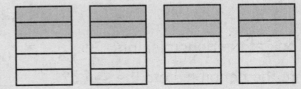

- **A.** $8 \times \frac{1}{5}$
- **B.** $4 \times \frac{1}{2}$
- **C.** $5 \times \frac{1}{4}$
- **D.** $4 \times \frac{1}{5}$

4. Multiply.

$$8 \times \frac{1}{4} = \boxed{}$$

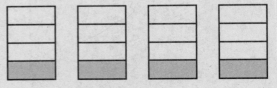

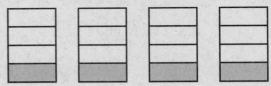

- **A.** $\frac{4}{8}$
- **B.** $\frac{1}{2}$
- **C.** 1
- **D.** 2

5. Multiply.

$$3 \times \frac{1}{12} = \boxed{}$$

A. $\frac{2}{12}$ **C.** $\frac{4}{12}$

B. $\frac{3}{12}$ **D.** 4

6. Multiply.

$$4 \times \frac{1}{2} = \boxed{}$$

A. 1

B. $\frac{3}{2}$

C. 2

D. $\frac{5}{2}$

7. Saul put $\frac{1}{2}$ bag of pretzels in his lunch box each day for 3 days. How many bags of pretzels did Saul put in his lunch box in all?

A. $\frac{2}{3}$ **C.** 2

B. $1\frac{1}{2}$ **D.** $2\frac{1}{2}$

8. Catalina decorated each of 5 shoeboxes with $\frac{1}{5}$ foot of ribbon. How many feet of ribbon did she use in all?

A. $\frac{2}{5}$ foot   **C.** $\frac{4}{5}$ foot

B. $\frac{3}{5}$ foot   **D.** 1 foot

9. Theresa has 9 baskets. Each basket is $\frac{1}{3}$ full of tomatoes.

A. Make a model to show the problem.

B. How many full baskets of tomatoes does Theresa have? Use multiplication. Show your work.

Lesson Practice • Part 2

Choose the correct answer.

1. Which is equivalent to $6 \times \frac{3}{5}$?

   A. $2 \times \frac{1}{5}$

   B. $3 \times \frac{2}{5}$

   C. $9 \times \frac{1}{5}$

   D. $18 \times \frac{1}{5}$

2. Each individual carton of milk contains $\frac{1}{4}$ quart. How many quarts are there in 12 cartons?

   A. 2 quarts

   B. $2\frac{1}{2}$ quarts

   C. 3 quarts

   D. $3\frac{1}{2}$ quarts

3. Each day Sparky, a dog, eats $\frac{3}{8}$ pound of food. Which describes the total amount of food that Sparky eats in 7 days?

   A. less than 2 pounds

   B. between 2 and 3 pounds

   C. between 3 and 4 pounds

   D. more than 4 pounds

4. Which explains how to multiply a whole number times a fraction?

   A. Multiply the numerator of the fraction times the whole number, which becomes the numerator. The denominator stays as is.

   B. Multiply the denominator of the fraction times the whole number, which becomes the numerator. The denominator stays as is.

   C. Multiply the numerator of the fraction times the whole number, which becomes the numerator. Then multiply the denominator of the fraction times the whole number, which becomes the denominator.

   D. Add the numerator of the fraction to the whole number, which becomes the numerator. The denominator stays as is.

5. Which number makes the sentence true?

   $$2 \times \frac{3}{4} = 6 \times \boxed{}$$

   A. $\frac{1}{4}$ **C.** $\frac{1}{2}$

   B. $\frac{1}{3}$ **D.** $\frac{9}{4}$

6. A whole number greater than 1 is multiplied by a fraction greater than 0 and less than 1. Which describes the relationship between the factors and the product?

   A. The product is less than both factors.

   B. The product is greater than both factors.

   C. The product is greater than the fraction and less than 1.

   D. The product is greater than the fraction and less than the whole number.

7. Multiply.

$$8 \times \frac{2}{3} = \boxed{}$$

   A. $1\frac{1}{3}$ **C.** $5\frac{1}{3}$

   B. $3\frac{1}{3}$ **D.** 12

8. Each lap around Finn Park is $\frac{3}{5}$ mile. Liam walked 4 laps around the park. How far did Liam walk around the park?

   A. $\frac{3}{20}$ mile

   B. $\frac{7}{9}$ mile

   C. $1\frac{2}{5}$ miles

   D. $2\frac{2}{5}$ miles

9. Which will result in a product that is a whole number?

   A. $5 \times \frac{1}{3}$

   B. $6 \times \frac{2}{3}$

   C. $7 \times \frac{1}{2}$

   D. $8 \times \frac{2}{5}$

10. Each juice glass at a table can hold $\frac{3}{4}$ cup. There are 8 juice glasses on a table.

   A. Jacob fills 5 of the glasses with orange juice. How many cups of orange juice did Jacob pour? Show your work.

   B. Jacob fills the other 3 glasses with apple juice. How many cups of apple juice did Jacob pour? Show your work.

11. Which has the same product as $3 \times \frac{2}{5}$? Circle all that apply.

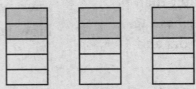

  A. $5 \times \frac{3}{2}$

  B. $6 \times \frac{1}{5}$

  C. $2 \times \frac{3}{5}$

  D. $5 \times \frac{2}{3}$

12. Select True or False for each sentence.

  A. $4 \times \frac{1}{8} = \frac{1}{4}$ ○ True   ○ False

  B. $6 \times \frac{1}{3} = 2$ ○ True   ○ False

  C. $5 \times \frac{3}{10} = \frac{8}{10}$ ○ True   ○ False

  D. $3 \times \frac{2}{12} = \frac{1}{2}$ ○ True   ○ False

13. Find each product. Write the problem in the correct box.

| $2 \times \frac{5}{8}$ | $7 \times \frac{3}{12}$ | $3 \times \frac{5}{12}$ | $2 \times \frac{7}{8}$ | $7 \times \frac{1}{4}$ | $5 \times \frac{1}{4}$ |

$1\frac{1}{4}$	$1\frac{3}{4}$

14. Draw a line from each multiplication problem to its product.

A. $4 \times \frac{1}{5}$ •   • $\frac{3}{5}$

B. $2 \times \frac{3}{10}$ •   • $\frac{4}{5}$

C. $3 \times \frac{2}{5}$ •   • $1\frac{1}{5}$

D. $4 \times \frac{6}{10}$ •   • $2\frac{2}{5}$

15. Manuel is making jars of homemade cookie mix to give as gifts. The table shows the volumes of some of the ingredients that go into each jar. Select True or False for each statement about the table.

Cookie Mix for 1 Jar

Ingredient	Volume
Salt	$\frac{1}{4}$ teaspoon
Chocolate chips	$\frac{1}{2}$ cup
Cocoa	$\frac{1}{3}$ cup

A. To make 12 jars, Manuel needs 3 teaspoons of salt. ○ True ○ False

B. To make 7 jars, Manuel needs $6\frac{1}{2}$ cups of chocolate chips. ○ True ○ False

C. To make 8 jars, Manuel needs $2\frac{2}{3}$ cups of cocoa. ○ True ○ False

D. To make 9 jars, Manuel needs $4\frac{1}{2}$ cups of chocolate chips. ○ True ○ False

Decimals

Getting the Idea

A **decimal** can name part of a whole or part of a group. A decimal can have a whole number part and a decimal part that are separated by a **decimal point (.).**

Each grid below represents 1 whole. The decimal shows the shaded part of the whole.

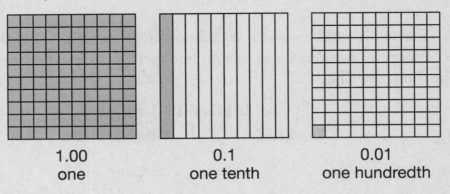

1.00
one

0.1
one tenth

0.01
one hundredth

Place values in decimals follow the same base-ten system as whole numbers.

Each place has 10 times the value of the place to its right.

　　1 tenth = 10 hundredths

　　1 one = 10 tenths

When you put a 0 to the right of the last digit of a decimal, it does not change the value of the decimal.

For example, 0.1 = 0.10 and 0.5 = 0.50.

You can use a place-value chart to show the value of each digit in a decimal. The decimal 2.35 has 2 ones, 3 tenths, and 5 hundredths, or 2 ones and 35 hundredths.

Ones	.	Tenths	Hundredths
2	.	3	5

Example 1

What decimal names the shaded part of the grid?

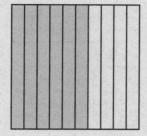

Strategy   **The entire grid equals 1 whole. Find the decimal for each part.**

Step 1   Find the decimal that represents each part of the grid.

There are 10 parts in the grid.

Each part is 0.1 or one tenth.

Step 2   Count the number of shaded parts.

There are 6 shaded parts.

So, six tenths, or 0.6, of the grid is shaded.

Solution   **The decimal 0.6 names the shaded part of the grid.**

To read or write the word name of a decimal less than 1, read the number to the right of the decimal point as you would read a whole number. Then read the least place value.

0.4 is read as *four tenths*.

0.23 is read as *twenty-three hundredths*.

To read or write the word name of a decimal greater than 1, read the whole number, use the word *and* for the decimal point, and then read the decimal part.

3.6 is read as *three and six tenths*.

1.27 is read as *one and twenty-seven hundredths*.

Example 2

What decimal names the shaded part of the grid?

Strategy **The entire grid equals 1 whole. Find the decimal for each part.**

Step 1   Find the decimal that represents each part of the grid.

There are 100 parts in the grid.

Each part is 0.01 or one hundredth.

Step 2   Count the number of shaded parts.

There are 57 shaded parts.

Step 3   Write the decimal in a place-value chart.

Ones	.	Tenths	Hundredths
0	.	5	7

Solution **The decimal 0.57, or fifty-seven hundredths, names the shaded part of the grid.**

Example 3

What decimal do the models show? What is the word name for the decimal?

Strategy   **Use a place-value chart.**

Step 1   Find the decimal represented by the models.

There is 1 whole grid shaded.

The other grid has 24 out of 100 parts shaded.

So, 0.24 of the other grid is shaded.

Step 2   Write the decimal in a place-value chart.

Ones	.	Tenths	Hundredths
1	.	2	4

Step 3   Write the part to the left of the decimal point in words.

The whole number part is *one*.

The decimal point is *and*.

Step 4   Write the part to the right of the decimal point in words.

The decimal part is *twenty-four*.

The least place value is *hundredths*.

Solution   **The models show the decimal 1.24.**
The word name is *one and twenty-four hundredths*.

You can represent decimals on a number line. Count the equal parts between marked numbers to decide what each tick mark represents.

Example 4

What decimal does point *H* represent on the number line?

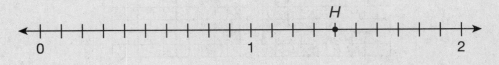

Strategy   **Decide what each tick mark represents.**

Step 1   Count the equal parts between marked numbers.

There are 10 equal parts between 1 and 2.

So, each tick mark represents 0.1 or one tenth.

Step 2   Count the spaces from 1 to point *H*.

Point *H* is at the fourth mark after 1.

Since each mark represents 0.1, point *H* is at 1.4.

Solution   **Point *H* represents 1.4.**

Example 5

What decimal does point *J* represent on the number line?

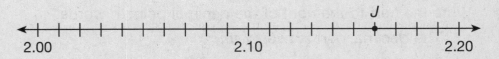

Strategy   **Decide what each tick mark represents.**

Step 1   Count the equal parts between marked numbers.

There are 10 equal parts between 2.10 and 2.20.

So, each tick mark represents 0.01 or one hundredth.

Step 2   Count the spaces from 2.10 to point *J*.

Point *J* is at the sixth mark after 2.10.

Since each mark represents 0.01, point *J* is at 2.16.

Solution   **Point *J* represents 2.16.**

Coached Example

What decimal do the models show? What is the word name for the decimal?

There are _____ whole grids shaded.

The other grid has _____ out of _____ parts shaded.

So, _____ of the other grid is shaded.

Write the decimal in a place-value chart.

Ones	.	Tenths	Hundredths

Write the part to the left of the decimal point in words.

The whole number part is _____.

The decimal point is _____.

Write the part to the right of the decimal point in words.

The decimal part is _____.

The least place value is _____.

The models show the decimal _____.

The word name is _____.

Lesson Practice • Part 1

Choose the correct answer.

1. What decimal names the shaded part of the grid?

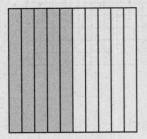

   A. 0.01

   B. 0.05

   C. 0.1

   D. 0.5

2. What decimal names the shaded part of the grid?

   A. 0.16

   B. 0.40

   C. 0.84

   D. 0.94

3. What is the word name of the decimal?

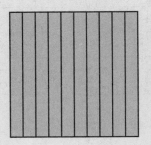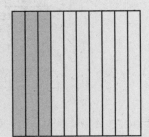

   A. three tenths

   B. one and three tenths

   C. one and three hundredths

   D. three and one tenth

4. Which digit is in the hundredths place in the decimal 1.73?

   A. 1   C. 4

   B. 3   D. 7

5. Which decimal is three and nine hundredths?

   A. 3.90   C. 0.93

   B. 3.09   D. 0.39

6. Which decimal has an 8 in the tenths place?

   A. 1.84   C. 8.19

   B. 3.28   D. 80.25

Use the number line for questions 7 and 8.

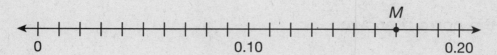

7. What decimal does point *M* represent on the number line?

   A. 0.07

   B. 0.17

   C. 0.7

   D. 1.7

8. How can you read the decimal that point *M* represents?

   A. seven hundredths

   B. seventeen tenths

   C. seventeen hundredths

   D. one and seven tenths

9. Mr. Tyler drew these grids on the board.

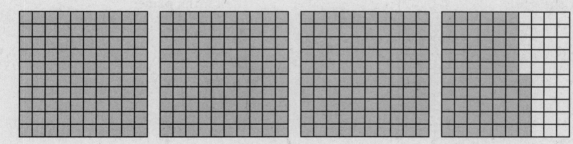

   A. What decimal do the grids show?

      3.55

   B. How many ones, tenths, and hundredths are in the decimal?

      3 1 5 5

   C. How can you write the word name of the decimal?

Lesson Practice • Part 2

Choose the correct answer.

1. Which decimal names the shaded part of the grid?

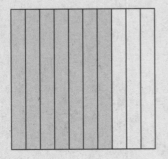

   A. 0.03
   B. 0.07
   C. 0.3
   D. 0.7

2. Which decimal names the shaded part of the grid?

   A. 0.38
   B. 0.48
   C. 0.52
   D. 0.62

3. Which decimal names the part of the grid that is shaded?

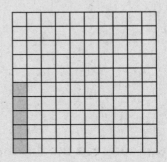

   A. 0.05
   B. 0.15
   C. 0.5
   D. 0.95

4. In the decimal 72.49, which digit is in the tenths place?

   A. 2
   B. 4
   C. 7
   D. 9

5. Which is sixty and four hundredths using base-ten numerals?

   A. 6.04
   B. 6.4
   C. 60.04
   D. 60.4

6. Which letter represents 1.6 on the number line?

    A. *E*

    B. *F*

    C. *G*

    D. *H*

7. Which decimal does point *J* represent?

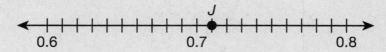

    A. 0.79

    B. 0.71

    C. 0.69

    D. 0.61

8. Use the grids for question 8.

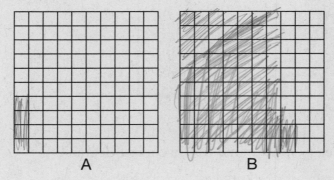

    A   B

    A. Shade grid A to represent 0.4.

    B. Shade grid B to represent 0.72.

9. In which place is the digit 5 in each decimal? Write the decimal in the correct box.

| 12.51 | 6.57 | 1.95 | 38.05 | 21.5 | 90.05 |

Hundredths Place	Tenths Place
12.51 38.05 21.5 90.05	6.57 1.95

10. Use numbers from the box to write the decimal that is seventy-eight and six hundredths.

7 8 . 0 6

| 0 |
| 6 |
| 7 |
| 8 |

11. Draw a line from each word name to the correct decimal.

A. twenty-six and five hundredths   20.35

B. two hundred six and five tenths   26.05

C. twenty and thirty-five hundredths   206.5

D. two hundred sixty and fifty-three hundredths   260.53

12. Draw a line from each set of grids to the decimal it shows.

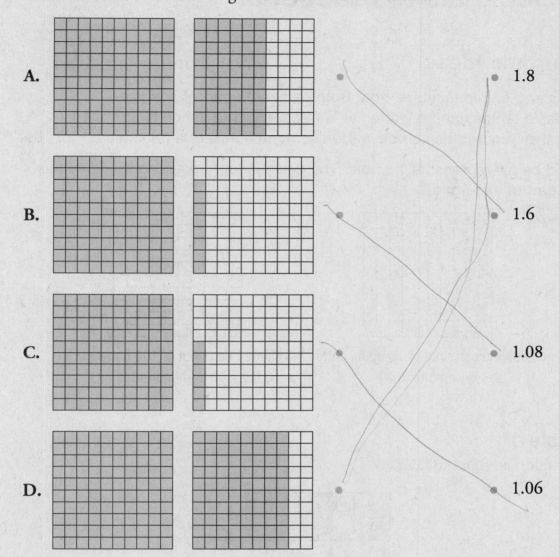

A.

B.

C.

D.

1.8

1.6

1.08

1.06

13. Which decimal is shown by point *A* on the number line? Circle all that apply.

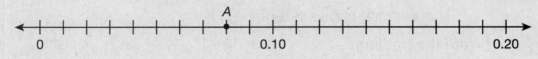

A. 0.12

B. eight tenths

C. 0.08

D. eight hundredths

Relate Decimals to Fractions

Getting the Idea

Decimals and fractions are related. Both can name part of a whole.
A decimal in tenths can be written as a fraction with a denominator of 10.
A decimal in hundredths can be written as a fraction with a denominator of 100.

Each grid below represents 1 whole. The decimal and fraction both name the shaded part of each grid.

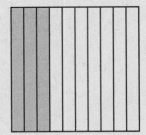

3 shaded parts out of 10 equal parts
$0.3 =$ three tenths $= \frac{3}{10}$

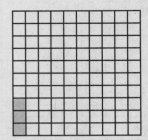

3 shaded parts out of 100 equal parts
$0.03 =$ three hundredths $= \frac{3}{100}$

Example 1

What fraction is equal to 0.8?

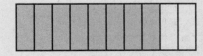

Strategy   **Use the place value of the decimal.**

Step 1   Find the place value of the decimal.

   The decimal shows 8 tenths.

Step 2   Write the fraction.

   The denominator is 10. The numerator is 8.

   $\frac{8}{10}$

Solution $0.8 = \frac{8}{10}$

Example 2

What fraction is equal to 0.07?

Strategy   **Use the place value of the decimal.**

Step 1   Find the place value of the decimal.

The decimal shows 7 hundredths.

Step 2   Write the fraction.

The denominator is 100. The numerator is 7.

$$\frac{7}{100}$$

Solution $0.07 = \frac{7}{100}$

You can express a fraction with a denominator of 10 as an equivalent fraction with a denominator of 100. Multiply the numerator and denominator by 10.

Example 3

What decimal is equivalent to the sum of $\frac{5}{10} + \frac{3}{100}$?

Strategy   **Rename the fraction and add.**

Step 1   Rename $\frac{5}{10}$, so that it has 100 as a denominator.

$$\frac{5}{10} \times \frac{10}{10} = \frac{50}{100}$$

$$\frac{5}{10} = \frac{50}{100}$$

Step 2   Add the fractions.

$$\frac{50}{100} + \frac{3}{100} = \frac{53}{100}$$

Step 3   Rename the sum as a decimal.

$$\frac{53}{100} = 0.53$$

Solution $\frac{5}{10} + \frac{3}{100} = 0.53$

Example 4

The shaded part of the grid shows 0.79.

What fraction is equal to that decimal? Write the fraction as an equation.

Strategy   **Break the shaded part into tenths and hundredths.**

  Step 1   Show the decimal in tenths and hundredths.

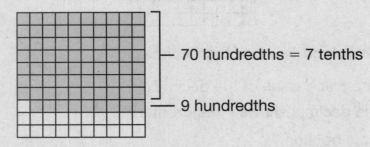

70 hundredths = 7 tenths

9 hundredths

$$0.79 = 79 \text{ hundredths} = 7 \text{ tenths } 9 \text{ hundredths}$$

  Step 2   Show the parts as fractions.

7 tenths $= \frac{7}{10}$

9 hundredths $= \frac{9}{100}$

So, 79 hundredths $= \frac{7}{10} + \frac{9}{100}$.

  Step 3   Show $\frac{7}{10}$ as an equivalent fraction with a denominator of 100.

$$\frac{7}{10} = \frac{7 \times 10}{10 \times 10} = \frac{70}{100}$$

  Step 4   Write the decimal as a sum of two fractions.

$$0.79 = 79 \text{ hundredths} = \frac{79}{100}$$

$$\frac{79}{100} = \frac{70}{100} + \frac{9}{100}$$

Solution   **The fraction $\frac{79}{100}$ is equal to 0.79.**

$$\frac{79}{100} = \frac{70}{100} + \frac{9}{100}$$

$$\frac{79}{100} = \frac{7}{10} + \frac{9}{100}$$

Coached Example

The shaded part of the grid shows 0.56.

What fraction is equal to that decimal? Write the fraction as an equation.

Show the decimal in tenths and hundredths.

0.56 = _____ hundredths = _____ tenths _____ hundredths

Show the parts as fractions.

5 tenths = _____

6 hundredths = _____

So, 56 hundredths = _____ + _____.

Show $\frac{5}{10}$ as an equivalent fraction with a denominator of 100.

$\frac{5}{10}$ = _____

Write the decimal as a sum of two fractions.

0.56 = 56 hundredths = _____

$\frac{56}{100}$ = _____ + _____

The fraction _____ is equal 0.56.

$\frac{56}{100} = \frac{}{100} + \frac{}{100}$

$\frac{56}{100} = \frac{}{10} + \frac{}{100}$

Lesson Practice • Part 1

Choose the correct answer.

1. What fraction is equal to 0.9?

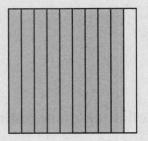

- **A.** $\frac{1}{9}$
- **B.** $\frac{9}{10}$
- **C.** $\frac{9}{100}$
- **D.** $\frac{90}{10}$

2. What fraction is equal to 0.04?

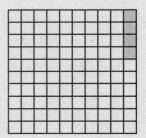

- **A.** $\frac{1}{4}$
- **B.** $\frac{4}{10}$
- **C.** $\frac{4}{100}$
- **D.** $\frac{40}{10}$

3. Rod's puppy ate 8 tenths of a can of dog food. Which model shows the amount of food the puppy ate?

A.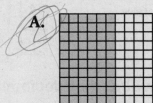

B.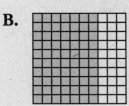

C.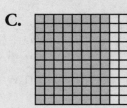

D.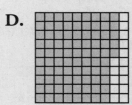

4. What fraction is equal to 0.19?

- **A.** $\frac{100}{19}$
- **B.** $\frac{19}{100}$
- **C.** $\frac{19}{10}$
- **D.** $\frac{1}{19}$

5. In simplest form, which fraction is equal to 0.5?

A. $\frac{5}{100}$ **C.** $\frac{1}{5}$

B. $\frac{10}{5}$ **D.** $\frac{1}{2}$

6. Which does **not** show the shaded part of the grid?

A. $\frac{1}{10}$

B. $\frac{1}{5}$

C. $\frac{2}{10}$

D. $\frac{20}{100}$

7. Which has a different value than all of the others?

A. $\frac{9}{100}$ **C.** 0.9

B. $\frac{9}{10}$ **D.** 0.90

8. The grid has 0.38 shaded.

Which sum of fractions shows 0.38?

A. $\frac{3}{10} + \frac{8}{10}$

B. $\frac{3}{10} + \frac{8}{100}$

C. $\frac{3}{100} + \frac{8}{100}$

D. $\frac{3}{100} + \frac{8}{10}$

9. Lamar shaded a grid.

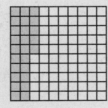

A. Write the decimal for the shaded part.
Write the fraction in simplest form for the shaded part.

_____

_____

B. Show the decimal as a sum of two fractions.

_____

Lesson Practice • Part 2

Choose the correct answer.

1. Which sentence about the shaded part of the grid is true?

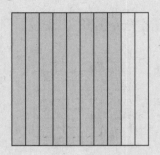

A. $\frac{8}{100} = 0.8$

B. $\frac{8}{100} = 0.08$

C. $\frac{8}{10} = 0.8$

D. $\frac{8}{10} = 0.08$

2. Which sentence about the shaded part of the grid is true?

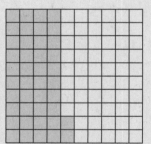

A. $\frac{42}{100} = 0.42$

B. $\frac{42}{10} = 4.2$

C. $\frac{52}{100} = 0.52$

D. $\frac{52}{10} = 5.2$

3. Which sum of fractions shows 0.95?

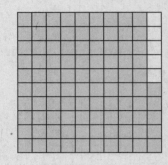

A. $\frac{5}{100} + \frac{9}{100}$ **C.** $\frac{5}{10} + \frac{9}{100}$

B. $\frac{9}{100} + \frac{5}{100}$ **D.** $\frac{9}{10} + \frac{5}{100}$

4. In simplest form, which fraction is equal to 0.25?

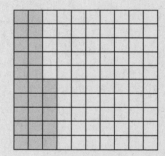

A. $\frac{1}{25}$ **C.** $\frac{1}{4}$

B. $\frac{1}{5}$ **D.** $\frac{1}{2}$

5. Which is the sum of $\frac{3}{10} + \frac{6}{100}$ written as a decimal?

A. 0.09   **C.** 0.63

B. 0.36   **D.** 0.9

6. Which has a different value than the others?

    A. 0.07

    B. $\frac{7}{100}$

    C. seven hundredths

    D. 0.7

7. In simplest form, which fraction is equal to 0.9?

    A. $\frac{9}{100}$

    B. $\frac{1}{11}$

    C. $\frac{1}{9}$

    D. $\frac{9}{10}$

8. Which sentence about fractions and decimals are true?

    A. The word name for a fraction and a decimal is always the same.

    B. If the denominator of a fraction is 10 or 100, the word name for a fraction and a decimal is always the same.

    C. The word name for a fraction and decimal is always the same unless the denominator of the fraction is 10 or 100.

    D. The word name for a fraction and a decimal is never the same.

---

9. Aaliyah was given $\frac{3}{100} + \frac{2}{10}$ to add.

    A. Write an equivalent expression using like denominators.

 $\frac{3}{100} + \frac{2}{10}$

    B. What is the sum written as a fraction? $\frac{32}{100}$

    C. What is the sum written as a decimal? 0.32

10. Draw a line from each grid to the fraction that shows the shaded part.

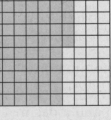

A.

B.

C.

D.

$\frac{35}{100}$

$\frac{43}{100}$

$\frac{57}{100}$

$\frac{65}{100}$

11. Which has the same value as 0.56? Circle all that apply.

A. $\frac{56}{100}$

B. $\frac{50}{100} + \frac{6}{100}$

C. $\frac{56}{10}$

D. $\frac{5}{10} + \frac{6}{100}$

12. Look at each decimal or fraction. Is it equal to $\frac{3}{10}$? Select Yes or No.

A. 0.03   ◯ Yes   ⊘ No

B. $\frac{30}{100}$ ◯ Yes   ⊘ No

C. 0.3   ⊘ Yes   ◯ No

D. 0.13   ◯ Yes   ⊘ No

13. Use numbers from the box to make the sum of fractions equal to 0.78.

$$\frac{7}{10} + \frac{8}{100}$$

7

8

70

80

14. Which shows the shaded part of the grid? Circle all that apply.

A. $\frac{1}{100} + \frac{6}{10}$

B. 0.16

C. $\frac{16}{100}$

D. $\frac{1}{10} + \frac{6}{100}$

E. $\frac{16}{10}$

F. 0.84

Compare and Order Decimals

Getting the Idea

Compare decimals as you would whole numbers. Refer to the same whole when comparing decimals.

Use the same symbols to compare decimals.

Example 1

What symbol makes this sentence true? Write >, <, or =.

0.62 ◯ 0.57

Strategy   **Make a model for each decimal.**

Step 1   Use 10-by-10 grids. Shade the squares to show each decimal.

Each grid represents 1 whole.

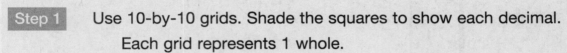

0.62 = 62 hundredths   0.57 = 57 hundredths

 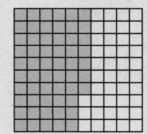

Step 2   Compare the shaded parts.

0.62 has more shaded parts.

0.62 is greater than 0.57.

Step 3   Choose the correct symbol.

> means *is greater than*.

Solution   **0.62 ⦥ 0.57**

You can compare decimals with different numbers of places. Align the numbers on the decimal point. You can write an equivalent decimal by writing a 0 to the right of the last decimal place. Then start comparing the digits in the greatest place.

Example 2

Which symbol makes this sentence true? Write >, <, or =

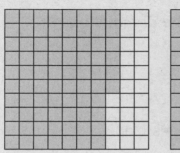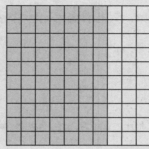

0.76 ◯ 0.7

Strategy   **Use a place-value chart.**

Step 1   Write an equivalent decimal for 0.7.

0.7 = 0.70

Step 2   Make a place-value chart.

Ones	·	Tenths	Hundredths
0	·	7	6
0	·	7	0

Step 3   Compare the digits in the ones place.

0 ones = 0 ones

Compare the next greatest place.

Step 4   Compare the digits in the tenths place.

7 tenths = 7 tenths

Compare the next greatest place.

Step 5   Compare the digits in the hundredths place.

6 hundredths > 4 hundredths

0.76 > 0.7.

Solution   **0.76 ⊛> 0.7**

When using place value to compare, line up the decimals on the decimal points. Compare the place values from left to right.

Example 3

List the decimals below in order from greatest to least.

0.81   1.03   0.88

Strategy   **Line up the decimals on the decimal points.**

0.81
1.03
0.88

Step 1 Compare the digits in the ones place.

0.81
1.03
0.88

1 > 0, so 1.03 is the greatest decimal.

Step 2 Compare the digits in the tenths place.

0.**8**1
0.**8**8

8 = 8, so compare the next place.

Step 3 Compare the digits in the hundredths place.

0.8**1**
0.8**8**

1 < 8, so 0.81 is the least decimal.

Solution   **From greatest to least, the order of the decimals is 1.03, 0.88, 0.81.**

Coached Example

Order the decimals below from least to greatest.

| 0.40 | 0.52 | 0.48 |

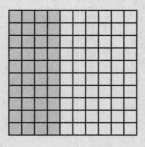  

Use place value to order the decimals.

Write the decimals in a place-value chart.

Ones	·	Tenths	Hundredths

Compare the digits in the greatest place, the _____.

_____ ones = _____ ones = _____ ones

All of the digits in the greatest place are _____.

Compare the digits in the next greatest place, the _____.

_____ tenths > _____ tenths, so _____ is the greatest decimal.

Compare the remaining two decimals.

Compare the digits in the next greatest place, the _____.

_____ hundredths < _____ hundredths, so _____ is the least decimal.

From least to greatest, the order of the decimals is

_____, _____, _____.

Lesson Practice • Part 1

Choose the correct answer.

1. What symbol makes this sentence true?

0.38 ◯ 0.36

A. >

B. <

C. =

D. +

2. Which sentence is true?

 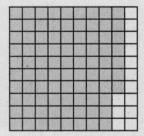

0.85   0.87

A. 0.85 = 0.87

B. 0.87 < 0.85

C. 0.85 > 0.87

D. 0.87 > 0.85

3. Which decimal makes this sentence true?

0.28 < ▢

A. 0.03

B. 0.27

C. 0.28

D. 0.30

4. Which decimal is less than 3.83?

A. 3.08

B. 3.83

C. 4.08

D. 4.80

5. Which list is in order from greatest to least?

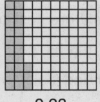  

0.23   0.42   0.22

A. 0.23   0.42   0.22

B. 0.22   0.23   0.42

C. 0.42   0.23   0.22

D. 0.22   0.42   0.23

6. Which is the greatest decimal?

    A. 2.02   **C.** 1.75

    B. 0.99   **D.** 1.68

7. Which list is in order from greatest to least?

    A. 0.97   1.62   1.68

    B. 1.62   1.68   0.97

    C. 1.68   1.62   0.97

    D. 0.97   1.68   1.62

8. Which list is in order from least to greatest?

    A. 0.44   0.34   0.30

    B. 0.30   0.44   0.34

    C. 0.44   0.30   0.34

    D. 0.30   0.34   0.44

9. Joseph bought 0.78 pound of roast beef. He also bought 0.52 pound of provolone cheese.

    A. Shade the grids below to show each decimal.

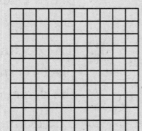 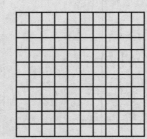

    B. Which item did Joseph buy more of, roast beef or provolone cheese?

    _____

Lesson Practice • Part 2

Choose the correct answer.

1. Which sentence is true?

   A. 0.48 > 0.44

   B. 0.56 < 0.53

   C. 0.74 > 0.78

   D. 0.87 < 0.83

Use the table for questions 2 and 3.

The table shows the mean density of four planets.

Planet Mean Density

Planet	Mean Density
Jupiter	0.24
Saturn	0.13
Uranus	0.23
Neptune	0.3

2. Which planet has the greatest mean density?

   A. Jupiter   **C.** Uranus

   B. Saturn   **D.** Neptune

3. Which planet has the least mean density?

   A. Jupiter   **C.** Uranus

   B. Saturn   **D.** Neptune

4. Which digit makes this sentence true?

   0.48 < 0.4☐

   A. 6   **C.** 8

   B. 7   **D.** 9

5. Payton is comparing a decimal with 2 decimal places to a decimal with 1 decimal place. Both decimals are greater than 0 and less than 1. Which sentence is true?

   A. The decimal with 2 decimal places is always greater than the decimal with 1 decimal place.

   B. The decimal with 2 decimal places is sometimes greater than the decimal with 1 decimal place.

   C. The decimal with 2 decimal places is never greater than the decimal with 1 decimal place.

   D. The decimal with 2 decimal places is equal to the decimal with 1 decimal place.

6. Which symbol makes this sentence true?

   0.2 ◯ 0.20

   A. >   **C.** =

   B. <   **D.** +

7. The table below shows the weights of four cats.

Weight of Cats

Cat	Weight (in pounds)
Gypsy	8.92
Roy	8.88
Shadow	9.1
Tippy	9.05

Which cat weighs the most?

A. Gypsy   C. Shadow

B. Roy   D. Tippy

8. The table below shows the ERA champions in the American League from 2011–2014.

A.L ERA Champions

Year	Pitcher	ERA
2011	Verlander	2.40
2012	Price	2.56
2013	Sanchez	2.57
2014	Hernandez	2.14

Which pitcher had the least ERA?

A. Verlander

B. Price

C. Sanchez

D. Hernandez

9. The currency of Malaysia is the ringgit. The table shows how many ringgits were worth $1 in different years.

Ringgits Worth $1

Year	Number of Ringgits
2011	3.22
2012	3.06
2013	3.09
2014	3.15

A. In which year could someone get the most ringgits for $1?

_____

B. In which year could someone get the least ringgits for $1?

_____

10. Circle the symbol that makes the sentence true.

0.67 $\begin{array}{c} > \\ < \\ = \end{array}$ 0.64

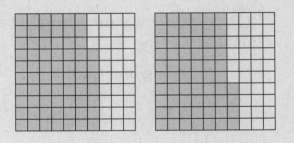

11. Select True or False for each sentence.

   A. 0.27 < 0.72   ○ True   ○ False

   B. 2.57 > 2.51   ○ True   ○ False

   C. 1.09 > 1.90   ○ True   ○ False

   D. 0.84 < 0.80   ○ True   ○ False

   E. 0.66 < 0.67   ○ True   ○ False

12. Which decimal is less than 3.38? Circle all that apply.

   A. 3.29

   B. 3.40

   C. 2.89

   D. 3.08

   E. 3.80

13. Is the list in order from least to greatest? Select Yes or No.

A. 0.97	1.26	1.20	○ Yes	○ No
B. 1.68	1.86	1.93	○ Yes	○ No
C. 2.51	2.15	1.52	○ Yes	○ No
D. 0.81	0.96	1.53	○ Yes	○ No
E. 1.26	1.62	2.16	○ Yes	○ No

14. Compare each decimal to 0.42. Write the decimal in the correct box.

| 0.38 | 0.24 | 0.62 | 0.40 | 0.50 | 0.14 |

Less than 0.42	Greater than 0.42

15. Which list shows the decimals in order from greatest to least? Circle all that apply.

A. 0.23   0.34   0.42

B. 0.85   0.57   0.39

C. 0.64   0.82   0.60

D. 0.71   0.59   0.45

E. 0.99   0.60   0.69

Domain 3: Cumulative Assessment for Lessons 18–27

1. Jessie has $\frac{8}{12}$ pound of cheese. Which shows an equivalent fraction to $\frac{8}{12}$?

   A.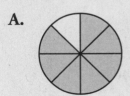

   B.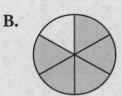

   C.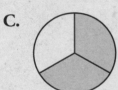

   D.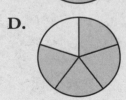

2. Cruz poured $\frac{2}{8}$ cup of milk into an empty pot. He then poured another $\frac{4}{8}$ cup of milk into the same pot. How much milk in all is in the pot?

   A. $\frac{3}{8}$ cup

   B. $\frac{5}{8}$ cup

   C. $\frac{6}{8}$ cup

   D. $\frac{7}{8}$ cup

3. In Nadine's class, $\frac{2}{8}$ of the students have summer birthdays. One-eighth of the students have autumn birthdays. What fraction more of Nadine's class has summer birthdays than autumn birthdays?

   A. $\frac{0}{4}$

   B. $\frac{1}{8}$

   C. $\frac{1}{4}$

   D. $\frac{3}{8}$

4. Multiply.

   $4 \times \frac{2}{3} = \boxed{}$

   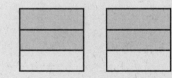
   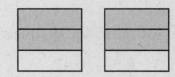

   A. $\frac{2}{3}$

   B. $1\frac{2}{3}$

   C. 2

   D. $2\frac{2}{3}$

5. Which sentence is true?

A. $\frac{2}{3} > \frac{4}{6}$

B. $\frac{3}{6} < \frac{5}{12}$

C. $\frac{2}{5} < \frac{3}{10}$

D. $\frac{5}{8} < \frac{3}{4}$

6. Which decimal represents the shaded part of the grids?

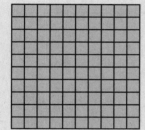 

A. 0.45

B. 1.45

C. 14.5

D. 145

7. This grid has 0.77 shaded.

Which sum of fractions shows 0.77?

A. $\frac{7}{10} + \frac{7}{10}$

B. $\frac{7}{100} + \frac{7}{100}$

C. $\frac{7}{10} + \frac{7}{100}$

D. $\frac{7}{1} + \frac{7}{10}$

8. Which decimal makes the sentence true?

$$0.17 < \boxed{}$$

A. 0.09

B. 0.15

C. 0.17

D. 0.20

9. Add.

$$2\frac{1}{6} + 3\frac{1}{6} = \boxed{}$$

10. There are $3\frac{1}{4}$ pints of ice cream in the freezer. Tori ate $\frac{3}{4}$ pint.

A. How much ice cream is left? Show your work.

_____

_____

_____

B. Show your answer for Part A in simplest form.

_____

_____

_____

Domain 4 Measurement and Data

Domain 4: Diagnostic Assessment for Lessons 28–36

Domain 4: Cumulative Assessment for Lessons 28–36

Domain 4: Diagnostic Assessment for Lessons 28–36

1. The point on the number line below shows the height of a table.

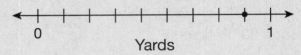

Yards

What is the height of the table?

A. $\frac{7}{8}$ yard

B. $\frac{7}{9}$ yard

C. $\frac{8}{9}$ yard

D. $\frac{9}{10}$ yard

2. Ebony started reading at 10:40 A.M. She stopped reading at 12:30 P.M. How long did Ebony spend reading?

A. 1 hour 30 minutes

B. 1 hour 50 minutes

C. 2 hours 30 minutes

D. 2 hours 50 minutes

3. A square has an area of 49 square inches. What is the length of one side of the square?

A. 6 inches

B. 7 inches

C. 9 inches

D. 11 inches

4. A chef needs 5 pounds of carrots for a salad. How many ounces are in 5 pounds?

A. 16 ounces   **C.** 64 ounces

B. 48 ounces   **D.** 80 ounces

5. A bathroom sink has a capacity of 4 liters. A bathtub has a capacity that is 50 times more than the sink. What is the capacity of the tub?

A. 54 liters   **C.** 240 liters

B. 200 liters   **D.** 450 liters

6. The area of this rectangle is 56 square centimeters.

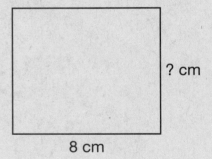

? cm

8 cm

What is the width of the rectangle?

A. 6 centimeters

B. 7 centimeters

C. 8 centimeters

D. 9 centimeters

7. The measure of angle *F* is 130°. A part of angle *F* measures 70°.

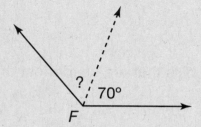

What is the measure of the other part of the angle?

A. 45°

B. 50°

C. 60°

D. 70°

8. What is the measure of this angle?

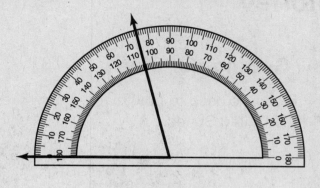

_____

9. Jamie recorded the number of miles he walked each day for a week. He made the line plot below.

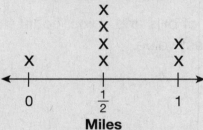

A. How many days did Jamie walk $\frac{1}{2}$ mile?

_____

B. What is the difference in miles between the longest distance and the shortest distance Jamie walked?

_____

Money

Getting the Idea

Money is used to buy things. Below are coins and bills that are used most often in the United States.

Penny	Nickel	Dime	Quarter	Half Dollar
1¢	5¢	10¢	25¢	50¢
$0.01	$0.05	$0.10	$0.25	$0.50

Dollar	Five Dollars	Ten Dollars	Twenty Dollars
$1.00 or $1	$5.00 or $5	$10.00 or $10	$20.00 or $20

There is also a dollar coin and a $2 bill, but they are not used often.

To find the value of a group of bills and coins, count from the bill with the greatest value to the coin with the least value.

Example 1

Eda has these bills and coins.

How much money does Eda have?

Strategy   **Start with the bill with the greatest value.**

Step 1	Count the bills from the greatest value to least value.

$20.00 → $25.00 → $26.00 → $27.00

Step 2	Count the coins from the greatest value to the least value.

Continue from $27.00.

$27.25 → $27.50 → $27.60 → $27.65

Solution   Eda has $27.65.

When you buy something at a store, you may not have the exact amount of money. You often give the cashier more money than the cost of your purchase and then get back change.

One way to make change is to count up from the price of the item to the amount of money you gave to the cashier.

Example 2

DeShawn bought a book for $8.59. He gave the cashier a $10 bill.
How much change should DeShawn receive from the cashier?

Strategy   Count up from the price of the book to the amount given.

Step 1	Start with the price of the book and count up to $10.

$8.59 → $8.60 → $8.65 → $8.75 → $9.00 → $10.00

Step 2	Count the coins and bill to find the value of the change.

$1.00   → $1.25 → $1.35 → $1.40 → $1.41

Solution   DeShawn should receive $1.41 in change.

You can also make change by subtracting the amount of a purchase from the amount given to the cashier.

Subtracting money amounts is similar to subtracting whole numbers, except that money amounts have decimal points. Line up the decimal points and subtract as you would with whole numbers. Be sure to include the decimal point and the dollar sign in the difference.

$$
\begin{array}{r}
9\ 9 \\
0\ \cancel{10}\ \cancel{10}\ 10 \\
\$ \cancel{1}\ \cancel{0}.\cancel{0}\ \cancel{0} \\
-\ \$\ \ \ 8.5\ 9 \\
\hline
\$\ \ \ 1.4\ 1
\end{array}
$$

Example 3

Lana bought a sweater for $27.36. She gave the cashier $30.00. How much change should Lana receive?

Strategy   **Subtract as you would with whole numbers.**

Step 1   Write the number sentence for the problem.

Lana used $30.00 to buy a sweater that costs $27.36.

Let c represent the change Lana should receive.

$\$30.00 - \$27.36 = c$

Step 2   Set up the problem.

$$
\begin{array}{r}
\$30.00 \\
-\ \$27.36 \\
\hline
\end{array}
$$

Line up the decimal points.

Step 3   Subtract from right to left. Regroup if necessary.

$$
\begin{array}{r}
9\ 9 \\
2\ \cancel{10}\ \cancel{10}\ 10 \\
\$ \cancel{3}\cancel{0}.\cancel{0}\cancel{0} \\
-\ \$27.36 \\
\hline
\$\ \ 2.64
\end{array}
$$

Solution   **Lana should receive $2.64 in change.**

Example 4

Kim has 4 library books that are all one day overdue. The library charges a late fee of $0.05 for each day a book is overdue. How much will Kim have to pay for the late fees?

Strategy   **Decide which operation to use.**

Step 1   Write the number sentence for the problem.

Kim has 4 books. Each book will be charged 5 cents.

Let *f* represent the total late fees.

$5 + 5 + 5 + 5 = f$ or $4 \times 5 = f$

Step 2   Multiply.

$4 \times 5 = 20$ cents

Step 3   Write the amount.

20 cents = $0.20

Solution   **Kim will have to pay $0.20 in late fees.**

Coached Example

Marvin has $20.00. He bought 2 books that cost $6.00 each and a bookmark that cost $1.50. How much money does Marvin have left?

Decide how to solve the problem.

Find the total amount Marvin spent.

Then subtract that amount from _____.

Marvin bought 2 books that cost _____ each.

So, 2 books cost _____.

Add the cost of 2 books to the cost of the bookmark.

_____ + _____ = _____

Marvin spent _____ in all.

Subtract the total amount from the amount Marvin has.

_____ – _____ = _____

Show your work.

Marvin has $_____ left.

Lesson Practice • Part 1

Choose the correct answer.

1. How much money is shown below?

   A. $16.30

   B. $20.30

   C. $21.30

   D. $21.50

2. Rico's dinner cost $6.35. He paid with a $10 bill. How much change should Rico receive?

   A. $3.65

   B. $3.75

   C. $4.65

   D. $4.75

3. Marcy bought a magazine for $3.75 and a carton of juice for $2.25. She paid with a $10 bill. How much change should Marcy receive?

   A. $16.00

   B. $6.00

   C. $5.00

   D. $4.00

4. George bought 7 erasers. Each eraser costs $0.25. How much money did George spend?

   A. $1.25

   B. $1.75

   C. $2.75

   D. $7.25

5. Elizabeth had $50.00. She bought a shirt for $12.50 and a pair of pants for $24.00. How much money does Elizabeth have left?

   A. $13.50

   B. $14.50

   C. $26.00

   D. $36.50

6. Angie makes $5.00 each hour. She worked for 3 hours yesterday. How much money did Angie make yesterday?

A. $8.00

B. $8.30

C. $10.00

D. $15.00

7. Peter spent a total of $3.00 on 6 pencils. Each pencil cost the same amount. What did 1 pencil cost?

A. $0.50

B. $0.60

C. $0.75

D. $1.25

8. Erin needs to buy some school supplies. She has $5.00 to spend on supplies. Prices for supplies are shown on the price list below.

School Supplies Price List

Item	Price
Pen	$2.50
Pencil	$1.20
Eraser	$0.50
Ruler	$2.25

A. Erin wants to buy a pen, a pencil, and 2 erasers. How much money will Erin spend in all? Show your work.

B. How much money will Erin have left? Show your work.

Lesson Practice • Part 2

Choose the correct answer.

1. Ellie bought a sweater for $22.75 and a pair of pants for $18.89. How much money did Ellie spend?

    A. $40.54

    B. $40.64

    C. $41.54

    D. $41.64

2. Ryker bought 5 packs of cards for $4.25. What was the cost of each pack of cards?

    A. $0.85

    B. $0.95

    C. $20.25

    D. $21.25

3. Paisley earns $6 each time she walks her neighbor's dog. She also earns $10 each time she dog sits. How much money would Paisley earn for 5 walks and dog-sitting twice?

    A. $62

    B. $50

    C. $42

    D. $40

4. Sanjay bought 4 pencils and a pen. The pencils cost $0.75 each and the pen cost $1.79. How much money did Sanjay spend?

    A. $2.54

    B. $4.79

    C. $5.54

    D. $7.91

5. Rosa had $7.42. She bought a magazine for $4.85. How much money does Rosa have left?

    A. $2.57

    B. $2.67

    C. $3.57

    D. $3.67

6. Grayson has $2.00 in a jar. He has only one type of coin in the jar. Which does **not** describe the number of coins he could have in the jar?

    A. 8 quarters

    B. 20 dimes

    C. 30 nickels

    D. 200 pennies

7. Evie has 3 bills that are all different. Which amount of money could she have?

A. $18

B. $24

C. $31

D. $36

8. The cost of menu items at Mama's Pizza and Pasta is shown.

Mama's Menu

Item	Price
Pizza Slice	$2.75
Topping	$0.75 each
Drink	$1.50
Side Salad	$3.25

A. What is the cost for 2 pizza slices with 1 topping on each slice, and a drink? Show your work.

_____

B. If you have $10, can you buy 2 pizza slices with no topping, a drink, and a side salad? Explain your reasoning.

_____

_____

_____

9. Randy bought 7 ride tickets at the carnival. Each ticket cost $0.30. Select True or False for each statement.

A. The total cost was $2.00.   ○ True   ○ False

B. The total cost was $2.10.   ○ True   ○ False

C. Randy could pay the total cost with   ○ True   ○ False
8 quarters and 2 nickels.

D. If Randy paid with three $1 bills, he   ○ True   ○ False
would get $0.80 in change.

10. Which group of coins and bills is equivalent to $24.52? Circle all that apply.

A.

B.

C.

D.

11. Caty put $40 in her purse to go shopping. At the end of the day she had $14.86 left in her purse. How much did Caty spend? Circle the amount of money that correctly completes the number sentence.

$$\$40.00 - \$14.86 = \boxed{\begin{array}{c} \$25.14 \\[2mm] \$25.24 \\[2mm] \$26.14 \end{array}}$$

12. Parker bought a CD for $13.25 and a DVD for $24.50. He gave the clerk a $50 bill. How much change did he receive? Use numbers from the box to complete the sentences.

$$\$13.25 + \$24.50 = \underline{\hspace{2cm}}$$

$$\$50.00 - \underline{\hspace{2cm}} = \underline{\hspace{2cm}}$$

Parker received _____ in change.

$$\boxed{\begin{array}{c} \$12.25 \\[2mm] \$12.75 \\[2mm] \$13.25 \\[2mm] \$37.50 \\[2mm] \$37.75 \end{array}}$$

13. Five friends ate lunch together. The total cost was $45. The friends decided to share the cost equally. Did each friend pay her share? Select Yes or No.

A. Adita paid with one $5 bill, two $1 bills, and 8 quarters. ○ Yes ○ No

B. Betty paid with one $5 bill and three $1 bills. ○ Yes ○ No

C. Carlotta paid with eight $1 bills and 4 quarters. ○ Yes ○ No

D. Debbie paid with one $5 bill, two $1 bills, 6 quarters, and 5 dimes. ○ Yes ○ No

E. Ellen paid with one $5 bill, three $1 bills, and 3 quarters. ○ Yes ○ No

Time

Getting the Idea

Elapsed time is the amount of time that has passed from a beginning time to an end time. To find the elapsed time, count the **hours (hr)** then the **minutes (min)**.

Example 1

Shawna started and finished her homework at the times shown on the clocks.

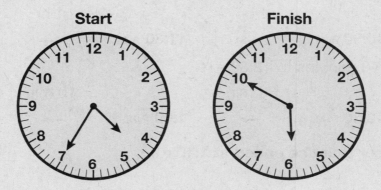

How long did it take Shawna to do her homework?

Strategy   **Find the elapsed time.**

Step 1   Read the start and finish times on the clocks.

The start time is 4:35. The finish time is 5:50.

Step 2   Count the hours.

1 hr

4:35   ⟶   5:35

There is one hour from 4:35 to 5:35.

Step 3   Count the minutes.

15 min

5:35   ⟶   5:50

There are 15 minutes from 5:35 to 5:50.

Step 4   Add the times.

1 hr + 15 min = 1 hr 15 min

Solution   **Shawna took 1 hour 15 minutes to do her homework.**

The time from midnight to noon is called A.M.
The time from noon to midnight is called P.M.

Example 2

Soccer practice began at 10:30 A.M. It lasted 2 hours 40 minutes.
At what time did soccer practice end?

Strategy   **Add the hours and minutes.**

Step 1   Add 2 hours to 10:30 A.M.

	1 hr		1 hr	
10:30 A.M.	⟶	**11:30 A.M.**	⟶	**12:30 P.M.**

Step 2   Add 40 minutes to 12:30 P.M.

	30 min		10 min	
12:30 P.M.	⟶	**1:00 P.M.**	⟶	**1:10 P.M.**

Solution   **Soccer practice ended at 1:10 P.M.**

The table shows the relationships of some units of time.

Units of Time
1 minute (min) = 60 seconds (sec)
1 hour (hr) = 60 minutes
1 **day (d)** = 24 hours
1 **week (wk)** = 7 days
1 **year (yr)** = 12 **months (mo)**

When you change from a larger unit to a smaller unit, use multiplication.

Example 3

Emily slept for 8 hours last night. How many minutes did Emily sleep last night?

Strategy   **Use multiplication to change from hours to minutes.**

Step 1   Find the relationship between hours and minutes.

1 hour = 60 minutes

Step 2   Multiply 8 hours by 60 minutes.

$8 \times 60 = 480$ minutes

So 8 hours = 480 minutes.

Solution   **Emily slept for 480 minutes.**

Example 4

The table shows the relationship between the number of days and the number of weeks. Complete the table.

Week	Days
1	7
2	14
3	
4	
5	

Strategy   **Use the relationship between weeks and days.**

Step 1   Find the relationship between weeks and days.

1 week = 7 days

Step 2   Multiply 2 weeks by 7 days.

$2 \times 7 = 14$ days

2 weeks = 14 days

Step 3   Find the number of days in 3 to 5 weeks.

Multiply the number of weeks by 7.

$3 \times 7 = 21$ days

$4 \times 7 = 28$ days

$5 \times 7 = 35$ days

Complete the table.

Week	Days
1	7
2	14
3	21
4	28
5	35

Solution   **The table is shown in Step 4.**

Some word problems use fractions to show amounts of time.
The table shows the relationships between hours and minutes.

Units of Time
$\frac{1}{4}$ hour = 15 minutes
$\frac{1}{2}$ hour = 30 minutes
$\frac{3}{4}$ hour = 45 minutes
1 hour = 60 seconds

Example 5

Malia had 5 workouts. They all lasted $\frac{1}{2}$ hour. How many minutes did Malia spend
doing yoga?

Strategy   **Rename hours to minutes.**

Step 1   Rename $\frac{1}{2}$ hour to minutes.

$\frac{1}{2}$ hour = 30 minutes

Each workout lasted 30 minutes.

Step 2   Multiply the number of minutes times the number of workouts.

5 × 30 min = 150 min

Solution   **Malia spent 150 minutes doing yoga.**

You can show intervals of time on a number line.

Example 6

Use the information in Example 5.
Show the time, in hours, that Malia spent doing yoga on a number line.

Strategy   **Label a number line in halves.**

Step 1   Draw a number line. Label it in halves.

Label the units.

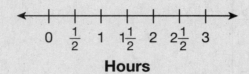

Hours

Step 2   Label the time Malia spent doing yoga.

She spent $2\frac{1}{2}$ hours doing yoga.

So label a point at $2\frac{1}{2}$ on the number line.

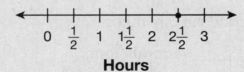

Hours

Solution   **The number line is shown in Step 2.**

Coached Example

A music video is 5 minutes long. How many seconds long is the music video?

Find the relationship between minutes and seconds.

1 minute = _____ seconds

Which is the larger unit? _____

Which is the smaller unit? _____

When you change from a larger unit to a smaller unit, which operation do you use?
_____

Show your work.

There are _____ seconds in 5 minutes.

The music video is _____ seconds long.

Lesson Practice • Part 1

Choose the correct answer.

1. Alana started studying at 3:30 P.M. and finished at 6:00 P.M. How much time did Alana spend studying?

   A. 2 hours 30 minutes

   B. 3 hours

   C. 3 hours 2 minutes

   D. 3 hours 30 minutes

2. A play started at 11:10 A.M. and ended at 12:50 P.M. How long was the play?

   A. 50 minutes

   B. 1 hour 30 minutes

   C. 1 hour 40 minutes

   D. 2 hours 20 minutes

3. Which is the missing number in the table?

Minutes	Seconds
4	240
6	360
9	?
12	720

   A. 420   C. 600

   B. 540   D. 660

4. Mark left his house at 1:05 P.M. He returned to his house at the time shown on the clock below.

   How long was Mark away from home?

   A. 4 hours 18 minutes

   B. 3 hours 18 minutes

   C. 3 hours 8 minutes

   D. 2 hours 8 minutes

5. At 7:15 P.M., Will finished watching a movie that lasted 1 hour 30 minutes. At what time did the movie start?

   A. 5:45 P.M.

   B. 6:45 P.M.

   C. 8:15 P.M.

   D. 8:45 P.M.

6. Samantha has 10 minutes to finish a puzzle. How many seconds are in 10 minutes?

    A. 60 seconds

    B. 100 seconds

    C. 160 seconds

    D. 600 seconds

7. When elected, a United States senator serves a 6-year term. How many months does a senator serve?

    A. 84 months

    B. 72 months

    C. 60 months

    D. 36 months

8. Peter walked the beach for $\frac{1}{2}$ hour each day of his vacation. His vacation lasted 8 days. How many hours did he walk on the beach during his vacation?

    A. 2 hours

    B. 3 hours

    C. 4 hours

    D. 5 hours

9. Sophie played a computer game 8 times. Each game took $\frac{1}{3}$ hour.

    A. How much time, in hours, did Sophie spend playing the computer game? Show your work. Then show the amount of time on the number line.

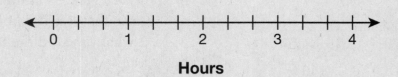

Hours

    B. How much time, in minutes, did Sophie spend playing the computer game? Show your work.

Lesson Practice • Part 2

Choose the correct answer.

1. Quinn finished reading a book at 7:15 P.M. She had been reading nonstop for 4 hours 40 minutes. At what time did Quinn start reading the book?

    A. 2:35 P.M.

    B. 3:35 P.M.

    C. 3:55 P.M.

    D. 11:55 P.M.

2. Leo left his home for a soccer tournament at 9:25 A.M. He returned home at 4:15 P.M. How long was Leo away?

    A. 4 hours 50 minutes

    B. 5 hours 10 minutes

    C. 6 hours 50 minutes

    D. 7 hours 10 minutes

3. The standard for running a mile is 4 minutes. Elite male runners can run a mile in 10 seconds fewer than 4 minutes. How many seconds does it take an elite male runner to run a mile?

    A. 410 seconds

    B. 390 seconds

    C. 250 seconds

    D. 230 seconds

4. A group is watching a movie that will run for 2 hours 20 minutes. How many minutes will the movie last?

    A. 120 minutes

    B. 140 minutes

    C. 180 minutes

    D. 220 minutes

5. Each day Kennedy jogs for $\frac{3}{4}$ hour. Which point on the number line represents the number of hours that Kennedy jogs in 5 days?

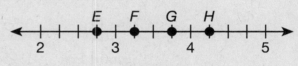

Hours

    A. E

    B. F

    C. G

    D. H

6. A concert started at 8:20 P.M. The concert lasted 2 hours 55 minutes. At what time did the concert end?

    A. 10:15 P.M.

    B. 10:25 P.M.

    C. 11:15 P.M.

    D. 11:25 P.M.

7. How many hours are there in a week?

   A. 140 hours

   B. 168 hours

   C. 350 hours

   D. 420 hours

8. The bumper cars ride at an amusement park takes 6 minutes including the loading and unloading of the cars. A total of 16 people can ride at one time. What is the greatest number of people that can ride in an hour?

   A. 10

   B. 26

   C. 80

   D. 160

9. The Wilson family is flying with a layover between legs of the flights. The planned flight schedule is shown.

Flight Schedule

Event	Departure	Arrival
First Leg	9:35 A.M.	12:10 P.M.
Second Leg	1:45 P.M.	4:00 P.M.

A. What is the scheduled elapsed time of the layover? Give your answer in hours and minutes.

_____

B. What is the scheduled total elapsed time of the flights, **not** including the layover? Give your answer in hours and minutes. Explain how you found your answer.

_____

_____

_____

10. D'Arcy cooked stew in a slow cooker for 3 hours, 45 minutes. Which choice shows the same elapsed time? Circle all that apply.

A. $3\frac{3}{4}$ hours

B. $3\frac{1}{2}$ hours

C. 205 minutes

D. 225 minutes

11. Ashton left the ranger's cabin at 1:25 P.M. It took him 2 hours, 15 minutes to hike the entire trail. Select True or False for each statement.

A. He finished the hike at 3:30 P.M.   ○ True   ○ False
B. The hike took 135 minutes in all.   ○ True   ○ False
C. He finished the hike at 3:40 P.M.   ○ True   ○ False
D. The hike took 125 minutes in all.   ○ True   ○ False

12. Mori is planning her schedule for the week. Draw a line from each event to its finish time.

A. practicing piano for 1 hour, 10 minutes starting at 7:35 P.M.   •   •   8:45 A.M.

B. volunteering for 4 hours, 25 minutes starting at 8:25 A.M.   •   •   12:50 P.M.

C. playing hockey for 3 hours, 12 minutes starting at 5:33 A.M.   •   •   1:55 P.M.

D. gardening for 2 hours, 40 minutes starting at 11:15 A.M.   •   •   8:45 P.M.

13. It is now 6:52 A.M. Juan has to leave for work at 7:30 A.M. Which activity does he have enough time to do before leaving for work? Write the activity in the correct box.

Shower: $\frac{1}{4}$ hour	Jog: 50 minutes	Walk dog: $\frac{3}{4}$ hour
Eat breakfast: 25 minutes	Clean house: 48 minutes	Watch news: $\frac{1}{2}$ hour

Has Enough Time	Does Not Have Enough Time

14. Jacqueline works 8 hours every day, 5 days a week. She worked 4 weeks this month. How many hours did she work this month? Use numbers from the box to complete the sentences.

_____ × 5 = _____

_____ × _____ = _____

Jacqueline worked _____ hours this month.

4
5
8
40
160
200

Weight and Mass

Getting the Idea

Weight is the measure of how heavy an object is. You can measure weight using a scale or a balance. Units of weight are in the **customary system**.

You can use these benchmarks to estimate weight.

A slice of bread weighs about 1 ounce.

A loaf of bread weighs about 1 pound.

Example 1

Kenika has a cell phone in her pocket. Does her cell phone weigh about 8 pounds or about 8 ounces?

Strategy   **Use benchmarks.**

Step 1   Think about something that weighs about 1 pound.
    A loaf of bread weighs 1 pound.

Step 2   Does a cell phone weigh as much as 8 loaves of bread?
    No, a cell phone weighs less than 8 pounds.

Step 3   Think about something that weighs about 1 ounce.
    A slice of bread weighs about 1 ounce.

Step 4   Does a cell phone weigh as much as 8 slices of bread?
    Yes, a cell phone weighs about 8 ounces.

Solution   **Kenika's cell phone weighs about 8 ounces.**

When you solve a word problem about weight, write a number sentence to represent the problem.

Example 2

Alex bought 2 bags of potatoes. Each bag weighs $2\frac{1}{2}$ pounds.

How many pounds of potatoes in all did Alex buy?

Strategy   **Write a number sentence.**

Step 1   Write a number sentence to represent the problem.

He bought 2 bags of potatoes that weighed $2\frac{1}{2}$ pounds each.

Let p represent the total weight of the potatoes.

$2\frac{1}{2} + 2\frac{1}{2} = p$

Step 2   Add the mixed numbers.

Add the fraction parts first.
Then add the whole number parts.

$$
\begin{array}{r}
2\frac{1}{2} \\
+\ 2\frac{1}{2} \\
\hline
4\frac{2}{2}
\end{array}
$$

Step 3   Simplify the mixed number $4\frac{2}{2}$.

Simplify $\frac{2}{2} = 1$.

Add to the whole number, $4 + 1 = 5$.

Solution   **Alex bought 5 pounds of potatoes in all.**

You can show a weight on a number line.

Example 3

Terry ordered $1\frac{1}{4}$ pounds of roast beef at the deli counter.

Show the amount of roast beef on a number line.

Strategy   **Label a number line in fourths.**

Step 1   Draw a number line from 0 to 2. Label it in fourths.
Label the units.

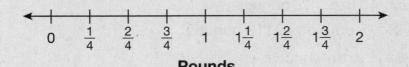

Pounds

Step 2   Label the amount of roast beef that Terry bought.
She bought $1\frac{1}{4}$ pounds of roast beef.
So label a point at $1\frac{1}{4}$ on the number line.

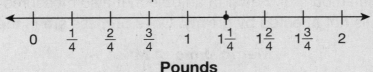

Pounds

Solution   **The number line is shown in Step 2.**

The table shows the relationship between pounds and ounces.

Customary Units of Weight
1 **pound (lb)** = 16 **ounces (oz)**

When you change from a larger unit to a smaller unit, use multiplication.

Example 4

Drew weighed 7 pounds 9 ounces when he was born.

How many ounces are in 7 pounds 9 ounces?

Strategy **Use multiplication to change from pounds to ounces.
Then add the extra ounces.**

Step 1   Find the relationship between pound and ounces.

1 pound = 16 ounces

Step 2   Multiply 7 pounds by 16 ounces.

$7 \times 16 = 112$ ounces

So, 7 pounds = 112 ounces.

Step 3   Add the extra ounces.

$112 + 9 = 121$ ounces

Solution   **There are 121 ounces in 7 pounds 9 ounces.**

Mass measures the amount of matter in an object. It also measures how heavy an object is, except it is not affected by gravity. Units of mass are in the **metric system.**

Metric Units of Mass
1 **kilogram (kg)** = 1,000 **grams (g)**

You can use these benchmarks to estimate mass.

A pen cap has a mass of about 1 gram.

A textbook has a mass of about 1 kilogram.

Example 5

The table shows the relationship between the number of kilograms and the number of grams. Complete the rest of the table.

Kilograms	Grams
1	1,000
2	2,000
3	
4	
5	

Strategy   **Use the relationship between kilograms and grams.**

Step 1   Find the relationship between kilograms and grams.

1 kilogram = 1,000 grams

Step 2   Multiply 2 kilograms by 1,000 grams.

2 × 1,000 = 2,000 grams

So, 2 kilograms = 2,000 grams.

Step 3   Find the number of grams in 3 to 5 kilograms.

Multiply the number of kilograms by 1,000 grams.

3 × 1,000 = 3,000 grams

4 × 1,000 = 4,000 grams

5 × 1,000 = 5,000 grams

Step 4   Complete the table.

Kilograms	Grams
1	1,000
2	2,000
3	3,000
4	4,000
5	5,000

Solution   **The table is shown in Step 4.**

Example 6

Jake caught a fish with a mass of 2 kilograms. Matthew caught a fish with a mass of 1,750 grams. Whose fish has a greater mass?

Strategy **Change 2 kilograms to grams. Then compare.**

Step 1 Multiply to change 2 kilograms to grams.

2 × 1,000 grams = 2,000 grams

Step 2 Compare the masses.

Jake's fish: 2 kilograms or 2,000 grams

Matthew's fish: 1,750 grams

2,000 grams > 1,750 grams

Solution **Jake's fish has a greater mass.**

Coached Example

Deanna has 3 pounds of peanuts and 45 ounces of raisins. Does she have more peanuts or raisins?

Which is the smaller unit, pounds or ounces? _____

Find the relationship between pound and ounces.

1 pound = _____ ounces

Multiply to change 3 pounds to ounces.

3 × _____ = _____ ounces

Compare the weights.

Peanuts: 3 pounds or _____ ounces

Raisins: 45 ounces

_____ ounces ◯ 45 ounces

Deanna has more _____ **than** _____.

Lesson Practice • Part 1

Choose the correct answer.

1. Which could be the weight of a desk?

   A. 4 ounces   C. 40 ounces

   B. 4 pounds   D. 40 pounds

2. Which is the best estimate for the mass of a cat?

   A. 30 kilograms

   B. 3 kilograms

   C. 30 grams

   D. 3 grams

3. A brick has a mass of 3 kilograms. A rock has a mass of 2,500 grams. Which sentence is true?

   A. The rock has more mass than the brick.

   B. The brick has less mass than the rock.

   C. The rock has less mass than the brick.

   D. The brick has the same amount of mass as the rock.

4. A chair has a mass of 7 kilograms. What is the mass, in grams, of the chair?

   A.   70 grams

   B.   112 grams

   C.   700 grams

   D. 7,000 grams

5. Which table shows the relationship between pounds and ounces?

A.

Pounds	Ounces
2	16
3	32
4	64

B.

Pounds	Ounces
2	32
3	48
4	64

C.

Pounds	Ounces
2	32
3	64
4	96

D.

Pounds	Ounces
2	20
3	30
4	40

6. Ruben buys a 3-pound 4-ounce bag of apples. How many ounces are there in 3 pounds 4 ounces?

   A. 52 ounces

   B. 48 ounces

   C. 44 ounces

   D. 34 ounces

7. The mass of a nickel is 5 grams. What is the mass, in grams, of 40 nickels?

   A.　20 grams

   B.　40 grams

   C. 200 grams

   D. 400 grams

8. A box of cards has 12 birthday cards. Each card weighs 2 ounces. How much do the 12 cards weigh?

   A. 1 pound 4 ounces

   B. 1 pound 8 ounces

   C. 2 pounds 4 ounces

   D. 2 pounds 8 ounces

9. Chelsea mailed 2 boxes and 2 bags to her uncle in the army. The two boxes weighed $8\frac{1}{2}$ pounds each and the two bags weighed $4\frac{1}{2}$ pounds each.

   A. How many pounds do all 2 boxes and 2 bags weigh? Show your work.

   _____

   _____

   B. What is the total weight, in ounces, of the two bags? Show your work.

   _____

   _____

Lesson Practice • Part 2

Choose the correct answer.

1. Which is the best estimate for the weight of a bicycle?

   A. 2 ounces

   B. 2 pounds

   C. 20 ounces

   D. 20 pounds

2. Which is the best estimate for the mass of a tennis ball?

   A. 6 grams

   B. 6 kilograms

   C. 60 grams

   D. 60 kilograms

3. A stack of cardboard weighs 6 pounds 9 ounces. What is the weight of the stack in ounces?

   A. 105 ounces

   B. 81 ounces

   C. 69 ounces

   D. 57 ounces

4. Each softball bat that London owns has a mass of 0.8 kilogram. She owns 3 bats. What is the total mass of the softball bats in grams?

   A. 110 grams

   B. 240 grams

   C. 1,100 grams

   D. 2,400 grams

5. Each portion of rice in a lunch special weighs $\frac{1}{4}$ pound. Which letter on the number line shows the amount of rice served to 14 people?

   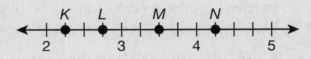

   Pounds

   A. *K*   **C.** *M*

   B. *L*   **D.** *N*

6. There are 8 identical books in a box. The total mass of the books inside the box is 4 kilograms. What is the mass of each book?

   A. 500 grams

   B. 1,000 grams

   C. 3,200 grams

   D. 5,000 grams

7. The mass of Aubrey's favorite stuffed animal is 825 grams. How many grams short of 1 kilogram is the stuffed animal?

A. 175 grams

B. 275 grams

C. 1,175 grams

D. 1,275 grams

8. Which symbol makes this sentence true?

5 lb ◯ 80 oz

A. >

B. <

C. =

D. +

9. Which sentence about weight and mass is true?

A. Only the mass of an object changes because of gravity.

B. Only the weight of an object changes because of gravity.

C. Both the mass and weight of an object changes because of gravity.

D. Neither the mass nor the weight of an object changes because of gravity.

10. Each team on a tug-o-war side is allowed to have 600 pounds. The Red team wants to have 8 students on its team. The Blue team wants to have 6 students on its team. Each team will have the maximum weight.

A. Which team will have the larger students? Explain how you know.

_____

_____

B. If each team's tug-o-war members weigh the same, how much more will the students from the team with the larger students weigh than the students from the other team? Show your work.

_____

_____

11. Use numbers from the box to make the sentence true.

3 pounds 6 ounces = _____ ounces

18
36
42
54

12. Draw a line from each object to the best estimate of its mass.

A. a nickel   •   •   5 grams

B. tennis ball   •   •   5 kilograms

C. adult Great Dane •   •   50 grams

D. bowling ball   •   •   50 kilograms

13. Select True or False for each sentence.

A. 3 pounds = 30 ounces   ○ True   ○ False

B. 5 pounds = 80 ounces   ○ True   ○ False

C. 4 pounds = 48 ounces   ○ True   ○ False

D. 6 pounds = 96 ounces   ○ True   ○ False

14. The table shows the weights of bags of four kinds of fruit. Draw a line from each amount of fruit to its weight.

Fruit Bag Weights

Fruit	Weight (in pounds)
Apples	$4\frac{1}{2}$
Pears	$2\frac{1}{2}$
Bananas	$2\frac{1}{2}$
Grapes	$3\frac{1}{2}$

A. 1 bag of apples and 1 bag of grapes   •   • 8 pounds

B. 2 bags of apples   •   • $8\frac{1}{2}$ pounds

C. 2 bags of pears and 1 bag of grapes   •   • 9 pounds

D. 1 bag of apples and 2 bags of pears   •   • $9\frac{1}{2}$ pounds

15. Which mass is greater than 5 kilograms? Circle all that apply.

A. 4,500 grams

B. 8,050 grams

C. 5,184 grams

D. 2,501 grams

16. Select True or False for each sentence.

A. 2 kilograms = 2,000 grams   ○ True   ○ False

B. 5 kilograms = 500 grams   ○ True   ○ False

C. 7 kilograms = 7,000 grams   ○ True   ○ False

D. 9 kilograms = 90 grams   ○ True   ○ False

Capacity

Getting the Idea

Capacity or **liquid volume** measures how much liquid a container holds. You can use these benchmarks to estimate capacity.

Customary Units of Capacity

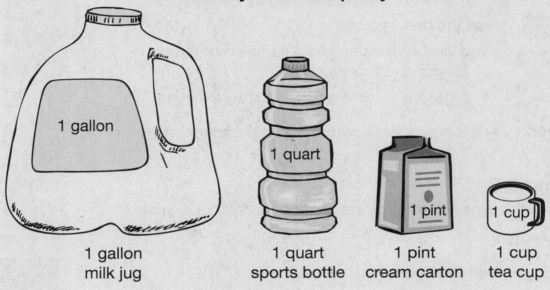

1 gallon
milk jug

1 quart
sports bottle

1 pint
cream carton

1 cup
tea cup

Metric Units of Capacity

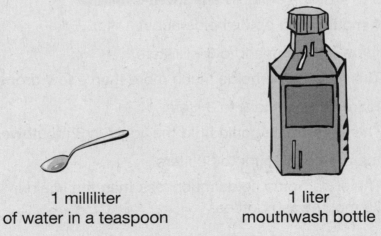

1 milliliter
of water in a teaspoon

1 liter
mouthwash bottle

Example 1

Which is the best estimate for the amount of water a kitchen sink can hold?

5 gallons   5 pints   5 cups

Strategy   **Compare an actual sink to 1 gallon.**

Step 1   Think about an actual kitchen sink.

A kitchen sink is big and can hold at least 1 gallon.

Step 2   Pick the best choice.

A kitchen sink can hold much more than 5 cups and 5 pints.

5 gallons is the most reasonable estimate.

Solution   **A kitchen sink can hold about 5 gallons of water.**

Example 2

Which is the best estimate for the capacity of this soda bottle?

3 milliliters   3 liters   30 liters

Strategy   **Use benchmarks.**

Step 1   Think about benchmarks for capacity.

3 to 4 drops of liquid are about 1 milliliter.

A mouthwash bottle holds about 1 liter.

Step 2   Compare a benchmark to 3 milliliters.

The soda bottle holds much more than a few drops of liquid.

Step 3   Compare a benchmark to 3 liters.

The soda bottle could hold the liquid in 3 mouthwash bottles.

Step 4   Compare a benchmark to 30 liters.

The soda bottle holds much less than the liquid in 30 mouthwash bottles.

Solution   **The best estimate for the capacity of the soda bottle is 3 liters.**

The table shows the relationships of the customary units of capacity.

Customary Units of Capacity
1 **pint (pt)** = 2 **cups (c)**
1 **quart (qt)** = 2 pints
1 **gallon (gal)** = 4 quarts

When you change from a larger unit to a smaller unit, use multiplication or addition.
When you change from a smaller unit to a larger unit, use division or subtraction.

Example 3

Jason has 8 quarts of water at home. He buys 2 gallons of water at the store.
How many gallons of water does Jason have now?

Strategy   **Use division to change from quarts to gallons.**
          Then add the gallons.

Step 1   Find the relationship between quarts and gallons.

4 quarts = 1 gallon

Step 2   Divide 8 quarts by 4 quarts.

$8 \div 4 = 2$ gallons

So, Jason bought 8 quarts or 2 gallons of water at the store.

Step 3   Add the gallons.

$2 + 2 = 4$ gallons

Solution   **Jason has 4 gallons of water now.**

The table shows the relationships of the metric units of capacity.

Metric Units of Capacity
1 **liter (L)** = 1,000 **milliliters (mL)**

Example 4

The table shows the relationship between the number of liters and the number of milliliters. Complete the table.

Liters	Milliliters
2	
4	
6	
8	

Strategy   **Use the relationship between liters and milliliters.**

Step 1   Find the relationship between liters and milliliters.

     1 liter = 1,000 milliliters

Step 2   How many milliliters are in 2 liters?

     Multiply 2 liters by 1,000 milliliters.

     $2 \times 1,000 = 2,000$ milliliters

Step 3   Find the number of milliliters in 4, 6, and 8 liters.

     Multiply the number of liters by 1,000 milliliters.

     $4 \times 1,000 = 4,000$ milliliters

     $6 \times 1,000 = 6,000$ milliliters

     $8 \times 1,000 = 8,000$ milliliters

Step 4   Complete the table.

Liters	Milliliters
2	2,000
4	4,000
6	6,000
8	8,000

Solution   The table is shown in Step 4.

Example 5

Mrs. O'Brien poured 3 liters of paint into 5 canisters. She poured the same amount of paint into each canister. About how much paint, in milliliters, is in each canister?

Strategy   **Multiply to change liters to milliliters. Then divide.**

Step 1   Use multiplication to change 3 liters to milliliters.

1 liter = 1,000 milliliters

$3 \times 1,000 = 3,000$ milliliters

So 3 liters = 3,000 milliliters.

Step 2   Find the amount of paint in each canister.

There is a total of 3,000 milliliters. There are 5 canisters.

Let c represent the amount of paint in each canister.

Find $3,000 \div 5 = c$.

$3,000 \div 5 = 600$ milliliters

Solution   **Each canister has about 600 milliliters of paint.**

Coached Example

A bottle has a capacity of 2 liters. A bucket has a capacity that is 4 times as great as the bottle. What is the capacity, in milliliters, of the bucket?

Write a number sentence for the problem.

The bottle has a capacity of _____ liters.

The bucket has a capacity that is _____ times more than the bottle.

Which operation should you use to find the capacity of the bucket? _____

Let b represent the capacity of the bucket.

Find _____ $\times$ _____ $= b$

Multiply.

_____ $\times$ _____ $=$ _____ liters

Change the capacity of the bucket in liters to milliliters.

1 liter = _____ milliliters

Multiply to change from liters to milliliters.

_____ $\times$ _____ $=$ _____ milliliters

The capacity of the bucket is _____ milliliters.

Lesson Practice • Part 1

Choose the correct answer.

1. Which is the best estimate for the amount of orange juice in the glass?

   A. 50 liters   **C.** 250 liters

   B. 50 milliliters   **D.** 250 milliliters

2. Which object holds about 1 liter of water?

   A.

   B.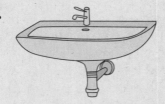

   C.

   D.

3. Which container's capacity would be best to measure in milliliters?

   A. bathtub

   B. coffee cup

   C. swimming pool

   D. water cooler

4. Michael bought 7 quarts of engine oil for his truck. How many pints are in 7 quarts?

   A. 12 pints

   B. 14 pints

   C. 28 pints

   D. 56 pints

5. Kate fills a tank with 5 liters of water. How many milliliters are in 5 liters?

   A.   5 milliliters

   B.   50 milliliters

   C.   500 milliliters

   D. 5,000 milliliters

6. A glass has a capacity of 750 milliliters. A pitcher has a capacity that is 5 times more than the capacity of the glass. What is the capacity of the pitcher?

    A. 3,750 milliliters

    B. 5,000 milliliters

    C. 5,750 milliliters

    D. 7,500 milliliters

7. Maria drank 6 cups of water yesterday and 8 cups of water today. How many pints of water did Maria drink in all?

    A. 2 pints

    B. 6 pints

    C. 7 pints

    D. 8 pints

8. Carol poured a total of 4 liters of iced tea into 8 tumblers. Each tumbler has the same amount of iced tea. How much iced tea, in milliliters, is in each tumbler?

    A. 200 milliliters

    B. 400 milliliters

    C. 450 milliliters

    D. 500 milliliters

9. Eliot has a 3-liter punch bowl. He poured 850 mL of pineapple juice, 900 mL of orange juice, and 250 mL of ginger ale into the bowl.

    A. What is the capacity of the punch bowl in milliliters? Show your work.

    _____

    B. How much liquid, in liters, did Eliot pour into the bowl in all? Show your work.

    _____

    _____

Lesson Practice • Part 2

Choose the correct answer.

1. Which is the missing number in the table?

Pints	Cups
2	4
6	12
9	?
12	24

   A. 15

   B. 16

   C. 18

   D. 21

2. A sports cooler holds 10 gallons. How many quarts does the sports cooler hold?

   A. 20 quarts

   B. 40 quarts

   C. 80 quarts

   D. 160 quarts

3. Which lists the units of customary capacity from greatest to least?

   A. gallons, quarts, pints, cups

   B. cups, pints, quarts, gallons

   C. gallons, pints, quarts, cups

   D. cups, quarts, pints, gallons

4. A bottle contains 1.5 liters. How many milliliters are in 2 such bottles?

   A. 150 milliliters

   B. 300 milliliters

   C. 1,500 milliliters

   D. 3,000 milliliters

5. Each serving makes 1 quart of soup. Which letter represents the number of pints there are in 4 servings of soup?

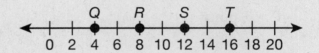

   A. Q

   B. R

   C. S

   D. T

6. Jim has a pitcher that contains 2 liters of lemonade. He pours 250 milliliters each for 3 people. How many milliliters are left in the pitcher?

   A. 250 milliliters

   B. 750 milliliters

   C. 1,250 milliliters

   D. 1,750 milliliters

7. A liter is slightly greater than a quart. Which sentence is true?

   A. A liter is slightly greater than 2 pints.

   B. A liter is slightly less than 2 pints.

   C. A liter is slightly greater than 2 cups.

   D. A liter is slightly less than 2 cups.

8. Which is the best estimate for the capacity of a kitchen sink?

   A. 200 milliliters

   B. 200 liters

   C. 20 milliliters

   D. 20 liters

9. Which symbol makes this sentence true?

$$6 \text{ c} \bigcirc 1 \text{ gal}$$

   A. >   **C.** =

   B. <   **D.** +

10. Travis tries to drink 3 quarts of water each day.

   A. How many pints of water does Travis try to drink each day?

   _____

   B. How many cups of water does Travis try to drink each day?

   _____

   C. Does Travis try to drink more or less than 7 gallons in a week? Explain your reasoning.

   _____

   _____

   _____

11. Draw a line from each object to the best estimate of its capacity.

A. teaspoon   •   •   5 milliliters

B. metal oil barrel   •   •   2 liters

C. water bottle   •   •   200 liters

D. paint bucket   •   •   500 milliliters

12. A container collects 12 quarts of rainwater. Which amount equals 12 quarts? Circle all that apply.

A. 48 cups

B. 22 pints

C. 26 pints

D. 3 gallons

13. The table shows the capacities of four different fish tanks. Draw a line from each description to the total capacity of the tanks described.

Capacities of Fish Tanks

Tank	Capacity (in gallons)
A	2
B	1
C	$2\frac{1}{2}$
D	$3\frac{1}{2}$

A. Tank A and Tank B   •   •   48 cups

B. Tank B and Tank D   •   •   56 cups

C. Tank A and Tank D   •   •   72 cups

D. Tank B and Tank C   •   •   88 cups

14. John poured 3 liters of water equally into several glasses. Select True or False for each statement.

    A. There would be 1,500 milliliters in each of 2 glasses.   ○ True   ○ False

    B. There would be 16 milliliters in each of 3 glasses.   ○ True   ○ False

    C. There would be 600 milliliters in each of 5 glasses.   ○ True   ○ False

    D. There would be 30 milliliters in each of 10 glasses.   ○ True   ○ False

15. How many cups are there in each amount? Write the amount in the correct box.

2 gallons	8 quarts	24 pints	16 pints	3 gallons	12 quarts

48 Cups	32 Cups

Length

Getting the Idea

Length measures how long, wide, or tall an object is. It also measures distances.

The table below shows some units of length in the customary system.

Customary Units of Length
1 **foot (ft)** = 12 **inches (in.)**
1 **yard (yd)** = 3 feet
1 **mile (mi)** = 1,760 yards

You can use these benchmarks to estimate lengths.

A 12-inch ruler measures 1 foot.

A yardstick measures 1 yard.

An adult can walk 1 mile in about 20 minutes.

Example 1

Which real object is most likely to be 150 feet long?

Strategy **Think about the length of 1 foot.**

Step 1 Think about how long 150 feet will be.

The length of this book is about 1 foot.

Imagine lining up 150 books to get 150 feet.

Step 2   Review the choices.

A pair of scissors is much shorter than 150 feet.

A 4-door car is shorter than 150 feet.

A building could be 150 feet long.

Solution   **The building is most likely about 150 feet.**

The table below shows some units of length in the metric system.

Metric Units of Length
1 **centimeter (cm)** = 10 **millimeters (mm)**
1 **meter (m)** = 100 centimeters
1 **kilometer (km)** = 1,000 meters

This line measures 1 centimeter. _____

1 meter is a little shorter than 1 yard.

An adult can walk 1 kilometer in about 10 minutes.

Example 2

Which real object is most likely to be 20 milliliters long?

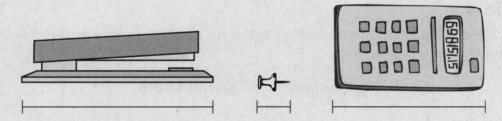

Strategy   **Think about the length of 1 millimeter.**

Step 1   Think about how long 20 millimeters will be.

1 millimeter is about the thickness of a dime.

20 millimeters will be about the height of 20 stacked dimes.

Step 2   Review the choices.

A stapler is longer than 20 millimeters.

The pushpin could be about 20 millimeters.

A calculator is about the length of a stapler, so it is longer
than 20 millimeters.

Solution   **The pushpin is most likely about 20 millimeters.**

You can use the relationship between units to change from one unit to another.

When you change a larger unit to a smaller unit, use multiplication.

To change 3 feet to inches, multiply 3 × 12.

So 3 feet = 36 inches.

Example 3

Mr. Conroy is 6 feet and 3 inches tall. How tall is Mr. Conroy in inches?

Strategy   **Multiply to change feet to inches. Then add the extra inches.**

Step 1   Find the relationship between feet and inches.

   1 foot = 12 inches

Step 2   Multiply 6 feet by 12 inches.

   6 × 12 = 72 inches

Step 3   Add the extra inches.

   72 + 3 = 75 inches

Solution   **Mr. Conroy is 75 inches tall.**

Example 4

The table shows the relationship between the number of meters and the number of centimeters. Complete the table.

Meters	Centimeters
2	
4	
6	
8	

Strategy   **Use the relationship between meters and centimeters.**

Step 1   Find the relationship between meters and centimeters.

   1 meter = 100 centimeters

Step 2   How many centimeters are in 2 meters?

Multiply 2 meters by 100 centimeters.

$2 \times 100 = 200$ centimeters.

So 2 meters = 200 centimeters.

Step 3   Find the number of centimeters in 4, 6, and 8 meters.

$4 \times 100 = 400$ centimeters

$6 \times 100 = 600$ centimeters

$8 \times 100 = 800$ centimeters

Step 4   Complete the table.

Meters	Centimeters
2	200
4	400
6	600
8	800

Solution   **The table is shown in Step 4.**

You can use a number line to represent length.

Example 5

Troy jogged $1\frac{2}{3}$ miles this morning.

Show the distance Troy jogged on a number line.

Strategy   **Make equal parts of fractional lengths on a number line.**

Step 1   Draw a number line from 0 to 2.

The denominator is 3, so draw the number line in thirds.

Step 2   Find $1\frac{2}{3}$ on the number line. Draw a point.

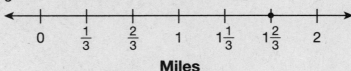

Miles

Solution   **The number line is shown in Step 2.**

When you solve a real world problem, write a number sentence to represent the problem.

Example 6

A window curtain is $3\frac{3}{8}$ feet wide. What is the total width of two window curtains side by side?

Strategy   **Write a number sentence for the problem.**

Step 1   Write a number sentence.

Each curtain is $3\frac{3}{8}$ feet wide.

To find the total width, use addition.

Let w represent the total width of two curtains.

Find $3\frac{3}{8} + 3\frac{3}{8} = w$.

Step 2   Find the sum.

Add the fraction parts.
Then add the whole number parts.

$$\begin{array}{r} 3\frac{3}{8} \\ + \ 3\frac{3}{8} \\ \hline 6\frac{6}{8} \end{array}$$

Step 3   Simplify.

$$\frac{6}{8} = \frac{6 \div 2}{8 \div 2} = \frac{3}{4}$$

So $6\frac{6}{8} = 6\frac{3}{4}$.

Solution   **The total width of two curtains is $6\frac{3}{4}$ feet.**

Coached Example

Nicole lives 3 kilometers from the mall and 1.6 kilometers from her school. How far, in meters, does Nicole live from the mall?
On the number line below, show the distance Nicole lives from her school.

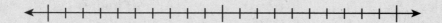

Kilometers

Find how far Nicole lives from the mall.

She lives _____ kilometers from the mall.

To change from kilometers to meters, should you use multiplication or division?
_____

1 kilometer = _____ meters

3 × _____ meters = _____ meters

So 3 kilometers = _____ meters.

Show the distance Nicole lives from school on the number line.

She lives _____ kilometers from the school.

The number line is in tenths. Label 0, 1, and 2 on the number line.

Find 1.6 on the number line. Draw a point.

Nicole lives _____ meters from the mall. The point on the number line above shows the distance, in kilometers, Nicole lives from school.

Lesson Practice • Part 1

Choose the correct answer.

1. Which measure is most likely the height of a ceiling?

   A. 10 miles

   B. 10 yards

   C. 10 feet

   D. 10 inches

2. Which measure is most likely the length of a digital camera?

   A. 12 millimeters

   B. 12 centimeters

   C. 12 meters

   D. 12 kilometers

3. Which measure is equal to 1,000 centimeters?

   A. 10 meters

   B. 10 millimeters

   C. 100 meters

   D. 100 millimeters

4. A lamp is 4 feet 8 inches tall. What is the height of the lamp in inches?

   A. 40 inches

   B. 48 inches

   C. 52 inches

   D. 56 inches

5. The point on the number line below shows the length of a piece of chalk.

   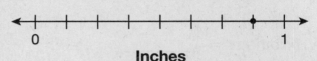

   Inches

   What is the length of the chalk?

   A. $\frac{1}{8}$ inch   C. $\frac{7}{8}$ inch

   B. $\frac{1}{4}$ inch   D. $\frac{9}{10}$ inch

6. The point on the number line below shows height of a ladder.

   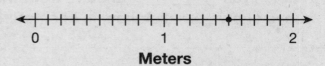

   Meters

   What is the height of the ladder?

   A. 1.5 meters

   B. 1.6 meters

   C. 2.1 meters

   D. 2.5 meters

7. A painting is 4 feet long. A photo frame is 10 inches long. How many inches longer is the painting than the photo frame?

   A. 6 inches

   B. 24 inches

   C. 30 inches

   D. 38 inches

8. LeAnne placed a box that is $1\frac{3}{4}$ feet high on top of another box that is $1\frac{1}{4}$ feet high. How many feet high are the boxes when stacked?

   A. $2\frac{3}{4}$ feet

   B. 3 feet

   C. $3\frac{1}{2}$ feet

   D. 4 feet

9. Daron has a cord that is 12 inches long and another one that is $2\frac{1}{2}$ feet. He connects the two cords.

   A. What is the total length, in inches, of the two cords? Show your work.

   _____

   _____

   _____

   B. In the number line below, show the total length, in feet, of the two cords. Explain how you found the total length in feet.

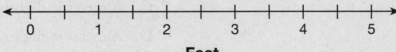

   Feet

   _____

   _____

Lesson Practice • Part 2

Choose the correct answer.

1. Which is the missing number in the table?

Feet	Inches
2	24
4	48
7	?
9	108

A. 96   **C.** 72

B. 84   **D.** 60

2. Each lap around a track is $\frac{1}{4}$ mile. Ross jogs 11 times around the track. How far did Ross jog?

A. $2\frac{1}{4}$ miles

B. $2\frac{3}{4}$ miles

C. $3\frac{1}{4}$ miles

D. $3\frac{3}{4}$ miles

3. Which is the best metric unit to use to measure the distance between Philadelphia and New York City?

A. millimeters

B. centimeters

C. meters

D. kilometers

4. Which is the missing number in the table?

Centimeters	Millimeters
1	?
3	30
5	50
7	70

A. 10   **C.** 28

B. 20   **D.** 32

5. A meter is slightly longer than a yard. Which sentence is true?

A. A meter is slightly greater than 3 inches.

B. A meter is slightly less than 3 inches.

C. A meter is slightly less than 3 feet.

D. A meter is slightly greater than 3 feet.

6. The length of the classroom floor is 8 meters. What is the length of the classroom floor in centimeters?

A.   8 centimeters

B.   80 centimeters

C.   800 centimeters

D. 8,000 centimeters

7. How many inches greater is a yard than a foot?

   A. 2 inches

   B. 12 inches

   C. 24 inches

   D. 35 inches

8. A football team must advance 10 yards in 4 plays to earn a first down. On first down, the Warriors advanced exactly 4 yards. How many more feet must the Warriors advance to earn a first down?

   A. 6 feet

   B. 18 feet

   C. 30 feet

   D. 72 feet

9. How many millimeters greater is a meter than a centimeter?

   A. 999 millimeters

   B. 990 millimeters

   C. 900 millimeters

   D. 99 millimeters

10. Main Street is 3 kilometers long. It runs parallel with 1st Avenue, which is 750 meters long. How many meters longer is Main Street than 1st Avenue?

    A. 2,250 meters

    B. 2,350 meters

    C. 3,000 meters

    D. 3,750 meters

11. The bases on a softball field are 20 yards apart. Including home plate, there are 4 bases.

    A. How many feet apart are the bases?

    _____

    B. How many inches apart are the bases?

    _____

    C. Liz hit a home run that she earned by running. What is the least distance, in feet, that she had to run?

    _____

12. Draw a line from each length to its value in feet.

A. 3 yards   •   •   2 feet

B. 24 inches   •   • $4\frac{1}{2}$ feet

C. $1\frac{1}{2}$ yards   •   • $6\frac{1}{2}$ feet

D. 78 inches   •   •   9 feet

13. Select True or False for each sentence.

A. 300 centimeters = 30 meters   ○ True   ○ False

B. 5,000 kilometers = 5 meters   ○ True   ○ False

C. 200 millimeters = 20 centimeters   ○ True   ○ False

D. 8 meters = 8,000 millimeters   ○ True   ○ False

14. Draw a line from each object to the best estimate of its length.

A. width of Rhode Island   •   •   12 millimeters

B. train car   •   •   15 meters

C. pencil   •   •   17 centimeters

D. raisin   •   •   60 kilometers

15. Which stack of boxes is at least 5 feet tall? Circle all that apply.

A. $2\frac{1}{4}$ feet + $1\frac{3}{4}$ feet

B. $3\frac{1}{2}$ feet + 2 feet

C. $1\frac{3}{4}$ feet + $3\frac{3}{4}$ feet

D. $1\frac{3}{4}$ feet + 3 feet

16. The ceiling in a room is 300 centimeters high. Write each height in the correct box.

250 centimeters	$5\frac{1}{2}$ meters	2,200 millimeters
4,700 millimeters	1 kilometer	2 meters

Can Fit in Room	Cannot Fit in Room

17. The number line shows the distances of several buildings from Lita's house. Is the statement correct? Select Yes or No.

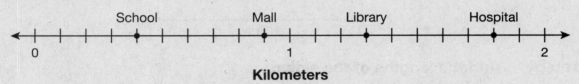

Kilometers

A. The mall is 0.5 kilometer farther from Lita's house than the school. ○ Yes ○ No

B. The library is 1,200 meters from Lita's house. ○ Yes ○ No

C. The hospital is 1.8 kilometers from Lita's house. ○ Yes ○ No

D. The hospital is twice as far from Lita's house as the mall. ○ Yes ○ No

Perimeter

Getting the Idea

Perimeter is the measure of the distance around a figure. The perimeter is measured in customary or metric units of length, such as inches, feet, centimeters, or meters.

To find the perimeter of a figure, add the lengths of all the sides.

Example 1

What is the perimeter of this rectangle?

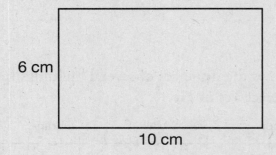

Strategy   **Add the lengths of the sides.**

Step 1   Find all the side lengths of the rectangle.

A rectangle has 4 sides, with opposite sides having equal lengths.

The length is 10 centimeters and the width is 6 centimeters.

So, two sides are 10 cm each and two sides are 6 cm each.

Step 2   Add the lengths of the four sides.

10 cm + 10 cm + 6 cm + 6 cm = 32 cm

Solution   **The perimeter of the rectangle is 32 centimeters.**

For Example 1, you could also use the formula for the perimeter of a rectangle.

Perimeter = (2 × length) + (2 × width)

$P = (2 \times 10) + (2 \times 6)$

$P = 20 + 12$

$P = 32$ cm

You can use a variable, such as *l* or *w*, to represent the length or the width of a rectangle.

Example 2

The rectangle below has a perimeter of 30 inches.

8 inches

$$P = 30 \text{ inches}$$

What is the width of the rectangle?

Strategy   **Use the formula for the perimeter of a rectangle.**

Step 1   Substitute the values into the formula for perimeter.

The perimeter is 30 feet.

The length is 8 feet.

Use *w* to represent the width.

Perimeter = (2 × length) + (2 × width)

$$30 = (2 \times 8) + (2 \times w)$$

Step 2   Multiply the values inside the parentheses.

$$30 = (2 \times 8) + (2 \times w)$$

$$30 = 16 + 2 \times w$$

Step 3   Subtract 16 on both sides of the equal sign.

$$30 = 16 + 2 \times w$$

$$30 - 16 = 16 - 16 + 2 \times w$$

$$14 = 2 \times w$$

Step 4   Divide both sides of the equal sign by 2 to solve for *w*.

$$14 = 2 \times w$$

$$14 \div 2 = 2 \div 2 \times w$$

$$7 = 1 \times w$$

$$7 = w$$

Solution   **The width of the rectangle is 7 inches.**

For Example 2, you can check the answer by substituting 7 inches for the width in the perimeter formula.

Perimeter = (2 × length) + (2 × width)

$$P = (2 \times 8) + (2 \times 7)$$

$$P = 16 + 14$$

$$P = 30 \text{ in.}$$

The perimeter is 30 inches. So, the answer is correct.

A square is a rectangle with all 4 sides equal in length. To find the perimeter of a square, add the lengths of all the sides. You could also multiply the length of one side by 4.

Here is the formula for the perimeter of a square:

Perimeter = 4 × length of a side

$$P = 4 \times s$$

Example 3

What is the perimeter of this square?

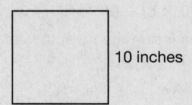

10 inches

Strategy   **Use the formula for the perimeter of a square.**

$$P = 4 \times s$$

$$P = 4 \times 10$$

$$P = 40 \text{ inches}$$

Solution   **The perimeter of the square is 40 inches.**

Example 4

A balcony has a perimeter of 28 meters. The balcony is in the shape of a square.
What is the length of one side of the balcony?

Strategy   **Use the formula for the perimeter of a square.**

Step 1   The balcony is a square. Write the formula for the perimeter.

$$P = 4 \times s$$

Step 2   Substitute the values you know into the formula.

The perimeter is 28 meters.

Use the variable s to represent the side length.

$$P = 4 \times s$$
$$28 = 4 \times s$$

Step 3   Divide both sides of the equal sign by 4 to solve for s.

$$28 = 4 \times s$$
$$28 \div 4 = 4 \div 4 \times s$$
$$7 = 1 \times s$$
$$7 = s$$

Solution   **The length of one side of the balcony is 7 meters.**

Coached Example

The rectangle below has a perimeter of 60 inches and a width of 10 inches.

P = 60 inches   10 inches

What is the length of the rectangle?

Write the formula for the perimeter of a rectangle.

$P = (2 \times$ _____$) + (2 \times$ _____$)$

Substitute the values you know into the formula.

Use the variable l to represent the _____.

$60 = (2 \times$ _____$) + (2 \times$ _____$)$

Solve for the length.

Check your answer by substituting _____ inches for the length in the formula.

$P = (2 \times$ _____$) + (2 \times$ _____$)$

$P =$ _____ $+$ _____

$P =$ _____

The length of the rectangle is _____ **inches.**

Lesson Practice • Part 1

Choose the correct answer.

1. What is the perimeter of this square?

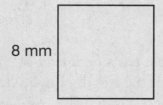

8 mm

   A. 16 mm

   B. 32 mm

   C. 48 mm

   D. 64 mm

2. What is the perimeter of this rectangle?

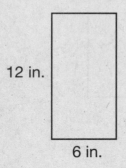

12 in.

6 in.

   A. 18 in.

   B. 30 in.

   C. 36 in.

   D. 72 in.

3. The square below has a perimeter of 36 meters.

P = 36 m

   What is the length of one side of the square?

   A. 4 m

   B. 8 m

   C. 9 m

   D. 12 m

4. The rectangle below has a perimeter of 72 centimeters and a length of 21 centimeters.

21 cm

P = 72 cm

   What is the width of the rectangle?

   A. 15 cm

   B. 30 cm

   C. 42 cm

   D. 51 cm

5. A rectangular playground has a length of 75 yards and width of 50 yards. What is the perimeter of the playground?

    A. 125 yards   **C.** 200 yards

    B. 175 yards   **D.** 250 yards

6. The floor of Jimmy's tree house is in the shape of a square. Each side of the floor is 15 feet. What is the perimeter of Jimmy's tree house?

    A. 30 feet   **C.** 90 feet

    B. 60 feet   **D.** 225 feet

7. Richie has a rug in his bedroom with a perimeter of 42 feet. The length of the rug is 12 feet. What is the width of the rug?

    A. 30 feet   **C.** 9 feet

    B. 18 feet   **D.** 6 feet

8. A square has a perimeter of 44 meters. What is the length of one side of the square?

    A. 9 meters   **C.** 11 meters

    B. 10 meters   **D.** 12 meters

9. Anna drew the square and the rectangle below.

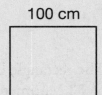

100 cm   13 km

P = 46 km

    A. What is the perimeter of the square? Show your work.

    B. What is the width of the rectangle? Show your work.

Lesson Practice • Part 2

Choose the correct answer.

1. A football field has a length of 120 yards and a width of 53 yards. What is the perimeter of the football field?

    A. 173 yards

    B. 226 yards

    C. 293 yards

    D. 346 yards

2. An 8-inch-by-6-inch rectangular photo is inside a 10-inch-by-8-inch rectangular frame. How much greater is the perimeter of the frame than the perimeter of the photo?

    A. 2 inches

    B. 8 inches

    C. 16 inches

    D. 32 inches

3. Jada's bedroom is rectangular. It has a perimeter of 52 feet. The length of her bedroom is 14 feet. What is the width?

    A. 12 feet

    B. 13 feet

    C. 19 feet

    D. 38 feet

4. Which is the missing number in the table?

Length of Square	Perimeter of Square
3	12
6	24
9	36
16	?

    A. 43

    B. 57

    C. 60

    D. 64

5. Which describes how to find the length of each side of a square if you know its perimeter?

    A. Add 4 to the perimeter.

    B. Multiply the perimeter by 4.

    C. Divide the perimeter by 4.

    D. Divide 4 by the perimeter.

6. Dylan's rectangular poster is 36 inches long and 24 inches wide. Neveah's square poster has the same perimeter. What is the length of each side of Neveah's poster?

    A. 15 inches

    B. 30 inches

    C. 50 inches

    D. 60 inches

7. A rectangle has a perimeter of 42 inches. Its width is 8 inches. How much longer is the length than the width?

    A. 5 inches

    B. 13 inches

    C. 26 inches

    D. 34 inches

8. Which describes a way to find the perimeter of a rectangle that is not a square if you know its length and width?

    A. Add the length and the width.

    B. Add the length and the width and multiply by 2.

    C. Add the length and the width and divide by 2.

    D. Multiply the length times 4.

9. A square playground has a perimeter of 240 yards. What is the length of each side?

    A. 60 yards

    B. 80 yards

    C. 120 yards

    D. 960 yards

10. The perimeter of Jase's basement is 28 yards. The length and width are at least 4 yards long and are whole numbers.

    A. If the basement is a square, what are the side lengths in yards?

    _____

    B. If the basement is a rectangle that is **not** a square, give all of the possible dimensions.

    _____

    _____

    _____

11. Draw a line from each rectangle to its perimeter.

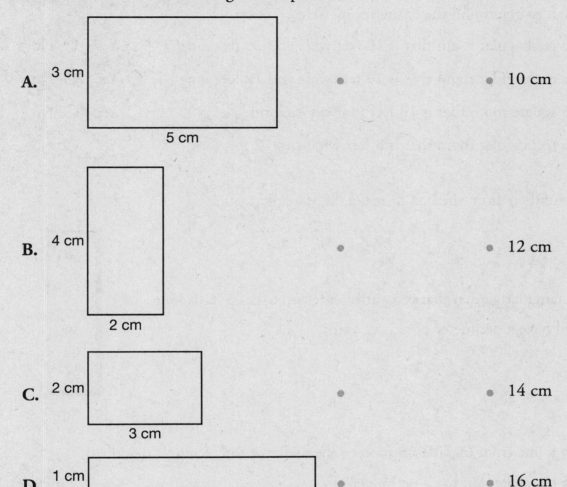

A.   3 cm   5 cm

B.   4 cm   2 cm

C.   2 cm   3 cm

D.   1 cm   6 cm

10 cm

12 cm

14 cm

16 cm

12. Which shape has a perimeter of 24 inches? Circle all that apply.

A.   a square that has a side length of 12 inches

B.   a rectangle that is 8 inches wide and 4 inches long

C.   a rectangle that is 3 inches wide and 9 inches long

D.   a rectangle that is 5 inches wide and 6 inches long

13. Kento has a string of lights that is 40 feet long. Will the string of lights be long enough to go around the entire room? Select Yes or No.

A. a rectangular room that is 10 feet wide and 20 feet long ○ Yes ○ No

B. a rectangular room that is 10 feet wide and 12 feet long ○ Yes ○ No

C. a square room that is 10 feet long on each side ○ Yes ○ No

D. a rectangular room that is 8 feet wide and 12 feet long ○ Yes ○ No

14. Use numbers from the box to make the statement true.

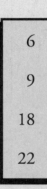

6

9

18

22

A rectangular garden that is 3 yards wide and _____ yards long would have a perimeter of _____ yards.

15. Draw a line from each description to the width of the rectangle described.

A. a rectangle that has a perimeter of 80 inches and a length of 25 inches • • 7 inches

B. a rectangle that has a perimeter of 60 inches and a length of 20 inches • • 10 inches

C. a rectangle that has a length of 20 inches and a perimeter of 54 inches • • 15 inches

D. a rectangle that has a length of 30 inches and a perimeter of 100 inches • • 20 inches

Area

Getting the Idea

Area is the measure of the region inside a figure. Area is measured in **square units**, such as square inches, square feet, and square centimeters. A square inch, for example, is a square with a side length of 1 inch.

To find the area of a figure, count the number of square units inside the figure. A scale tells what each square unit represents.

Example 1

What is the area of this rectangle?

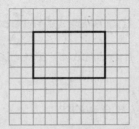

Scale: ☐ = 1 square meter

Strategy   **Count the number of square units inside the figure.**

Step 1   Count the square units.

There are 24 square units inside the rectangle.

Step 2   Look at the scale to find what each square unit represents.

Each square unit is 1 square meter.

So, 24 square units = 24 square meters.

Solution   **The area of the rectangle is 24 square meters.**

You can use formulas to find the areas of rectangles and squares.

To find the area of a rectangle, multiply the length by the width.

Area = length × width

$A = l \times w$

Example 2

What is the area of this rectangle?

8 cm

5 cm

Strategy   **Use the formula for the area of a rectangle.**

Step 1   Write the formula for the area of a rectangle.

$A = l \times w$

Step 2   Multiply the length by the width.

The length is 5 centimeters.

The width is 8 centimeters.

$A = 5 \times 8 = 40$ square centimeters

Solution   **The area of the rectangle is 40 square centimeters.**

To find the area of a square, multiply the length of one side by itself.

Area = side × side

$A = s \times s$

Example 3

What is the area of this square?

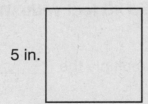

5 in.

Strategy   **Use the formula for the area of a square.**

Step 1   Write the formula for the area of a square.

$A = s \times s$

Step 2   Multiply the length of one side by itself.

The length is 5 inches.

$A = 5 \times 5 = 25$ square inches

Solution   **The area of the square is 25 square inches.**

Example 4

The floor of Winnie's bedroom is a rectangle. It has an area of 108 square feet. The length is 9 feet. What is the width of Winnie's bedroom?

Strategy   **Use the formula for the area of a rectangle.**

Step 1   The bedroom floor is a rectangle, so write the formula for the area.

$A = l \times w$

Step 2   Substitute the values into the formula.

The area is 108 square feet.

The length is 9 feet.

$108 = 9 \times w$

Step 3   Divide both sides of the equal sign by 9 to solve for w.

$108 = 9 \times w$

$108 \div 9 = 9 \div 9 \times w$

$12 = 1 \times w$

$12 = w$

Solution   **The width of Winnie's bedroom is 12 feet.**

Coached Example

A playground is 80 feet long and 45 feet wide. What is the area of the playground?

To find the area of the rectangle, multiply the _____ by the _____.

Write the area formula. Use *l* for length and *w* for width.

$A =$ _____ $\times$ _____

Substitute the values into the formula.

$A =$ _____ $\times$ _____

Multiply.

$A =$ _____

Label the product with the correct units.

The units are _____ _____.

The playground has an area of _____.

Lesson Practice • Part 1

Choose the correct answer.

1. What is the area of this rectangle?

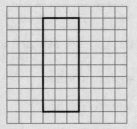

Scale: ☐ = 1 square inch

   A. 24 square inches

   B. 22 square inches

   C. 12 square inches

   D. 11 square inches

2. What is the area of this rectangle?

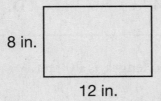

8 in.

12 in.

   A. 20 square inches

   B. 40 square inches

   C. 48 square inches

   D. 96 square inches

3. Each side of a square poster measures 12 inches. What is the area of the poster?

   A. 48 square inches

   B. 96 square inches

   C. 144 square inches

   D. 288 square inches

4. A rectangular table has an area of 42 square feet. The width is 3 feet. What is the length of the table?

   A. 7 feet

   B. 14 feet

   C. 18 feet

   D. 39 feet

5. A square has an area of 36 square inches. What is the length of its sides?

   A. 6 inches

   B. 9 inches

   C. 12 inches

   D. 18 inches

6. Lisa made a drawing of her kitchen. What is the area of Lisa's kitchen?

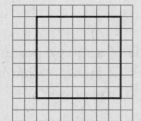

Scale: □ = 1 square foot

A. 14 square feet

B. 28 square feet

C. 49 square feet

D. 70 square feet

7. What is the area of the figure below?

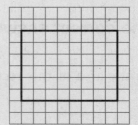

Scale: □ = 1 square inch

A. 48 square inches

B. 36 square inches

C. 28 square inches

D. 24 square inches

8. A patio is in the shape of a rectangle. It has an area of 120 square feet. The length is 8 feet. What is the width of the patio?

A. 13 feet   C. 15 feet

B. 14 feet   D. 16 feet

9. Logan's office floor has an area of 700 square feet. The length is 20 feet.

A. Write an equation that can be used to find the width. Let *w* represent the width.

_____

B. What is the width of the office floor? Show your work.

_____

_____

_____

Lesson Practice • Part 2

Choose the correct answer.

1. The floor of Hayden's rectangular bedroom is 15 feet long and 12 feet wide. What is the area of the floor in the bedroom?

   A. 27 square feet

   B. 54 square feet

   C. 160 square feet

   D. 180 square feet

2. A square has a perimeter of 32 inches. What is its area?

   A. 64 square inches

   B. 128 square inches

   C. 256 square inches

   D. 1,024 square inches

3. Which sentence about the perimeter and area of rectangles is true?

   A. A rectangle will always have an area that is greater than its perimeter.

   B. A rectangle will always have a perimeter that is greater than its area.

   C. The perimeter and area of a rectangle can be equal.

   D. The two measures cannot be compared because they are measured in different units.

4. Which is the missing number in the table?

Length of Square	Area of Square
3	9
4	16
5	25
6	?

   A. 26

   B. 30

   C. 36

   D. 41

5. A rectangular 8-inch-by-6-inch photo is inside a frame that is 1 inch around all sides. What is the area of the frame?

   A. 52 square inches

   B. 63 square inches

   C. 80 square inches

   D. 120 square inches

6. A square and a rectangle that is not a square have the same perimeter. Which sentence is true?

   A. The rectangle will always have the greater area.

   B. The square will always have the greater area.

   C. The rectangle and the square can have the same area.

   D. The rectangle can have the greater area depending on its shape.

7. The cover of Zoe's rectangular book has an area of 88 square inches. The width of the book is 8 inches. What is the length of the book?

   A. 11 inches

   B. 22 inches

   C. 36 inches

   D. 80 inches

8. A rectangular garden bed has an area of 8 square yards. The width of the garden bed is 1 yard. What is the length of the garden bed?

   A. 1 yard

   B. 3 yards

   C. 7 yards

   D. 8 yards

9. A rectangle has an area of 24 square centimeters. The length of the rectangle is 8 centimeters. What is the perimeter of the rectangle?

   A. 64 centimeters

   B. 22 centimeters

   C. 11 centimeters

   D. 3 centimeters

10. Mr. Peterson will buy 80 feet of fencing. The pieces of fence come in whole numbers of feet. His enclosure will be a rectangle and have 4 sides.

   A. If he wants to enclose the greatest area, what should be the length, width, and area?

   _____

   B. If he wants to enclose the least area, what should be the length, width, and area?

   _____

11. Draw a line from each rectangle to its area.

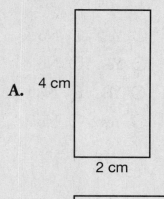

A.   4 cm

2 cm

●   ● 6 square centimeters

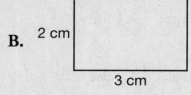

B.   2 cm

3 cm

●   ● 8 square centimeters

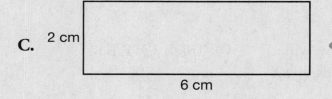

C.   2 cm

6 cm

●   ● 12 square centimeters

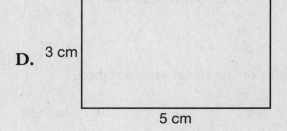

D.   3 cm

5 cm

●   ● 15 square centimeters

12. Which shape has an area of 48 square inches? Circle all that apply.

A. a rectangle that is 3 inches wide and 14 inches long

B. a rectangle that is 4 inches wide and 12 inches long

C. a square that has a side length of 24 inches

D. a rectangle that is 6 inches wide and 8 inches long

E. a rectangle that is 2 inches wide and 24 inches long

13. Julie has enough paint to cover 96 square feet. Will the paint be enough to cover the wall? Select Yes or No.

   A. a rectangular wall that is 8 feet wide and 12 feet long   ○ Yes ○ No

   B. a rectangular wall that is 9 feet wide and 10 feet long   ○ Yes ○ No

   C. a square wall that is 10 feet long on each side   ○ Yes ○ No

   D. a rectangular wall that is 6 feet wide and 16 feet long   ○ Yes ○ No

14. Select True or False for each statement.

   A. A square has an area of 36 square meters.   ○ True ○ False
   One side of the square is 6 meters.

   B. A rectangle has an area of 30 square meters   ○ True ○ False
   and a width of 5 meters. The length of the
   rectangle is 6 meters.

   C. A rectangle is 8 feet long and 2 feet wide.   ○ True ○ False
   The area of the rectangle is 10 square feet.

   D. A square has a side length of 2 yards. The   ○ True ○ False
   area of the square is 4 square yards.

15. Draw a line from each description to the width of the rectangle described.

   A. a rectangle that has an area of 64 square   •   • 2 inches
   inches and a length of 16 inches

   B. a rectangle that has an area of 18 square   •   • 3 inches
   inches and a length of 6 inches

   C. a rectangle that has a length of 10 inches   •   • 4 inches
   and an area of 20 square inches

   D. a rectangle that has a length of 9 inches   •   • 8 inches
   and an area of 72 square inches

Angles

Getting the Idea

An **angle** (∠) is formed by two **rays** that meet at the same **endpoint**. That endpoint is the **vertex** of the angle. An angle can be named by its vertex. The angle below can be named as angle Y or ∠Y.

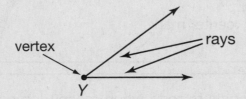

The vertex of an angle can be at the center of a **circle**. A **degree** (°) is the angle made by $\frac{1}{360}$ of a full turn around a circle. A full turn around a circle is 360 degrees.

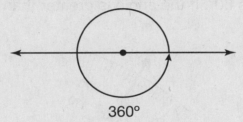

360°

The measure of an angle is the fraction of the circle between the points where the two rays intersect the circle. Below are some examples.

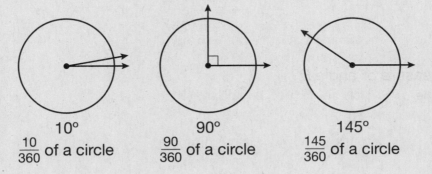

10°	90°	145°
$\frac{10}{360}$ of a circle	$\frac{90}{360}$ of a circle	$\frac{145}{360}$ of a circle

You can use a **protractor** to measure angles. A protractor often has two scales. The scales increase from 0° to 180°, but in opposite directions.

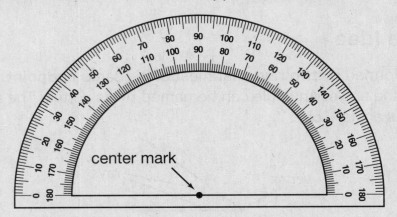

center mark

To help you decide which scale to read when measuring an angle, compare the angle to 90°.

For example, if the scales read 120° and 60°, and the angle is less than 90°, then the measure of the angle is 60°. If the angle is greater than 90°, then the measure of the angle is 120°.

Example 1

What is the measure of angle *B*?

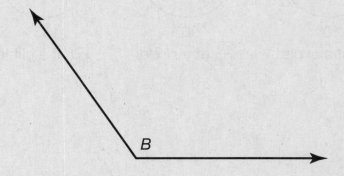

B

Strategy   **Use a protractor.**

Step 1   Place the center mark of the protractor on the vertex of the angle.

Line up one ray of the angle with the 0° mark on one of the scales.

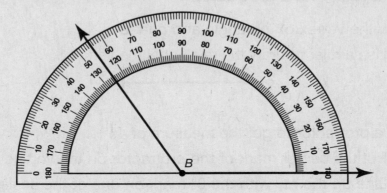

Step 2   Look at the scale at the point where the other ray of the angle crosses it.

Read the degree mark on the same scale used in Step 1.

The ray crosses the scale at 125°.

It crosses the other scale at 55°.

Step 3   Decide which scale to use.

Angle *B* appears greater than 90°, so it makes sense that the measure would be 125°, not 55°.

Solution   **The measure of angle *B* is 125°.**

Example 2

Draw an angle *S* that measures 45°.

Strategy   **Use a ruler and a protractor.**

> **Step 1**   Draw the vertex of the angle and one ray.
>
> Use a ruler to draw the ray. Label the vertex *S*.

> **Step 2**   Use a protractor to get the measure of 45°.
>
> Put the center mark of the protractor on the vertex.
>
> Line up the ray with the 0° mark on one of the scales.
>
> Then find the 45° mark. Place a dot above the protractor.

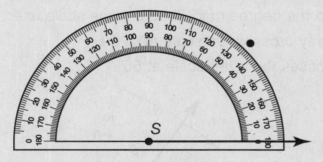

> **Step 3**   Remove the protractor. Draw the other ray.
>
> Use a ruler to draw a ray from the vertex to the dot.

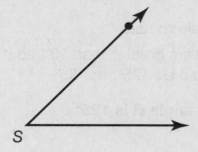

Solution   **Angle *S* is shown in Step 3.**

Example 3

The measure of angle *D* is 135°. A part of angle *D* measures 65°.

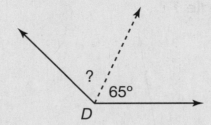

What is the measure of the other part of angle *D*?

Strategy   **Write a number sentence.**

Step 1   Use a variable to represent the measure of the missing part.

Choose the letter *m* for the missing part.

Step 2   Write a number sentence.

$$65° + m = \angle D$$
$$65° + m = 135°$$

Step 3   Solve for *m*.

Subtract 65° from both sides of the equal sign.

$$65° + m = 135°$$
$$65° - 65° + m = 135° - 65°$$
$$0 + m = 70°$$
$$m = 70°$$

Solution   **The measure of the other part of angle *D* is 70°.**

What is the measure of angle *T*?

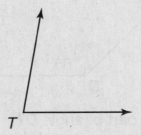

Put the center mark of the protractor on the _____ of the angle.

Line up one ray of the angle with the _____° mark on one of the scales.

Look at the scale where the other ray of the angle crosses it.

The ray crosses the scale at _____°.

It crosses the other scale at _____°.

Check your answer.

Angle *T* appears _____ than 90°, so the measure is _____°,
not _____°.

The measure of angle *T* is _____°.

Lesson Practice • Part 1

Choose the correct answer.

1. What is the measure of this angle?

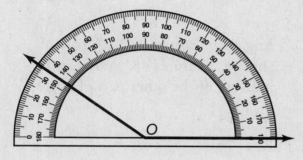

    A.   45°

    B.   55°

    C.   135°

    D.   145°

2. What is the measure of this angle?

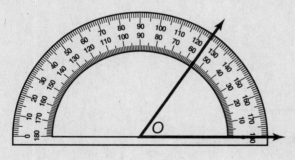

    A.   55°

    B.   60°

    C.   120°

    D.   125°

3. Which angle could measure 130°?

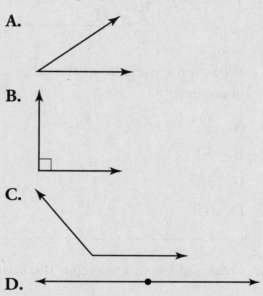

4. The measure of angle *A* is 90°. A part of angle *A* measures 35°.

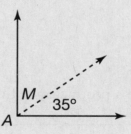

What is the measure of the other part of angle *A*?

    A.   65°

    B.   55°

    C.   45°

    D.   35°

5. The measure of angle *R* is 155°. A part of angle *R* measures 105°.

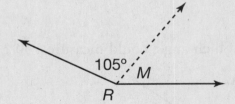

What is the measure of the other part of angle *R*?

A. 45°

B. 50°

C. 55°

D. 65°

6. A 45° angle turns through what fraction of a circle?

A. $\frac{315}{360}$ C. $\frac{45}{90}$

B. $\frac{45}{100}$ D. $\frac{45}{360}$

7. Angle *K* measures 112°. A part of angle *K* measures 48°. What is the measure of the other part of angle *K*?

A. 64°

B. 74°

C. 76°

D. 160°

8. Gabriel drew this angle on the board.

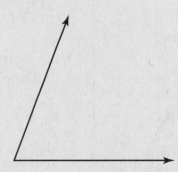

A. Use a protractor to find the measure of Gabriel's angle. _____

_____

B. Draw an angle that measures 45° more than Gabriel's angle.

Lesson Practice • Part 2

Choose the correct answer.

1. Use a protractor. What is the measure of this angle?

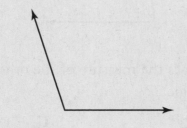

   A. 68°   **C.** 108°

   B. 72°   **D.** 112°

2. Use a protractor. What is the measure of this angle?

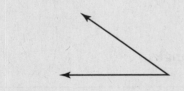

   A. 36°   **C.** 136°

   B. 44°   **D.** 144°

3. What fraction of a circle does 1° represent?

   A. $\frac{1}{360}$

   B. $\frac{1}{180}$

   C. $\frac{1}{90}$

   D. $\frac{1}{2}$

4. Which angle measures 70°?

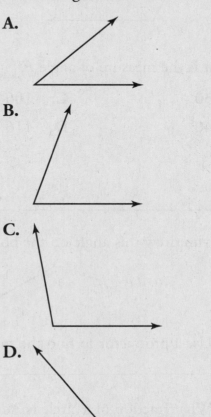

5. An angle that forms a square corner measures 90°. The angle is split into two unequal parts. The greater part measures 60°. Which equation can be used to find the measure, *m*, of the lesser part?

   A. $60 + 90 = m$

   B. $60 + m = 90$

   C. $m - 90 = 60$

   D. $m - 60 = 90$

6. Angle *F* is split into two parts.

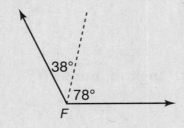

What is the measure of angle *F*?

A. 30°   **C.** 106°

B. 40°   **D.** 116°

7. The measure of angle *T* is 84°. A part of angle *T* measures 57°.

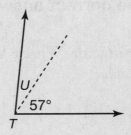

What is the measure of the other part of angle *T*?

A. 27°   **C.** 131°

B. 37°   **D.** 141°

8. Adalynn drew this angle on the board.

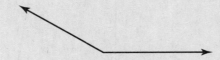

A. Use a protractor to find the measure of Adalynn's angle.

_____

B. What fraction of a circle is Adalynn's angle?

_____

C. Draw an angle that is 60° less than Adalynn's angle.

9. Draw a line from each angle to its measure.

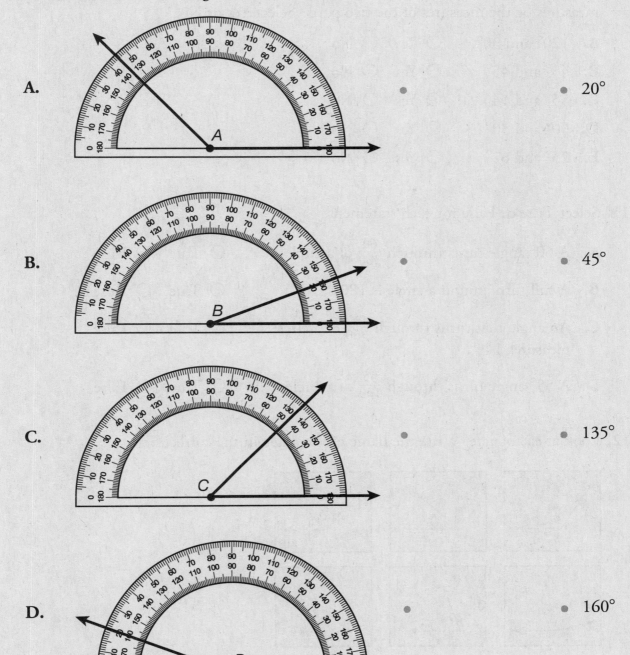

A.

B.

C.

D.

20°

45°

135°

160°

10. Angle *C* has a measure of 90°. Angle *C* is divided into two parts. Can the angle measures be the measures of the two parts? Select Yes or No.

A. 120° and 30°   ○ Yes ○ No

B. 45° and 45°   ○ Yes ○ No

C. 55° and 145°   ○ Yes ○ No

D. 60° and 30°   ○ Yes ○ No

E. 23° and 67°   ○ Yes ○ No

11. Select True or False for each statement.

A. A 60° angle turns through $\frac{60}{360}$ of a circle.   ○ True ○ False

B. A full turn around a circle is 180°.   ○ True ○ False

C. An angle that turns through $\frac{145}{360}$ of a circle measures 145°.   ○ True ○ False

D. A 55° angle turns through $\frac{55}{180}$ of a circle.   ○ True ○ False

12. Look at each angle. Write the name of the angle in the correct box.

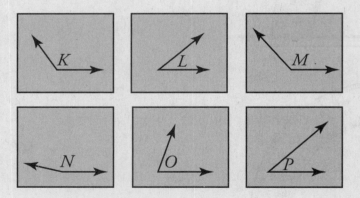

Less than 90°	Greater than 90°

Line Plots

Getting the Idea

A **line plot** is a graph that uses Xs above a number line to record data. To read a line plot, count the number of Xs above the number on the number line.

Example 1

Dana and Josiah measured the widths of books in a shelf. They made the line plot below.

Book Thickness

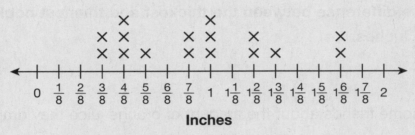

Inches

How many books were less than $\frac{7}{8}$ inch thick?

Strategy	Count the number of Xs above each number less than $\frac{7}{8}$.

Step 1 Determine which Xs to count.

The fractions less than $\frac{7}{8}$ are to the left of it on the number line.

Do not count the Xs above $\frac{7}{8}$.

Step 2 Count the number of Xs above the numbers that are less than $\frac{7}{8}$.

There are 2 Xs above $\frac{3}{8}$.

There are 3 Xs above $\frac{4}{8}$.

There is 1 X above $\frac{5}{8}$.

Step 3 Add to find the total.

$2 + 3 + 1 = 6$

Solution There were 6 books that were less than $\frac{7}{8}$ inch thick.

Example 2

Use the line plot in Example 1.

What is the difference in thickness between the thickest and thinnest books?

Step 1   Find the thickness of the thickest book.

The thickest book is $1\frac{6}{8}$ inches thick.

Step 2   Find the thickness of the thinnest book.

The thinnest book is $\frac{3}{8}$ inches thick.

Step 3   Subtract

$$1\frac{6}{8} - \frac{3}{8} = 1\frac{3}{8}$$

Solution   **The difference between the thickest and thinnest books is $1\frac{3}{8}$ inches.**

Example 3

Janelle asked some friends about the amount of orange juice they drank one day. She listed the results below.

0 cups	$\frac{1}{2}$ cup	1 cup	1 cup	0 cups	1 cup
$\frac{1}{2}$ cup	1 cup	$\frac{1}{2}$ cup	1 cup	$\frac{1}{2}$ cup	1 cup

Make a line plot of Janelle's results.

Strategy   **Count each amount. Draw a number line to make the line plot.**

Step 1 Look at the amounts of juice.

There are also $\frac{1}{2}$ cups.

The greatest amount is 1 cup. The least amount is 0 cups.

Step 2 Make a number line from 0 to 1 in halves.

Label the number line.

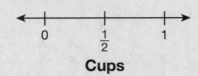

Cups

Step 3 Count the number for each amount.

2 friends drank 0 cups of juice.

4 friends drank $\frac{1}{2}$ cup of juice.

6 friends drank 1 cup of juice.

Step 4 Draw an X to represent each friend above each amount.

Write a title for the line plot.

Orange Juice Amounts

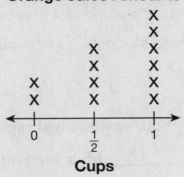

Cups

Solution **The line plot is shown in Step 4.**

Coached Example

Isaac asked some students how long they spent reading last night. He made the line plot below.

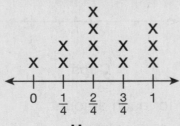

Time Spent Reading

Hours

How many students spent $\frac{1}{4}$ hour reading last night?

How much time in all did those students spend reading?

Count the number of Xs above the time of _____ hour on the number line.

There are _____ Xs above that time.

So, _____ students spent $\frac{1}{4}$ hour reading last night.

To find how much time in all those students spent reading, which operation should you use? _____

$\frac{1}{4}$ + _____ = _____

So, _____ students spent $\frac{1}{4}$ hour reading last night.

In all, those students spent _____ hour reading.

Lesson Practice • Part 1

Choose the correct answer.

1. The list shows the distances that 10 students ran in gym class.

0 miles, $\frac{1}{2}$ mile, 1 mile, 1 mile, $\frac{1}{2}$ mile, $\frac{1}{2}$ mile, 0 miles, 1 mile, 1 mile, $\frac{1}{2}$ mile

Which line plot shows the results?

A.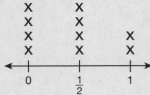

B.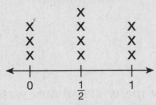

C.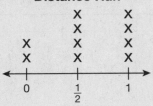

D.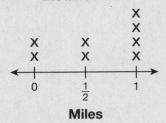

Use the line plot for questions 2–4.

William measured the lengths of some stickers. He recorded the results in a line plot.

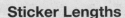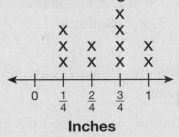

2. How many stickers were $\frac{3}{4}$ inch long or longer?

   A. 7   C. 5

   B. 6   D. 4

3. What is the difference in length between the longest stickers and the shortest stickers?

   A. $\frac{1}{4}$ inch   C. $\frac{3}{4}$ inch

   B. $\frac{2}{4}$ inch   D. 1 inch

4. William placed all of the $\frac{1}{4}$-inch stickers side by side. What is the total length of the stickers?

   A. $\frac{1}{4}$ inch   C. $\frac{4}{4}$ inch

   B. $\frac{3}{4}$ inch   D. $\frac{5}{4}$ inches

Use the line plot for questions 5–8.

The line plot shows the capacity of 12 containers.

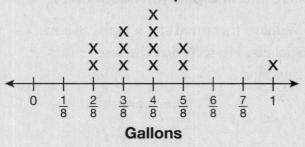

Container Capacities

Gallons

5. How many $\frac{1}{8}$-gallon containers are there?

    A. 0   **C.** 2

    B. 1   **D.** 3

6. How many containers are $\frac{4}{8}$ gallon or greater?

    A. 2   **C.** 6

    B. 4   **D.** 7

7. What is the combined capacity of all of the $\frac{2}{8}$-gallon containers?

    A. $\frac{2}{8}$ gallon   **C.** $\frac{4}{8}$ gallon

    B. $\frac{3}{8}$ gallon   **D.** $\frac{8}{8}$ gallon

8. What is the difference in capacity between the largest containers and the smallest containers?

    A. $\frac{5}{8}$ gallon   **C.** $\frac{7}{8}$ gallon

    B. $\frac{6}{8}$ gallon   **D.** $\frac{8}{8}$ gallon

9. Michelle asked some classmates how much time they spent watching a 1-hour special on TV. The list below shows the times, in hours, her classmates watched the special.

    $\frac{1}{4}, \frac{2}{4}, 1, \frac{2}{4}, \frac{1}{4}, 1, 0, 1, \frac{2}{4}, 0$

    A. Make a line plot of Michelle's results. Be sure to include a title and label the number line.

    B. How many classmates watched $\frac{2}{4}$ hour or more of the TV special?

    _____

Lesson Practice • Part 2

Choose the correct answer.

1. Makayla recorded the lengths of 15 movies on her DVR to the nearest $\frac{1}{4}$ hour.

$1\frac{3}{4}$, $1\frac{1}{2}$, $1\frac{3}{4}$, 2, $2\frac{1}{4}$, $1\frac{3}{4}$, $1\frac{1}{2}$, $1\frac{3}{4}$,

$2\frac{1}{4}$, 2, $1\frac{1}{2}$, $1\frac{1}{4}$, $1\frac{1}{2}$, $2\frac{1}{2}$, 2

Which line plot shows the data?

A.
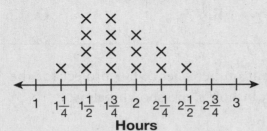

C.
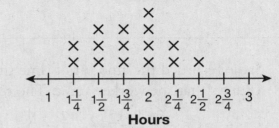

B.
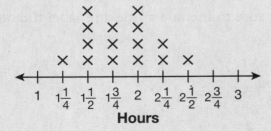

D.
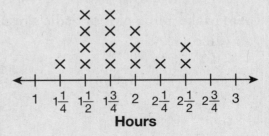

Use the line plot for questions 2 and 3.

Coach Williams recorded the heights of the high jumps of his students.

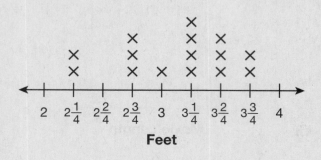

High Jumps

Feet

2. What is the difference between the greatest and least high jumps?

   A. 2 feet   **C.** $1\frac{1}{2}$ feet

   B. $1\frac{3}{4}$ feet   **D.** $1\frac{1}{4}$ feet

3. How many more students high jumped at least 3 feet than high jumped less than 3 feet?

   A. 8   **C.** 6

   B. 7   **D.** 5

4. Sadie recorded the amount of time she spent on her science fair project for the 18 days that she worked on it. The results, in hours, are shown below.

   $1\frac{2}{4}$, $2\frac{1}{4}$, $2\frac{2}{4}$, $2\frac{3}{4}$, $\frac{3}{4}$, $2\frac{3}{4}$, $2\frac{2}{4}$, $\frac{2}{4}$, $2\frac{1}{4}$,

   2, $1\frac{2}{4}$, $2\frac{2}{4}$, $2\frac{1}{4}$, $1\frac{3}{4}$, 2, $2\frac{1}{4}$, $1\frac{1}{4}$, $2\frac{3}{4}$

   A. Make a line plot of Sadie's results. Be sure to include a title and label the number line.

   B. In how many more days did Sadie work at least 2 hours on her science fair project than less than 2 hours?

   _____

   C. What is the difference between the greatest and least amount of times that Sadie spent working on her science fair project? Show your work.

   _____

5. The line plot shows the masses of the rocks in Leon's collection. Draw a line from each description to the correct mass.

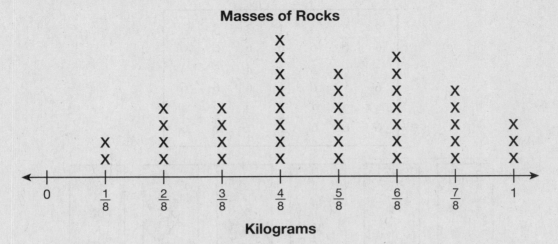

Masses of Rocks

Kilograms

A. the mass of the least number of rocks •   • 1 kilogram

B. the difference between the masses of the rock with the greatest mass and the rock with the least mass •   • $\frac{7}{8}$ kilogram

C. the mass of the greatest number of rocks •   • $\frac{4}{8}$ kilogram

D. the total mass of all the $\frac{2}{8}$-kilogram rocks •   • $\frac{2}{8}$ kilogram

E. the mass of the rocks that has the same number of rocks as $\frac{3}{8}$-kilogram rocks •   • $\frac{1}{8}$ kilogram

6. The list shows the capacities in liters of several glasses in Tony's cupboard. Draw the correct number of Xs above the numbers on the line plot to show the data in the list.

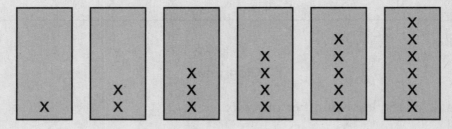

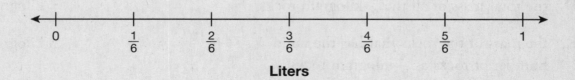

Capacities of Tony's Glasses

0          $\frac{1}{6}$ $\frac{2}{6}$ $\frac{3}{6}$ $\frac{4}{6}$ $\frac{5}{6}$ 1

Liters

Domain 4: Cumulative Assessment for Lessons 28–36

1. The point on the number line below shows the length of a ribbon.

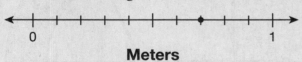

   Meters

   What is the length of the ribbon?

   A. 0.5 meter

   B. 0.6 meter

   C. 0.7 meter

   D. 0.8 meter

2. A rock concert lasted 2 hours and 30 minutes. How many minutes did the concert last?

   A. 60 minutes

   B. 90 minutes

   C. 120 minutes

   D. 150 minutes

3. The area of a square is 64 square meters. What is the length of one side of the square?

   A. 8 meters

   B. 9 meters

   C. 12 meters

   D. 16 meters

4. Kareem's backpack has a mass of 6 kilograms. What is the mass of the backpack in grams?

   A. 60,000 grams

   B. 6,000 grams

   C. 600 grams

   D. 60 grams

5. The length of a living room is 9 meters. How many centimeters is that?

   A. 9 centimeters

   B. 90 centimeters

   C. 900 centimeters

   D. 9,000 centimeters

6. Mitch is painting a wall in his bedroom. He knows that the area of the wall is 99 square feet. The length of the wall is 11 feet. What is the width of the wall?

   A. 11 feet

   B. 10 feet

   C. 9 feet

   D. 8 feet

7. Three children shared 4 pints of juice. How many cups are in 4 pints?

    A. 6 cups   **C.** 10 cups

    B. 8 cups   **D.** 16 cups

8. The angle below measures 110°. A square is placed on the angle.

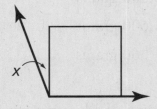

What is the measure of angle *x*?

    A. 20°   **C.** 45°

    B. 35°   **D.** 90°

9. What is the measure of this angle?

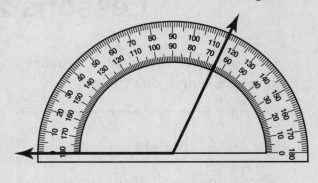

_____

10. Ron recorded the heights of some candles.

$\frac{2}{4}$ foot $\frac{1}{4}$ foot $\frac{3}{4}$ foot $\frac{3}{4}$ foot   1 foot

1 foot $\frac{3}{4}$ foot $\frac{2}{4}$ foot $\frac{2}{4}$ foot $\frac{3}{4}$ foot

    A. Create a line plot of Ron's results. Be sure to include a title and label the number line.

    B. What is the difference in height between the tallest candles and the shortest candles?

_____

Domain 5

Geometry

Domain 5: Diagnostic Assessment for Lessons 37–39

Domain 5: Cumulative Assessment for Lessons 37–39

Domain 5: Diagnostic Assessment for Lessons 37–39

1. Which shows parallel lines?

   A.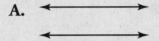

   B.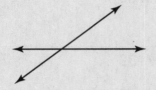

   C.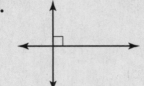

   D.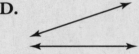

2. Which is an obtuse angle?

   A.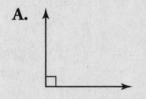

   B.

   C.

   D.

3. How many pairs of parallel sides does this figure have?

   A. 3   **C.** 6

   B. 4   **D.** 8

4. How many right angles does this triangle have?

   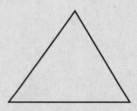

   A. 0   **C.** 2

   B. 1   **D.** 3

5. Jackie drew a quadrilateral.

   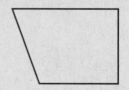

   What type of quadrilateral did she draw?

   A. parallelogram

   B. rectangle

   C. trapezoid

   D. square

6. Which best describes angle *B*?

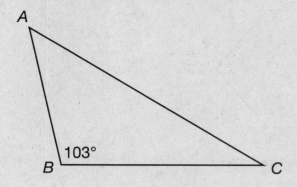

A. It is an acute angle.

B. It is a right angle.

C. It is an obtuse angle.

D. It is a straight angle.

7. Which appears to be a right triangle?

A.

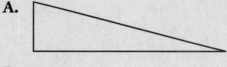

B.

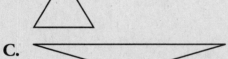

C.

D.

8. Which has exactly 1 line of symmetry?

A.
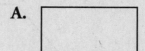

B.

C.

D.

9. How many lines of symmetry does this figure have?

10. Look at the figure below.

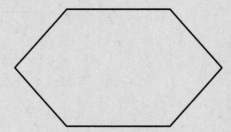

    A. How many lines of symmetry does the figure have?

_____

    B. Draw all the lines of symmetry on the figure below.

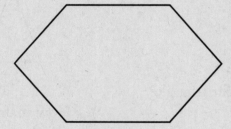

Lines and Angles

Getting the Idea

A **point** is a particular place or location.

A **line** is a straight path that goes in two directions without end.

This line with points S and T can be written as $\overleftrightarrow{ST}$ or $\overleftrightarrow{TS}$.

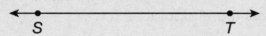

A **ray** is part of a line with one endpoint and goes in the other direction without end. A ray is named by its endpoint first. This ray is named $\overrightarrow{YZ}$.

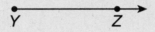

A **line segment** is part of a line with two endpoints.

This line segment can be named $\overline{MN}$ or $\overline{NM}$.

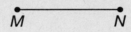

Example 1

How can you name this figure?

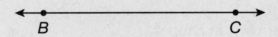

Strategy   **Look for endpoints or arrows.**

Step 1   Identify the figure.

    The figure has arrows on both sides.

    It shows a straight path without end in both directions.

    The figure is a line.

Step 2   Identify points on the line.

    The points B and C are on the line.

Step 3   Name the line.

    Use the points on the line to name the figure.

Solution   **The figure is line *BC* or line *CB*.**

Example 2

Draw $\overrightarrow{DE}$.

Strategy   **Identify the symbol. Then use the definition to draw the figure.**

Step 1   Identify the symbol in the name.

The symbol above $\overrightarrow{DE}$ is ⟶.

The figure is a ray with points *D* and *E*.

Step 2   Draw and label the endpoint.

The endpoint is the first point listed in the name.

Point *D* is the endpoint.

•
D

Step 3   Draw the ray.

Draw an arrow pointing away from the endpoint.

•——————————▶
D

Step 4   Draw and label the second point on the ray.

The other point is point *E*.

•——————•——▶
D   *E*

Solution   **Ray *DE* is shown in Step 4.**

Pairs of lines or line segments can be identified as parallel, intersecting, or perpendicular.

Parallel lines are lines that remain the same distance apart and never meet.

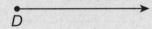
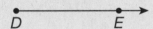

Intersecting lines are lines that cross at exactly one point.

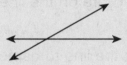

Perpendicular lines are intersecting lines that cross to form 4 square corners.

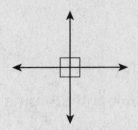

Example 3

Which street is parallel to 2nd Avenue?

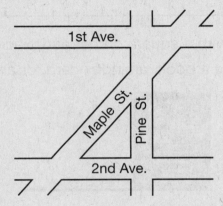

Strategy	Use the definition of parallel lines.
Step 1	Define parallel lines.
	Parallel lines are lines that remain the same distance apart.
Step 2	Find the street that is parallel to 2nd Avenue.
	1st Avenue and 2nd Avenue do not intersect.
	They appear to remain the same distance apart.

Solution   **1st Avenue is parallel to 2nd Avenue.**

You can draw parallel or perpendicular lines by using a ruler.

Example 4

Draw a pair of perpendicular lines.

Strategy   **Use a ruler and an object that forms a square corner.**

Step 1   Use a ruler to draw a straight line.

Step 2   Use an object with a square corner and place it on the line.

You can use a book, an index card, or an envelope.

Step 3   Draw a straight line that crosses the first line and forms a square corner.

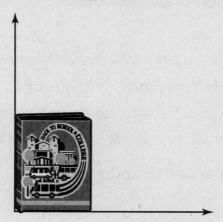

Solution   **A pair of perpendicular lines is shown in Step 3.**

Angles can be identified as acute, right, or obtuse.

A **right angle** forms a square corner.
It measures exactly 90°.

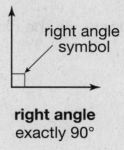

right angle
exactly 90°

An **acute angle** forms an angle less than a right angle.
It measures more than 0°, but less than 90°.

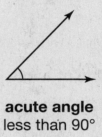

acute angle
less than 90°

An **obtuse angle** forms an angle greater than a right angle.
It measures more than 90°, but less than 180°.

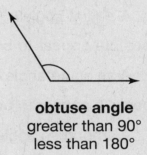

obtuse angle
greater than 90°
less than 180°

Example 5

Name the angle shown below.

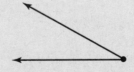

Strategy   **Compare the angle to a right angle.**

Step 1   Think about a right angle.

A right angle measures 90° and forms a square corner.

Step 2   Compare this angle to a right angle.

This angle is smaller than a right angle.

Solution   **The angle is an acute angle.**

The hands on the clock form an angle.

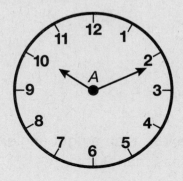

What type of angle is ∠A?

Compare the angle to a right angle.

Does ∠A appear to be exactly 90°? _____

Is ∠A a right angle? _____

Does ∠A appear to be less than 90°? _____

Is ∠A an acute angle? _____

Does ∠A appear to be greater than 90°? _____

Is ∠A an obtuse angle? _____

Angle A is a(n) _____ angle.

Lesson Practice • Part 1

Choose the correct answer.

1. Which is shown below?

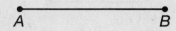

   A. line segment *AB*

   B. line *AB*

   C. ray *AB*

   D. ray *BA*

2. Which shows line *XY*?

3. Which appears to be a pair of perpendicular lines?

4. Which shows ray *AB*?

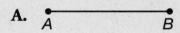
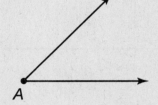

5. Which is an obtuse angle?

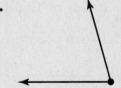
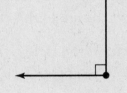
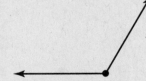
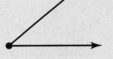

6. Which pair of lines is intersecting, but **not** perpendicular?

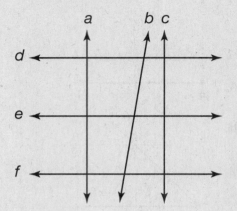

A. lines *a* and *c*

B. lines *d* and *e*

C. lines *a* and *f*

D. lines *b* and *f*

7. Which type of angle is shown below?

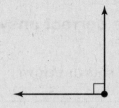

A. acute

B. right

C. obtuse

D. straight

8. Think about the hands of an analog clock.

A. Name a time when the minute hand and hour hand form a right angle.

_____

B. In the clock on the left below, show a time where the hands would form an acute angle. Label the angle *A*.

In the clock on the right, show a time where the hands would form an obtuse angle. Label the angle *O*.

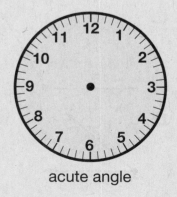

acute angle

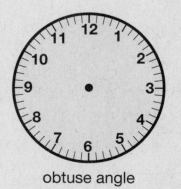

obtuse angle

Lesson Practice • Part 2

Choose the correct answer.

1. How many acute angles does this figure appear to have?

   A. 0   **C.** 2

   B. 1   **D.** 3

2. Which sentence is true?

   A. A line is part of a line segment.

   B. A ray is part of a line segment.

   C. A line is part of a ray.

   D. A ray is part of a line.

3. Which letter contains parallel and perpendicular line segments?

   A. A

   B. E

   C. K

   D. T

4. Which describes the angle?

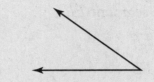

   A. acute   **C.** obtuse

   B. right   **D.** straight

5. How many right angles does this figure appear to have?

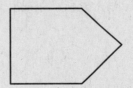

   A. 1   **C.** 3

   B. 2   **D.** 4

6. Which appears to be a pair of parallel lines?

   A.

   B.

   C.

   D.

7. Which is **not** a way to name this figure?

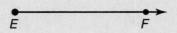

E   F

  A. line segment *EF*

  B. line segment *FE*

  C. ray *EF*

  D. ray *FE*

8. Which describes the angles in this figure?

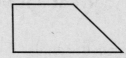

  A. 4 right angles

  B. 2 acute angles and 2 obtuse angles

  C. 2 right angles, 1 acute angle, and 1 obtuse angle

  D. 2 acute angles, 1 right angle, and 1 obtuse angle

9. Use a ruler.

  A. Draw an acute angle.

  B. Draw line *TU*.

  C. Draw a pair of perpendicular line segments.

10. Draw a line from each figure to the name that best describes it.

A. •   • intersecting lines

B.  •   • perpendicular lines

C. 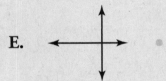 •   • obtuse angle

D. •   • line

E. •   • parallel lines

11. Select True or False for each statement.

A. At 3:00, the hands of a clock form a right angle.   ○ True   ○ False

B. At 12:28, the hands of a clock form an acute angle.   ○ True   ○ False

C. At 1:42, the hands of a clock form an obtuse angle.   ○ True   ○ False

D. At 5:17, the hands of a clock form an acute angle.   ○ True   ○ False

E. At 9:15, the hands of a clock form a right angle.   ○ True   ○ False

12. Look at each angle. Write the letter for the angle in the correct box.

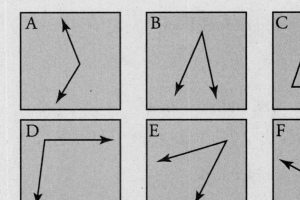

Acute	Obtuse

13. Which figure appears in the diagram? Circle all that apply.

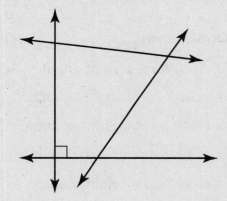

A. intersecting lines

B. perpendicular lines

C. parallel lines

D. acute angle

E. obtuse angle

F. right angle

Two-Dimensional Shapes

Getting the Idea

A **two-dimensional shape** is a flat figure. A **polygon** is a closed two-dimensional shape with straight sides. Polygons are classified, or sorted, by the number of sides and angles. Each side of a polygon is a line segment. The line segments meet at points that form the angles of the polygon.

triangle	quadrilateral	pentagon	hexagon	octagon
3 sides 3 angles	4 sides 4 angles	5 sides 5 angles	6 sides 6 angles	8 sides 8 angles

A circle is a two-dimensional shape in which all points are an equal distance from the center. A circle is not a polygon because it does not have straight sides.

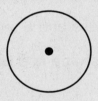

Example 1

What is the name of this two-dimensional shape?

Strategy   **Count the number of sides and angles.**

Step 1   Decide if the shape is a polygon.

Yes, it is a polygon because it has all straight sides.

Step 2   Count the number of sides and angles.

There are 3 sides and 3 angles.

Step 3   Identify the shape.

A polygon with 3 sides and 3 angles is a triangle.

Solution   **The two-dimensional shape is a triangle.**

Look at the three angles in the triangle in Example 1. There is 1 right angle and 2 angles that are smaller than right angles. Any triangle with a right angle is called a **right triangle**.

Example 2

What is the name of this two-dimensional shape?

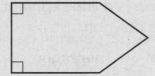

Strategy **Count the number of sides and angles.**

Step 1   Decide if the shape is a polygon.

Yes, it is a polygon because it has all straight sides.

Step 2   Count the number of sides and angles.

There are 5 sides and 5 angles.

Step 3   Identify the shape.

A polygon with 5 sides and 5 angles is a pentagon.

Solution **The two-dimensional shape is a pentagon.**

Example 3

Describe the sides and angles of the pentagon in Example 2.

Strategy **Identify the types of angles and sides.**

Step 1   Describe the types of angles.

The angles on the left side of the pentagon form square corners.

So, there are 2 right angles.

There are also 2 obtuse angles.

The angle on the right side is an acute angle.

Step 2	Describe the sides.

The top and bottom sides are parallel.

The left side meets the top and bottom sides at right angles. So, there are 2 pairs of perpendicular sides.

The 2 right sides of the pentagon intersect.

They form 2 obtuse angles and 1 acute angle.

Solution **The pentagon has 2 right angles, 2 obtuse angles, and 1 acute angle. It has parallel, perpendicular, and intersecting sides.**

Quadrilaterals have 4 sides and 4 angles. They are classified by the lengths of their sides and the types of angles. Here are some quadrilaterals you should know.

Name	Diagram	Properties
Parallelogram		It has two pairs of parallel sides. The opposite sides are equal.
Rhombus		It is a parallelogram with 4 equal sides.
Rectangle		It is a parallelogram with 4 right angles.
Square		It is a rectangle with 4 equal sides.
Trapezoid		It has exactly 1 pair of parallel sides.

Example 4

What is the name of this polygon? Be as specific as possible.

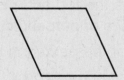

Strategy **Look at the sides and angles.**

Step 1 Decide if the polygon is a quadrilateral.

The polygon has 4 straight sides.

It is a quadrilateral.

Step 2 Decide if the polygon is a parallelogram.

The polygon has 2 pairs of parallel sides.

It is a parallelogram.

Step 3 Look at the angles.

The polygon does not have any right angles.

It has 2 angles that are smaller than right angles.

It also has 2 angles that are greater than right angles.

So, there are 2 acute angles and 2 obtuse angles.

Step 4 Decide if the sides are the same length.

The polygon appears to have 4 equal sides.

Step 5 Name the polygon.

A rhombus is a quadrilateral with 4 sides that are the same length and 2 pairs of parallel sides.

Solution **The polygon is a rhombus.**

Coached Example

What is the name of this two-dimensional shape? Be as specific as possible.

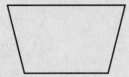

Decide if the shape is a polygon.

Does the shape have straight sides? _____

Is the shape a polygon? _____

Count the number of sides and angles.

How many straight sides does the shape have? _____

How many angles does the shape have? _____

Is the shape a quadrilateral? _____

Does the shape have any right angles? _____

Is the shape a rectangle? _____

What types of angles does the shape have?

_____ angles and _____ angles

Does the shape have parallel sides? _____

How many pairs of parallel sides does the shape have? _____

Which quadrilateral has only 1 pair of parallel sides? _____

The name of this two-dimensional shape is _____.

Lesson Practice • Part 1

Choose the correct answer.

1. Which is **not** a polygon?

   A.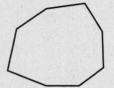

   B.

   C.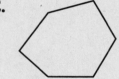

   D.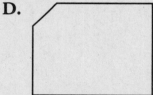

2. Which best describes this shape?

   A. quadrilateral

   B. square

   C. rhombus

   D. hexagon

3. Which of these shapes has right angles?

   A.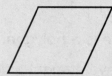

   B.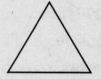

   C.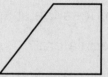

   D.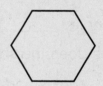

4. Wendy was driving when she passed a yield sign.

   Which best describes the angles in the sign?

   A. 3 right angles

   B. 3 acute angles

   C. 3 obtuse angles

   D. 2 acute angles and 1 right angle

5. How many pairs of parallel lines are in this shape?

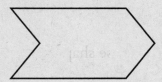

    A. 1

    B. 3

    C. 4

    D. 5

6. How many angles does an octagon have?

    A. 6

    B. 7

    C. 8

    D. 10

7. Which appears to be a right triangle?

    A.

    B.

    C.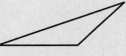

    D.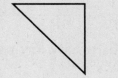

8. Which is the name of this two-dimensional shape?

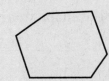

    A. octagon

    B. hexagon

    C. pentagon

    D. trapezoid

9. Jessica drew the shape below.

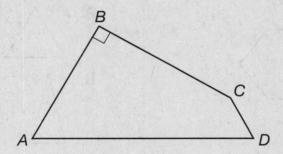

A. Describe all of the angles in the shape.

_____

_____

B. Does the shape have any parallel or perpendicular sides? Explain your answer.

_____

_____

_____

C. Name the shape that Jessica drew.

_____

Lesson Practice • Part 2

Choose the correct answer.

1. Which quadrilateral can have exactly 2 right angles?

   A. rectangle   C. square

   B. rhombus   D. trapezoid

2. Which describes a combination of 3 angles that does **not** form a triangle?

   A. 1 acute angle, 1 right angle, and 1 obtuse angle

   B. 2 acute angles and 1 right angle

   C. 2 acute angles and 1 obtuse angle

   D. 3 acute angles

3. Which sentence about the sides of triangles is true?

   A. A triangle can have a pair of parallel sides.

   B. A triangle can have a pair of perpendicular sides.

   C. A triangle can have parallel and perpendicular sides.

   D. A triangle can not have parallel or perpendicular sides.

4. Which is the greatest number of acute angles a quadrilateral can have?

   A. 1   C. 3

   B. 2   D. 4

5. Which shape has the greatest number of pairs of opposite sides parallel?

   A.   C.

   B.   D.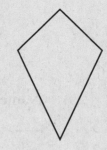

6. A quadrilateral has two pairs of opposite sides parallel. Without knowing the angle measures, how can the quadrilateral be classified?

   A. parallelogram   C. rhombus

   B. rectangle   D. square

7. Which is **not** a way to name this figure?

   A. parallelogram

   B. rectangle

   C. rhombus

   D. trapezoid

8. What is the least number of obtuse angles a quadrilateral can have?

A. 0

C. 2

B. 1

D. 3

9. How can a quadrilateral with exactly 1 right angle be classified?

A. parallelogram

B. quadrilateral only

C. rectangle

D. trapezoid

10. Sue drew the quadrilaterals below.

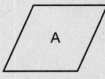

A. Name each quadrilateral.

_____

B. Other than having 4 sides, describe how the quadrilaterals are alike.

_____

_____

C. Describe how the quadrilaterals are different.

_____

_____

11. Circle the names that describe the angles in the triangle.

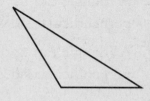

The triangle has 2 | obtuse / acute / right | angles and 1 | obtuse / acute / right | angle.

12. Which shape is a polygon? Circle all that apply.

A.

B.

C.

D.

E.

13. Select Yes or No to answer each question about the shape.

		Yes	No
A.	Does the shape appear to have parallel sides?	○ Yes	○ No
B.	Does the shape appear to have perpendicular sides?	○ Yes	○ No
C.	Does the shape appear to be a trapezoid?	○ Yes	○ No
D.	Does the shape appear to have right angles?	○ Yes	○ No
E.	Does the shape appear to have acute angles?	○ Yes	○ No
F.	Does the shape appear to be a rectangle?	○ Yes	○ No
G.	Does the shape appear to be a square?	○ Yes	○ No

14. Draw a line from each shape to the name that best describes it.

A.   •   •   trapezoid

B.   •   •   pentagon

C.   •   •   octagon

D.   •   •   rhombus

15. Decide whether each shape is a quadrilateral. Write the name of the shape in the correct box.

triangle	parallelogram	rhombus
octagon	trapezoid	hexagon

Quadrilateral	Not a Quadrilateral

Symmetry

Getting the Idea

A figure with **line symmetry** can be divided into two matching parts.

The line that divides the figure is a **line of symmetry**. Some figures have 1 line of symmetry and others have more than 1 line of symmetry.

The equilateral triangle below has 3 lines of symmetry.

Lines of Symmetry

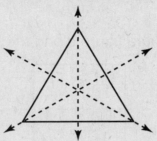

Example 1

Which figure(s) shows a line of symmetry?

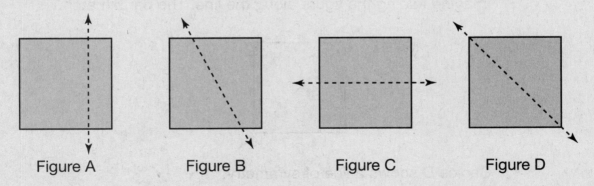

| Figure A | Figure B | Figure C | Figure D |

Strategy   Imagine folding each figure along the line so that the parts match exactly.

Step 1   Look at Choice A.

Imagine folding the figure along the line.
The parts do not match.

Choice A does not show a line of symmetry.

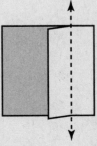

Step 2   Look at Choice B.

Imagine folding the figure along the line. The parts do not match.

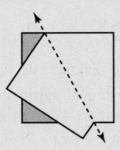

Choice B does not show a line of symmetry.

Step 3   Look at Choice C.

Imagine folding the figure along the line. The parts match.

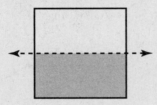

Choice C shows a line of symmetry.

Step 4   Look at Choice D.

Imagine folding the figure along the line. The parts match.

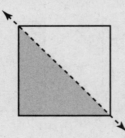

Choice D shows a line of symmetry.

Solution   **Figures C and D show a line of symmetry.**

Example 2

Which figure has line symmetry?

  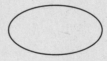

Strategy   **Draw lines on each figure.**
Imagine folding on the lines to see if the parts match.

Step 1   Draw different lines on the first figure.

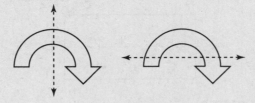

The parts do not match.

The figure does not have line symmetry.

Step 2   Draw different lines on the second figure.

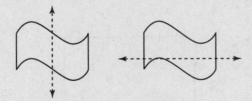

The parts do not match.

The figure does not have line symmetry.

Step 3   Draw different lines on the third figure.

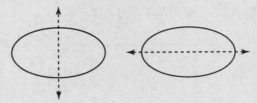

The parts match.

Both dashed lines are lines of symmetry.

The figure has line symmetry.

Solution   **The third figure has line symmetry.**

Example 3

Does this figure have line symmetry? If so, how many lines of symmetry does it have?

Strategy   **Test different lines on the rectangle.**
Imagine folding on the lines to see if the parts match.

Step 1   Draw a horizontal line through the middle of the figure.

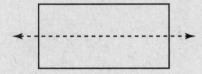

The parts match.

The dashed line is a line of symmetry.

The figure has line symmetry.

Step 2   Draw a vertical line through the middle of the figure.

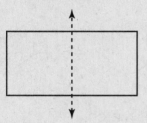

The parts match.

The dashed line is a line of symmetry.

Step 3   Draw a diagonal line across the figure.

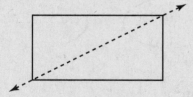

When folded across the line, the parts do not match.

The dashed line is not a line of symmetry.

Solution   **The rectangle has 2 lines of symmetry.**

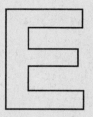 **Coached Example**

Which block letters have line symmetry?

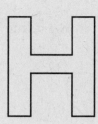

E S H

Look at the letter E.

Draw lines to see if it has line symmetry.

It has _____ line of symmetry.

Does the letter E have line symmetry? _____

Look at the letter S.

Draw lines to see if it has line symmetry.

It has _____ lines of symmetry.

Does the letter S have line symmetry? _____

Look at the letter H.

Draw lines to see if it has line symmetry.

It has _____ lines of symmetry.

Does the letter H have line symmetry? _____

The letters _____ and _____ have line symmetry.

Lesson Practice • Part 1

Choose the correct answer.

1. Which figure shows a line of symmetry?

   A.

   B.

   C.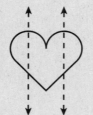

   D.

2. Which triangle has only 1 line of symmetry?

   A.

   B.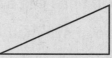

   C.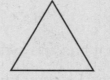

   D.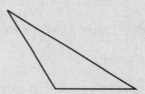

3. Which block letter has exactly 2 lines of symmetry?

   A.

   B.

   C.

   D.

4. How many lines of symmetry does this figure have?

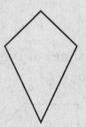

A. 0   **C.** 2

B. 1   **D.** 4

5. How many lines of symmetry does this figure have?

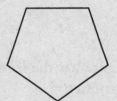

A. 3   **C.** 5

B. 4   **D.** 7

6. Which figure has the most lines of symmetry?

A.   **C.**

B. 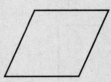   **D.**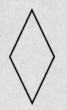

7. How many lines of symmetry does this block letter have?

A. 0

B. 1

C. 2

D. 3

8. Trevon drew the figure below.

A. Draw a line of symmetry on the figure.

B. Does the figure have line symmetry? Explain how you know.

_____

_____

_____

Lesson Practice • Part 2

Choose the correct answer.

1. How many lines of symmetry does a square have?

  A. 0   **C.** 2

  B. 1   **D.** 4

2. Which figure shows a line of symmetry?

  A.
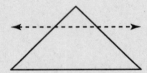

  B.
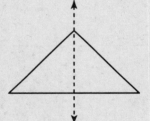

  C.
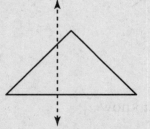

  D.
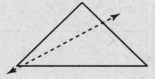

3. How many lines of symmetry does this figure have?

  A. 0

  B. 1

  C. 2

  D. 5

4. Which figure has the least number of lines of symmetry?

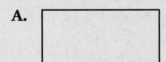

5. How many lines of symmetry is it impossible for a triangle to have?

   A. 0

   B. 1

   C. 2

   D. 3

6. How many lines of symmetry does this block letter have?

   A. 0

   B. 1

   C. 2

   D. 3

7. How many lines of symmetry does this figure have?

   A. 0   **C.** 2

   B. 1   **D.** 3

8. Which describes the greatest number of lines of symmetry that a polygon can have?

   A. the same as the number of sides it has

   B. 1 more than the number of sides it has

   C. 1 fewer than the number of sides it has

   D. there is no limit to the number of lines of symmetry

9. Adrienne drew this arrow.

   A. How many lines of symmetry does the arrow have?

   B. Draw any lines of symmetry on the arrow.

10. Count the lines of symmetry for each figure. Write the number of the figure in the correct box.

Only One Line of Symmetry	More Than One Line of Symmetry

11. Draw a line from each figure to the number of lines of symmetry it has.

A. •   • 0

B. •   • 1

C. •   • 2

D. •   • 3

12. Look at each figure. Does it show all the possible lines of symmetry? Select Yes or No.

A. 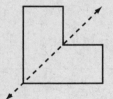   ○ Yes   ○ No

B. 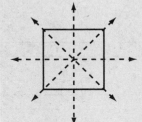   ○ Yes   ○ No

C. 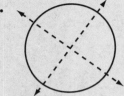   ○ Yes   ○ No

D. 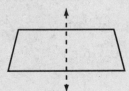   ○ Yes   ○ No

13. Look at the figures below. Use letters from the box to complete the statements.

A   B   C

Figure _____ has no lines of symmetry.

Figure _____ has two lines of symmetry.

Figure _____ has one line of symmetry.

A

B

C

Domain 5: Cumulative Assessment for Lessons 37–39

1. Which shows perpendicular lines?

A.

B.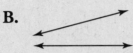

C.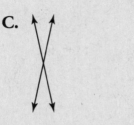

D.

2. What type of angle is shown below?

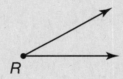

- **A.** It is an obtuse angle.
- **B.** It is a straight angle.
- **C.** It is an acute angle.
- **D.** It is a right angle.

3. Look at the map below.

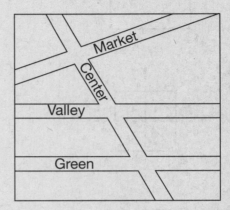

Which streets appear to be parallel to each other?

- **A.** Green and Valley
- **B.** Valley and Market
- **C.** Market and Center
- **D.** Center and Green

4. Which is **not** true about this shape?

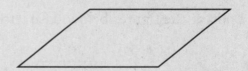

- **A.** It is a quadrilateral.
- **B.** The opposite sides are parallel.
- **C.** Two angles are greater than right angles.
- **D.** It has perpendicular line segments.

5. Emily drew a polygon with 2 pairs of parallel sides and 4 right angles. The length is twice as long as the width. What shape best describes the polygon Emily drew?

   A. rectangle

   B. square

   C. rhombus

   D. trapezoid

6. Which shape does **not** have any parallel sides?

   A.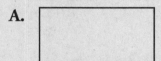

   B.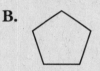

   C.

   D.

7. Which is a right triangle?

   A.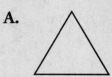

   B.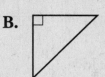

   C.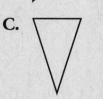

   D.

8. Which figure has the most lines of symmetry?

   A.

   B.

   C.

   D.

9. How many lines of symmetry does this figure have?

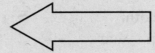

_____

10. Look at the figure below.

A. How many lines of symmetry does the figure have?

_____

B. Draw all the lines of symmetry on the figure below.

Glossary

acute angle an angle with a measure less than 90 degrees (Lesson 37)

add (addition) to find the total when two or more groups are joined (Lesson 12)

addend a number to be added (Lesson 12)

A.M. the time between 12 midnight and 12 noon (Lesson 29)

angle a figure formed by two rays that have the same endpoint (Lesson 35)

area the number of square units needed to cover a figure (Lesson 34)

array an arrangement of objects in equal rows and columns (Lesson 3)

associative property of multiplication a property that states that when you multiply, the grouping of the factors does not change the product (Lesson 5)

base-ten numeral a number written using only its digits (Lesson 1)

benchmark a common number that can be compared to another number (Lesson 20)

capacity the measure of how much liquid a container holds; also called liquid volume (Lesson 31)

centimeter (cm) a metric unit of length; 1 centimeter = 10 millimeters (Lesson 32)

circle a two-dimensional shape in which all points are an equal distance from the center (Lesson 35)

common denominator the same denominator in two or more fractions (Lesson 20)

commutative property of multiplication a property that states that when you multiply, the order of the factors does not change the product (Lesson 5)

compatible numbers numbers that are close in value to the exact numbers and that are easy to compute with (Lesson 16)

composite number a whole number that has more than one factor pair (Lesson 11)

cup a customary unit of capacity; 2 cups = 1 pint (Lesson 31)

customary system a system of measure that includes feet, pounds, and gallons (Lesson 30)

day (d) a unit of time; 1 day = 24 hours (Lesson 29)

decimal a number with a decimal point (Lesson 25)

decimal point (.) a period separating the ones from the tenths in a decimal (Lesson 25)

degree (°) a unit for measuring angles (Lesson 35)

denominator the bottom number in a fraction that tells how many equal parts in the whole or group (Lesson 18)

difference the answer in a subtraction problem (Lesson 13)

distributive property of multiplication a property that states that when you multiply a number by a sum, you can multiply the number by each addend of the sum and then add the products (Lesson 6)

divide (division) to find the number of equal groups or the number in each group (Lesson 7)

dividend the number to be divided (Lesson 7)

divisor the number by which the dividend is divided (Lesson 7)

elapsed time the amount of time that has passed from a beginning time to an end time (Lesson 29)

endpoint a point on the end of a line segment or ray (Lesson 35)

equivalent fractions two or more fractions that name the same value, but have different numerators and denominators (Lesson 18)

estimate a number that is close to the exact amount (Lesson 15)

expanded form a way of writing a number that shows the sum of the values of each digit (Lesson 1)

fact family a group of related addition and subtraction facts or multiplication and division facts that use the same numbers (Lesson 7)

factor a number that is multiplied to get a product (Lessons 3, 11)

foot (ft) a customary unit of length; 1 foot = 12 inches (Lesson 32)

fraction a number that names part of a whole or part of a group (Lesson 18)

gallon a customary unit of capacity; 1 gallon = 4 quarts (Lesson 31)

gram (g) a metric unit of mass; 1,000 grams = 1 kilogram (Lesson 30)

greatest common factor (GCF) the greatest factor that is common to two or more numbers (Lesson 18)

hexagon a two-dimensional shape with 6 sides and 6 angles (Lesson 38)

hour (hr) a unit of time; 1 hour = 60 minutes (Lesson 29)

improper fraction a fraction with a numerator that is equal to or greater than its denominator (Lesson 19)

inch (in.) a customary unit of length; 12 inches = 1 foot (Lesson 32)

intersecting lines lines that cross (Lesson 37)

inverse operations operations that undo each other, such as addition and subtraction, and multiplication and division (Lesson 7)

is equal to (=) a symbol that shows that two quantities have the same value (Lesson 2)

is greater than (>) a symbol that shows that the first quantity is greater than the second quantity (Lesson 2)

is less than (<) a symbol that shows that the first quantity is less than the second quantity (Lesson 2)

kilogram (kg) a metric unit of mass; 1 kilogram = 1,000 grams (Lesson 30)

kilometer (km) a metric unit of length; 1 kilometer = 1,000 meters (Lesson 32)

least common multiple (LCM) the least number that is a common multiple of two or more numbers (Lesson 20)

length the measure of how long, wide, or tall something is (Lesson 32)

like denominators two or more denominators that are the same (Lesson 21)

line a straight path that goes in two directions without end (Lesson 37)

line of symmetry a line that divides a figure in which the halves match exactly (Lesson 39)

line plot a graph that uses Xs above a number line to record data (Lesson 36)

line segment a part of a line that has two endpoints (Lesson 37)

line symmetry a property of a figure in which a figure can be divided into 2 matching halves (Lesson 39)

liquid volume the measure of how much liquid a container holds; also called capacity (Lesson 31)

liter a metric unit of capacity; 1 liter = 1,000 milliliters (Lesson 31)

mass the amount of matter in an object (Lesson 30)

meter (m) a metric unit of length; 1 meter = 100 centimeters (Lesson 32)

metric system a system of measure that includes meters, grams, and liters (Lesson 30)

mile (mi) a customary unit of length; 1 mile = 1,760 yards (Lesson 32)

milliliter (mL) a metric unit of capacity; 1,000 milliliters = 1 liter (Lesson 31)

millimeter (mm) a metric unit of length; 10 millimeters = 1 centimeter (Lesson 32)

minuend the number being subtracted from in a subtraction problem (Lesson 13)

minute (min) a unit of time; 60 minutes = 1 hour (Lesson 29)

mixed number a number with a whole number part and a fraction part (Lesson 19)

month (mo) a unit of time; 12 months = 1 year (Lesson 29)

multiple the product of a number and another number (Lessons 10, 11)

multiplicative identity property of 1 a property that states that when you multiply a number by 1, the product is that number (Lesson 5)

multiply (multiplication) to find a total when there are equal groups; a shortcut for repeated addition (Lesson 3)

number name a way of writing numbers using words (Lesson 1)

numerator the top number in a fraction that tells how many equal parts are being considered (Lesson 18)

obtuse angle an angle with a measure greater than 90 degrees, but less than 180 degrees (Lesson 37)

octagon a two-dimensional shape with 8 sides and 8 angles (Lesson 38)

ounce (oz) a customary unit of weight; 16 ounces = 1 pound (Lesson 30)

parallel lines lines that remain the same distance apart and never meet (Lesson 37)

parallelogram a quadrilateral with 2 pairs of parallel sides; the opposite sides are equal (Lesson 38)

pattern a series of numbers or figures that follows a rule (Lesson 17)

pentagon a two-dimensional shape with 5 sides and 5 angles (Lesson 38)

perimeter the distance around a figure, measured in units (Lesson 33)

perpendicular lines intersecting lines that cross to form 4 right angles (Lesson 37)

pint a customary unit of capacity; 1 pint = 2 cups (Lesson 31)

place value the value of a digit based on its position in a number (Lesson 1)

P.M. the time between 12 noon and 12 midnight (Lesson 29)

point a particular place or location (Lesson 37)

polygon a type of two-dimensional shape with straight sides (Lesson 38)

pound a customary unit of weight; 1 pound = 16 ounces (Lesson 30)

prime number a whole number that has exactly one factor pair, 1 and itself (Lesson 11)

product the answer in a multiplication problem (Lesson 3)

protractor a tool used to measure angles (Lesson 35)

quadrilateral a two-dimensional shape with 4 sides and 4 angles (Lesson 38)

quart a customary unit of capacity; 1 quart = 2 pints (Lesson 31)

quotient the answer in a division problem (Lesson 7)

ray a part of a line that has an endpoint at one end and goes on forever in the other direction (Lessons 35, 37)

rectangle a parallelogram with 4 right angles (Lesson 38)

regroup to rename a number, such as 10 tens as 1 hundred (Lesson 12)

remainder a number that is left after division has been completed (Lesson 9)

rhombus a parallelogram with 4 equal sides (Lesson 38)

right angle an angle that measures exactly 90° (Lesson 37)

right triangle a triangle with one right angle (Lesson 38)

round to replace a number with one that tells about how much or about how many (Lesson 14)

rule a description of how the terms are related in a pattern (Lesson 17)

simplest form a form of a fraction whose numerator and denominator have only 1 as a common factor (Lesson 18)

square a rectangle with 4 equal sides (Lesson 38)

square unit a square with a side length of 1 unit; used to measure area (Lesson 34)

subtract (subtraction) to find how many are left when a quantity is taken away (Lesson 13)

subtrahend the number that is subtracted in a subtraction problem (Lesson 13)

sum the answer in an addition problem (Lesson 12)

term a number in a number pattern (Lesson 17)

trapezoid a quadrilateral with exactly 1 pair of parallel sides (Lesson 38)

triangle a two-dimensional shape with 3 sides and 3 angles (Lesson 38)

two-dimensional shape a flat figure (Lesson 38)

unit fraction a fraction that has a numerator of 1 (Lesson 21)

variable a letter or symbol used to represent a value that is unknown (Lesson 3)

vertex the common endpoint where two rays meet in an angle (Lesson 35)

week (wk) a unit of time; 1 week = 7 days (Lesson 29)

weight a measurement that tells how heavy an object is (Lesson 30)

whole number any of the numbers 1, 2, 3, and so on (Lesson 1)

yard (yd) a customary unit of length; 1 yard = 3 feet (Lesson 32)

year (yr) a unit of time; 1 year = 12 months (Lesson 29)